No free Government or the Blessing of Liberty can be preserved to any People but by a firm adherence to Justice Moderation Temperance Frugality and Virtue and by frequent recurrence to fundamental Principles.
—George Mason, Article 15, Virginia Declaration of Rights, *1776*

•

It may be a reflection on human nature, that . . . devices should be necessary to controul the abuses of government. But what is government itself but the greatest of all reflections on human nature? If men were angels, no government would be necessary. If angels were to govern men, neither external nor internal controuls on government would be necessary. In framing a government . . . the great difficulty lies in this: You must first enable the government to controul the governed; and in the next place, oblige it to controul itself. A dependence on the people is no doubt the primary controul on the government; but experience has taught mankind the necessity of auxillary precautions.
—James Madison, *The Federalist*, No. 51, *1788*

•

It is impossible that {the Constitution} shou'd ever continue perverted to bad purposes untill it is dangerous—unless the great mass of the people shou'd become Corrupt*! ignorant of their Birthright—and regardless of their posterity. Shou'd such at any period be the unhappy Characterisk of My fellow Citizens . . . it will not be in the power of Folios of Bills of rights to maintain their Liberties. The rights of Freemen are only to be maintain'd by Freemen—and when the Spirit of Freedom (that has ever elevated those who felt its influence amongst Mankind) becomes extinct in the bosoms of men Liberty itself will be a curse to them.*
—George Lee Tuberville to James Madison, *1788*

The Bill of Rights
A Lively Heritage

Edited by Jon Kukla

Essays by *Lawrence Delbert Cress, William Cuddihy, B. Carmon Hardy, Charles F. Hobson, John P. Kaminski, Jon Kukla, Martin E. Marty, John M. Murrin, David M. O'Brien, A. G. Roeber, Robert A. Rutland, Brent Tarter,* and *Richard A. Williamson*

Virginia State Library and Archives
Richmond 1987

For the children who inherit
the rights we preserve and expand

Library of Congress Cataloging-in-Publication Data
The Bill of Rights.
    Includes bibliographical references and index.
    1. United States—Constitutional law—Amendments—
1st–10th—History. 2. Civil Rights—United States—
History. I. Kukla, Jon, 1948–   II. Cress,
Lawrence Delbert.
KF4749.B5   342.73′085   87–10514
ISBN 0–88490–141–6   347.30285

Contents

The Bill of Rights: A Lively Heritage has been recognized
as a bicentennial project and authorized to bear the emblem of the
Virginia Commission on the Bicentennial of the United States Constitution.
A. E. DICK HOWARD, Chairman
TIMOTHY G. O'ROURKE, Executive Director

U.S. CONSTITUTION
It has Virginia written all over it.

Preface

NO DOCUMENT IN OUR HISTORY has seen more recurrent controversy than the Bill of Rights. By their nature, the first ten amendments to the Constitution of the United States stand bravely as thin lines of ink defending freedom and civilization from tyranny and barbarism. Violent conflicts shaped the historical antecedents of all ten amendments, argument and debate marked their drafting and ratification, and heated controversies testify to their importance in the lives of Americans today. Daily headlines in a complex late-twentieth-century world of rapid communication and sophisticated technologies chronicle disagreements—on subjects both profound and seemingly mundane—in which these eighteenth-century statements of fundamental rights continue to guide the administration of justice and shaping of public policy. The historical essays in this volume are intended to illuminate contemporary life by allowing expert scholars to describe the major elements of the Bill of Rights in terms that ordinary citizens (including the editor) can understand and appreciate. Published serially in *Virginia Cavalcade* from October 1982 through January 1986, the essays reminded thousands of *Cavalcade*'s subscribers of those Virginians whose wisdom, enunciated in the Bill of Rights, has a lasting influence in American life. Every generation must heed Patrick Henry's advice "to be extremely cautious, watchful, jealous of your liberty; for, instead of securing your rights, you may lose them forever. If a wrong step be now made, the republic may be lost forever. . . . I repeat it again, and I beg gentlemen to consider, that a wrong step, made now, will plunge us into misery, and our republic will be lost." The heritage of freedom embodied in our Bill of Rights is lively, vital, and deserving of eternal vigilance.

•

Fittingly, the idea for *The Bill of Rights: A Lively Heritage* developed during a conversation about contemporary events one Saturday morning while my then-toddling daughter, Amy, gleefully stomped on ants and chinaberries in Brent Tarter's backyard. Soon thereafter The Library Board endorsed my proposal, and talented scholars accepted my invitations to contribute articles in their special fields of research. I am grateful to Mr. Tarter and to Sandra

Gioia Treadway for advice and critical judgment; to the editors of *Virginia Cavalcade*, the late Patricia L. Faust and Edward D. C. Campbell, Jr., for helping prepare the essays for their serial publication; to Emily Jones Salmon for gracing both the texts and notes with editorial consistency; and to W. Donald Rhinesmith for guiding the volume through the press. Cynthia H. Spindle and Brenda M. White ably shared the secretarial work of word processing and of correspondence during the publication of these essays. Coordinating a jointly written book is an experience that some editors try to forget, but my experience with the contributors to *The Bill of Rights: A Lively Heritage* has been delightful. I am profoundly grateful to them for all that I learned in the course of editing their essays for publication. Finally, my preparation of the index during a blizzard that kept us snowbound was enhanced by Jennifer and Amy's vocal exercise of First Amendment rights despite futile parental efforts at prior restraint.

JON KUKLA

Short Titles and Symbols

Annals of Congress	Joseph Gales, Sr., comp., *The Debates and Proceedings in the Congress of the United States* (Washington, D.C., 1834–1856) ("Gales & Seaton's History of Debates in Congress")
BL	British Library, London
CO	Colonial Office, Public Record Office, London
Elliot, *Debates*	Jonathan Elliot, ed., *The Debates in the Several State Conventions on the Adoption of the Federal Constitution*, 2d ed., rev. (Philadelphia, 1836–1845)
English Reports	A. Wood Renton, Max A. Robertson, and Geoffrey Ellis, eds., *English Reports* (Edinburgh and London, 1900–1932)
Gage Correspondence	Clarence Edwin Carter, ed., *Correspondence of General Thomas Gage with the Secretaries of State {and} with the War Office and the Treasury, 1763–1775* (New Haven, 1931–1933)
Hening, *Statutes*	William Waller Hening, ed., *Statutes at Large; Being a Collection of All the Laws of Virginia, from the First Session of the Legislature in the Year 1619* (Richmond, Philadelphia, and New York, 1809–1823)
Huntington Library	Huntington Library, Art Collections, and Botanical Gardens, San Marino, Calif.
Jefferson Papers	Julian P. Boyd et al., eds., *Papers of Thomas Jefferson* (Princeton, 1950–)
Kenyon, *Antifederalists*	Cecelia M. Kenyon, ed., *The Antifederalists* (Indianapolis, 1966)

MCGC	H. R. McIlwaine, ed., *Minutes of the Council and General Court of Colonial Virginia*, 2d ed. (Richmond, 1979)
Madison Papers	Robert A. Rutland et al., eds., *Papers of James Madison* (Chicago and Charlottesville, 1962–)
Mason Papers	Robert A. Rutland, ed., *Papers of George Mason, 1725–1792* (Chapel Hill, 1970)
PRO	Public Record Office, London
Ratification	Merrill Jensen et al., eds., *Documentary History of the Ratification of the Constitution* (Madison, Wis., 1976–)
Schwartz, *Bill of Rights*	Bernard Schwartz, ed., *The Bill of Rights: A Documentary History* (New York, 1971)
Schwartz, *Roots*	Bernard Schwartz, ed., *The Roots of the Bill of Rights: An Illustrated Source Book of American Freedom* (New York, 1971)
State Trials	W. Cobbett et al., eds., *Cobbett's Complete Collection of State Trials* (London, 1809–1828)
U.S. Reports	A. J. Dallas et al., *Reports of Cases Argued and Adjudged in the Supreme Court of the United States* (Philadelphia, New York, Washington, D.C., and Boston, 1806–)
University of Michigan	William L. Clements Library, University of Michigan, Ann Arbor
VMHB	*Virginia Magazine of History and Biography*
VSL	Archives Branch, Virginia State Library and Archives, Richmond
WMQ	*William and Mary Quarterly*

The Bill of Rights

A Lively Heritage

Virginians and the Bill of Rights

BRENT TARTER

IN MAY 1776 Thomas Jefferson was in Philadelphia as a member of the Continental Congress about to compose the Declaration of Independence. He wanted to be in Williamsburg, where a convention of Virginians met from 6 May through 5 July to write a constitution for the new commonwealth of Virginia. "It is a work of the most interesting nature," Jefferson told a friend, "and such as every individual would wish to have his voice in. In truth it is the whole object of the present controversy; for should a bad government be instituted for us in future it had been as well to have accepted at first the bad one offered to us from beyond the water without the risk and expence of contest."[1]

Never before 1776 had citizen-legislators met in conventions to devise written constitutions of government. This novel activity engrossed the attentions of Americans as much as news of battles or of the decision taken in Congress on 2 July 1776 (and explained by the declaration passed on the fourth) to separate from the British empire.

On 15 May 1776 the delegates of the Virginia convention had unanimously adopted resolutions drafted by Edmund Pendleton instructing the Virginia members of Congress to propose a declaration of independence. Pendleton's resolves also charged a committee of the Virginia convention to "prepare a Declaration of Rights and such a plan of government as will be most likely to maintain peace and order . . . and secure substantial and equal liberty to the people."[2]

Pendleton, president of the convention, named a twenty-eight-member committee with Archibald Cary as chairman and such distinguished veterans of the House of Burgesses as Richard Bland, Patrick Henry, and Robert Carter Nicholas as members. In time he enlarged the committee to thirty-six

---

1. *Jefferson Papers*, 1:292.
2. William J. Van Schreeven, Robert L. Scribner, and Brent Tarter, eds., *Revolutionary Virginia, The Road to Independence: A Documentary Record* (Charlottesville, 1973–1983), 7:143.

members and appointed a few promising first-term legislators such as James Madison and Edmund Randolph. The most important of the additional appointees was George Mason, whose ill health had delayed his arrival at the convention.[3]

Mason ranked thirty-second in seniority, but when the work began he ranked first. He drafted both the Declaration of Rights and the first constitution of the commonwealth. Mason's proposals, Edmund Randolph later recalled, "swallowed up all the rest by fixing the grounds and plan, which after great discussion and correction" the convention unanimously adopted.[4]

Mason began with the Declaration of Rights. He and his contemporaries believed that the purpose of government was to protect the safety and liberty of the people. They insisted upon guaranteeing their rights before granting any powers to their new governments. Mason spelled out their convictions in his opening sentences:

> That all Men are born equally free and independant, and have certain inherent natural Rights, of which they can not by any Compact, deprive or divest their Posterity; among which are the Enjoyment of Life and Liberty, with the Means of acquiring and possessing Property, and pursueing and obtaining Happiness and Safety.
>
> That Power is, by God and Nature, vested in, and consequently derived from the People; that Magistrates are their Trustees and Servants, and at all times amenable to them.
>
> That Government is, or ought to be, instituted for the common Benefit and Security of the People, Nation, or Community.[5]

The similarity of Mason's language to that of Jefferson's Declaration of Independence is striking but not surprising. Both men drew upon the same rich heritage. They looked back at the centuries of English history and saw a torturous struggle to secure fundamental liberties from the hands of grasping kings or corrupt parliaments. The fruits of that struggle were clearly seen in the Glorious Revolution of 1689 that had deposed James II and produced the English Bill of Rights; in the English Civil War and the execution of a divine-right king; in the grudging acceptance by Charles I in 1628 of the Petition of Right; in Magna Carta of 1215; and even, in

---

3. Ibid., 7:143, 158, 182–183.

4. Edmund Randolph, *History of Virginia*, ed. Arthur H. Shaffer (Charlottesville, 1970), 252.

5. *Mason Papers*, 1:277

Jefferson's opinion, in the presumed golden age of Saxon liberty before the Norman Conquest.

The rights of Englishmen had formed the cornerstone of Americans' objections to the Stamp Act of 1765 and had been invoked repeatedly during the 1770s. Americans believed that their English liberties were being threatened by George III and Parliament, and, acting in what they believed to be the great tradition of their English ancestors, first they protested and then they rebelled. When in 1776 they wrote their own constitutions, they sought to codify their liberties with declarations of rights so that no officers of government could unjustly restrict their freedom.

In composing the Virginia Declaration of Rights, George Mason spelled out the fundamental rights so that, as Edmund Randolph explained, "the legislature should not in their acts violate any of those canons" and that "in all the revolutions of time, of human opinion, and of government, a perpetual standard should be erected, around which the people might rally and by a notorious record be forever admonished to be watchful, firm, and virtuous."[6]

As revised by the committee, Mason's declaration abolished all hereditary officeholding; provided for the separation of the legislative, executive, and judicial branches of government; institutionalized the principle of no taxation without representation; prohibited the passage of bills of attainder and ex post facto laws; guaranteed the right to jury trials in civil and criminal cases; required the government to adhere to the principles of "Justice, Moderation, Temperance, Frugality, and Virtue"; granted the vote to almost all adult white men; decreed that "excessive bail ought not to be required, nor excessive fines imposed, nor cruel and unusual punishments inflicted"; outlawed general warrants; enshrined the militia as the guardian of the public liberty; declared that the "freedom of the press is one of the great bulwarks of liberty, and can never be restrained but by despotick governments"; and secured to all people the "fullest Toleration in the Exercise of Religion."

The committee reported the amended draft to the full convention on 27 May 1776, and the delegates debated it, amended it, and finally adopted the Declaration of Rights on 12 June. The convention's amendments included stylistic improvements and deletion of the prohibition against bills of attainder after Patrick Henry frightened the delegates with a "terrifying" speech in which he painted a dramatic "picture of some towering public offender against whom the ordinary laws would be impotent."

---

6. Randolph, *History of Virginia*, 255.

The delegates also substantially revised the paragraph on religious liberty. James Madison composed an amendment to change Mason's reluctant grant of toleration into a bold assertion that all men possessed a natural right to believe and worship, or not to believe, as they wished. Unpracticed in parliamentary debate and shy in his first term as a legislator, Madison prevailed upon Patrick Henry to offer the amendment and advocate its adoption. Henry was immediately charged with undermining the established Church of England, and he promptly and ungraciously dropped Madison's amendment and let it die. Madison thereupon drafted language that did not offend conservative Anglicans or threaten the establishment and persuaded another member to introduce it. The convention adopted Madison's second proposal and proclaimed that all men had a natural right to "the free exercise of religion." Boldly taking the first such step in modern Western civilization, Virginia removed all legal pretense for persecution or discrimination based upon religious differences.[7]

The Virginia Declaration of Rights stood as the lone beacon to the conventions of other states as they defined their rights and wrote their constitutions, but those who believed they were faithfully following the Virginia example were slightly deceived. The text of the document adopted on 12 June 1776 was not widely available then or for many years thereafter. What was available was a printed copy of the draft declaration introduced by the committee on 27 May—that is, without the additions made by the full convention, with the prohibition against bills of attainder, and without Madison's amendment guaranteeing religious freedom. This unfinished text had been printed as a handbill in Williamsburg in May and in the *Virginia Gazette* on 1 June 1776. Copies of the documents had found their way rapidly to Philadelphia, where in June the committee's proposals were printed in city newspapers, and from them copied in nearly every major newspaper in the United States by the end of the summer. Before the end of December the committee's draft had been printed in London, and within a short time it had been translated into French and printed in Paris, as well.

Benjamin Franklin employed the committee's text as the basis for the bill of rights he wrote for the Pennsylvania Constitution of 1776. John Adams used it as the outline for the one he wrote for the Massachusetts Constitution of 1780. The French translation formed the basic text from which the Declaration of the Rights of Man and Citizen was compiled in 1789. And

---

7. Van Schreeven, Scribner, and Tarter, *Revolutionary Virginia*, 7:270–272, 449–450, 453–458.

numerous American state conventions copied all or parts of the committee's text into their constitutions during the nineteenth century.[8]

The Virginia Declaration of Rights represented a distillation of the rights British Americans believed that as free men they naturally possessed. Just as the documents of English history had been the immediate ancestors of the text of the declaration, it in turn was the parent of the Bill of Rights that was added to the Constitution of the United States in 1791.

•

The constitution written in Philadelphia in 1787 changed the character of the United States government and, for many Americans of the day, made necessary a national bill of rights. Supporters of the new constitution won its ratification in 1788 with the argument that the central government under the old Articles of Confederation had insufficient authority to preserve the prosperity, security, and union of the states: the nation needed a stronger central government and the new constitution provided it. Congress was given power to regulate foreign and interstate commerce, power to raise a peacetime army and navy, power to coin money and regulate its value, and power to levy taxes, excises, and tariffs instead of requesting state legislatures voluntarily to provide the national revenue. The new constitution also created a potentially powerful federal chief executive and a system of courts accountable neither to Congress nor to the states. With this consolidation of power came limitations upon the states' freedom of action, an elastic clause giving Congress all "necessary and proper" powers to carry out its broad new responsibilities, and a declaration that the laws and treaties made by the national government were to be the "supreme law of the land" in federal courts and take precedence over state laws.

The new constitution bolstered the national government with sufficient power to keep the federation of states from falling into disarray, but it also raised the specter of governmental invasions of the liberties that the Virginia Declaration of Rights and its counterparts in other states had forbidden state governments from infringing. This potential abuse of power—more than the strengthening of the national government itself—worried many members of the revolutionary generation. George Mason, one of Virginia's delegates to the Philadelphia convention, refused to sign the Constitution and returned

---

8. Gilbert Chinard, "Notes on the French Translations of the 'Forms of Government or Constitutions of the Several United States,' 1778 and 1783," in *American Philosophical Society Year Book, 1943* (Philadelphia, 1944), 98–106; Durand Echeverria, "French Publications of the Declaration of Independence and the American Constitutions, 1776–1783," *Papers of the Bibliographical Society of America* 47 (1953): 333–337; R. Carter Pittman, review of Richard L. Perry, ed., *Sources of Our Liberties* in *VMHB* 68 (1960): 110–112.

to Virginia determined to prevent its ratification. "There is no Declaration of Rights," thundered the first sentence of a critique of the Constitution that Mason wrote before he left Philadelphia. "The laws of the general government being paramount to the laws and constitution of the several States," Mason continued, "the Declarations of Rights in the separate States are no security. Nor are the people secured even in the enjoyment of the benefit of the common law. . . . There is no declaration of any kind, for preserving the liberty of the press, or the trial by jury in civil causes; nor against the danger of standing armies in time of peace."[9]

Edmund Randolph, then the governor of Virginia, also took exception to the Constitution, even though early in the convention's deliberations he had introduced the Virginia Plan, which had formed the first draft of the document. Randolph also refused to sign the Constitution, and he went back to Virginia hoping to summon a second convention to remove the provisions that he and others thought dangerous to liberty. Randolph's comments alarmed George Washington, president of the convention, and James Madison, who is known to posterity as the Father of the Constitution. Both feared that selfishness and parochialism throughout the union would fatally weaken the proposed constitution if the opportunity existed for rewriting the document. Immediately after the convention adjourned Madison hurried to the sessions of the moribund Confederation Congress in New York, but he worked hard to persuade his fellow Virginians that no new convention could devise a government half as good as the plan that he had guided through the Convention of 1787.

From New York on 24 October 1787 Madison sent a copy of the proposed constitution to his friend Thomas Jefferson, then United States minister to France. Jefferson found much to admire in the new framework, particularly the delicate system of checks and balances designed to separate the branches of government and prevent the accumulation of too much power in any one branch. Jefferson objected to other features of the plan, especially, he told Madison, "the omission of a bill of rights providing clearly and without the aid of sophisms for freedom of religion, freedom of the press, protection against standing armies, restriction against monopolies, the eternal and unremitting force of the habeas corpus laws, and trials by jury in all matters of fact." To another friend Jefferson suggested that nine states ratify the Constitution but that the remaining four states hold out for a satisfactory bill of rights. "Let me add," Jefferson reminded Madison, "that a bill of rights is what the people are entitled to against every government on

---

9. *Mason Papers*, 3:991–993.

earth . . . and what no just government should refuse, or rest on inference."[10]

Almost every clause in the Constitution provoked controversy. The advocates and opponents of ratification waged a spirited propaganda campaign during the winter of 1787–1788, disputing everything from the preamble's assertion that "We the people" formed the compact to the mode of ratification specified in article 7 of the text. They engaged in learned (and some not-so-learned) discussions of political theory as each side broadcast its darkest fears. Pointing to the absence of a bill of rights, opponents of ratification predicted that a powerful new government, unrestrained by a binding prohibition, would inevitably transgress against the liberties of the people. Advocates argued that the Constitution created a government powerful enough to maintain national unity and security but that the system of checks and balances and the independent judiciary protected the people from abuse. The government was to have specifically delegated powers, supporters asserted, and nothing in the Constitution gave the government power to interfere with any fundamental liberty.

This latter assertion was put most forcefully in the newspaper articles now known as *The Federalist*, eighty-five essays written by Alexander Hamilton, John Jay, and James Madison under the pen name Publius. In number eighty-four, Hamilton stated flatly "that bills of rights, in the sense and in the extent in which they are contended for, are not only unnecessary in the proposed constitution, but would even be dangerous. They would contain various exceptions to powers which are not granted; and on this very account, would afford a colourable pretext to claim more than were granted. For why declare that things shall not be done which there is no power to do? Why for instance, should it be said, that the liberty of the press shall not be restrained, when no power is given by which restrictions may be imposed?"[11] Hamilton's argument carried weight both with Federalists and Antifederalists (as the advocates and opponents of ratification came to be known) who feared that a list of rights in the Constitution would cast unenumerated rights into doubt. The Antifederalist fear that the government would expand its delegated powers by infringing upon rights that the Constitution did not protect was an issue strongly debated during the Massachusetts convention in January and February 1788. Some of the delegates wished to add a bill of rights to the Constitution before ratifying it, but

---

10. *Jefferson Papers*, 12:440, 558.

11. Alexander Hamilton, John Jay, and James Madison, *The Federalist*, ed. Jacob E. Cooke (Middletown, Conn., 1961), 579.

the Massachusetts Federalists successfully argued that if each state convention amended the document it would be virtually impossible to get the requisite nine states to agree to one text. The Massachusetts convention ratified the Constitution and proposed a list of amendments, including a declaration that the people and states retained all rights not prohibited by the Constitution, prohibition of monopolies, and a provision for grand jury indictments before criminal trials.[12]

The most important debate on the Constitution was held in the ratification convention in Richmond, Virginia, in June 1788. By then eight states had approved the document, and word was expected any day that New Hampshire's ratification would put the Constitution into force. Nevertheless, the outcome in Virginia was uncertain, and if Virginia and New York (where a convention was also meeting in June) refused to join the union the new government had little chance to succeed.

James Madison led the Federalists in the Virginia convention. His allies in debate included John Marshall; Edmund Pendleton, president of the convention; and Governor Edmund Randolph, who announced that despite his reservations about the Constitution he intended to vote for ratification as the best means to preserve the faltering union. Madison's explanations of the Constitution and Randolph's pleas for the salvation of the new nation formed the heart of the Federalist argument. Patrick Henry led the Antifederalist orators, assisted by the able debaters William Grayson and George Mason. Henry and Mason spoke repeatedly, descrying pernicious tendencies in the strengthened national government and depicting the lack of a bill of rights as a fatal omission.

For three weeks the debates raged. Henry ridiculed George Wythe's proposal of a single amendment to guarantee freedom of religion, freedom of the press, and other essential liberties. "Other essential rights," Henry cried! "What are they? The world will say that you intended to give them up. When you go into an enumeration of your rights, and stop that enumeration, the inevitable conclusion is, that what is omitted is intended to be surrendered." Edmund Randolph replied that by prohibiting bills of attainder and ex post facto laws and by establishing checks and balances the Constitution provided a government competent only to exercise its delegated powers. Randolph thought Wythe's proposal was neither dangerous nor essential, but "that it was in vain to provide against the exercise of a power which did not exist."[13] Neither side persuaded the other, and Virginia's ratification

---

12. Elliot, *Debates*, 2:177.
13. Ibid., 3:594, 600.

turned on the votes of a few undecided members, many from the western parts of the state, who were more interested in protecting American navigation on the Mississippi River than in anything else. The test of strength came on 25 June on the question of whether Virginia should ratify upon the condition that the other states agree to the Virginia convention's proposed amendments. The Antifederalists lost eighty to eighty-eight, and a motion for unconditional ratification then passed eighty-nine to seventy-nine. Wythe's motion to suggest amendments to the new Congress came back to the floor, and convention president Pendleton named Wythe chairman of a committee that met on 26 June to draw up the amendments.

On 27 June Wythe reported a series of amendments that went further than Madison liked. One proposed amendment limited the new government's authority to tax the people directly, a power that Madison thought fundamentally important but that Pendleton, Randolph, and a number of other Federalists thought needed curtailment. Over Patrick Henry's opposition, the convention adopted Wythe's committee report and list of suggested amendments, which included almost the entire text of the Virginia Declaration of Rights of 1776 and three substantial additions. The first guaranteed the rights "peaceably to assemble together to consult for the common good" and "to petition or apply to the legislature for redress of grievances." The second protected "freedom of speech, and of writing and publishing." And the third provided that the states "respectively retain every power, jurisdiction, and right, which is not by this Constitution delegated to the Congress of the United States, or to the departments of the federal government."[14]

•

On 21 June 1788 New Hampshire became the ninth state to ratify the Constitution, and on 26 July, a month after the Virginia convention had adjourned, New York approved the Constitution. Eleven states having ratified it, the Constitution was scheduled to go into operation in March 1789. During the winter the states chose presidential electors, senators, and congressmen. As anticipated, George Washington was unanimously elected president of the United States. Dominated by Patrick Henry, the General Assembly of Virginia named former Antifederalists William Grayson and Richard Henry Lee to the United States Senate. Voters in Virginia's ten congressional districts sent a mixture of former Federalists and Antifederalists to the House of Representatives. James Madison was conspicuous among the former.

---

14. Ibid., 3:657–662.

Soon after the First Congress met, Madison announced that he would propose amendments to the Constitution. Proposals for changes, he told a friend, "would have come *within three days*, from the adverse side," and it was "certainly best that they should appear to be the free gift of the friends of the Constitution rather than to be extorted by . . . its enemies." Madison had argued against the necessity for a bill of rights during the Virginia convention, but he yielded to those who wished one to be added to the Constitution. A bill of rights, he wrote in the summer of 1789, "is a thing not improper in itself and was always viewed in that light by myself. It may be less necessary in a republic, than in a Monarchy, & in a fedl Govt. than the former, but it is in some degree rational in every Govt." Besides, the Virginia convention had proposed amendments, and during his campaign for Congress he had promised that he would adhere to the "tacit compact" by which the convention had ratified the Constitution with the understanding that amendments would be submitted to the state legislatures.[15]

Seven state conventions had proposed amendments to the Constitution, and Madison reviewed all the proposals before he introduced a list of nineteen in the House of Representatives on 8 June 1789. He carefully ignored proposals that would have altered the substance of the Constitution, especially the Virginia convention's attempt to curtail the congressional power to levy direct taxes. Madison aimed instead at protecting fundamental liberties from the power of Congress or the judiciary, basing his amendments upon the Virginia Declaration of Rights as enlarged by Wythe's committee in June 1788. The House of Representatives approved seventeen of Madison's amendments on 24 August and sent them to the Senate, which consolidated those seventeen into twelve. After the two houses compromised on differences of phrasing, Congress on 25 September 1789 submitted twelve amendments to the state legislatures for approval according to the amendment procedure specified in article 5 of the Constitution.

The first two—restricting the size of the House of Representatives to between one and two hundred members and preventing Congress from altering the salaries of "Senators and Representatives . . . until an election of Representatives shall have intervened"—were never approved by enough state legislatures to become part of the Constitution. The third proposal, destined to become the First Amendment to the Constitution, contained Madison's pet proposal to prohibit the national government from legislating "respecting an establishment of religion, or prohibiting the free exercise thereof," and to forbid Congress from "abridging the freedom of speech, or

---

15. *Madison Papers*, 12:57–59, 193–210, 347.

of the press; or the right of the people peaceably to assemble, and to petition the Government for a redress of grievances."

What became the Second Amendment had originated in the prohibition of standing armies in the Virginia Declaration of Rights. This Congress had reduced to a right "to keep and bear Arms" for militia service in times of emergency. The Third Amendment prevented recurrence of the British practice of billeting soldiers in private buildings. The Fourth Amendment, again based on the Virginia Declaration of Rights, outlawed general warrants for searching the private homes of citizens. The Fifth Amendment preserved the rights of persons charged with committing crimes or whose property was taken for public use, and was rooted in British common law, the Virginia Declaration of Rights, and the Massachusetts convention's call for grand jury indictments before trials. The Sixth and Seventh amendments guaranteed the right to jury trials in criminal and civil cases and the rights of accused persons in criminal cases. The Eighth Amendment prevented judicial abuses such as persecution, excessive bail or fines, and cruel and unusual punishments. The Ninth Amendment responded to doubts raised during the ratification debates by declaring that "the enumeration in the Constitution of certain rights, shall not be construed to deny or disparage others retained by the people." Finally, to make it clear that the strong powers granted to the national government were limited and that the rights not specified in the other amendments were also protected, the Tenth Amendment declared "that powers not delegated to the United States by the Constitution, nor prohibited by it to the States, are reserved to the States respectively or to the people."[16]

By March 1790 eight state legislatures had approved all but the first, respecting the number of representatives. By November 1791 Rhode Island and Vermont had followed suit. Approval by one more state was needed.

Ironically, in Virginia, where the loudest cry about the absence of a bill of rights had been heard in 1788, the proposed amendments encountered stiff opposition in the General Assembly. Angered that Congress had not suggested amendments to reduce the strength of the national government, Senators Grayson and Lee, in a public letter to the General Assembly, condemned the amendments as inadequate. Grayson and Lee feared that a strong national government would eventually swallow up the sovereignties of the states and the liberties of the people, and they urged the General

---

16. Linda Grant De Pauw et al., eds., *Documentary History of the First Federal Congress of the United States of America, March 4, 1789–March 3 1791* (Baltimore, 1972–), 1:134, 135–139, 155–156, 158–168, 198; 3:84, 166, 228–229.

Assembly to reject the proposals and demand stronger restrictions upon the government.[17]

Few members of the House of Delegates who heard their senators' letter read on 19 October 1789 still hoped for a second convention to revise the Constitution; most were willing to give the new institutions a fair chance. They viewed the amendments as prudent guarantees, and on 30 November the delegates voted overwhelmingly to ratify the proposals, with a majority of about a dozen favoring the eleventh and twelfth.[18]

When the amendments came before the upper house only fifteen of the twenty-four senators were present, and by a vote of eight to seven the former Antifederalists postponed final action until after the next election so that the voters could let their representatives know of their disapproval of the amendments. Taking their cue from Grayson and Lee, the former Antifederalists in the state Senate declared that the amendments were "far short of what the people of Virginia wish" and "by no means sufficient to secure the rights of the people, or to render the government safe and desirable." The Senate faction warned their countrymen "not to be put off with amendments so inadequate."[19]

Led by Patrick Henry, the General Assembly procrastinated, as though waiting for a public reaction to undermine the new government. Not until autumn 1791, after two intervening elections, did the Virginia proponents again push for ratification of the twelve amendments. Francis Corbin, who had been a Federalist member of the 1788 convention, obtained the approval of the House of Delegates on 25 October to the first proposed amendment, dealing with the size of the House of Representatives, and the state Senate followed suit on 3 November. Then on 5 December Corbin persuaded the lower house to approve the eleven remaining amendments by an almost unanimous vote. Ten days later, with only three of the eight die-hard senators from the 1789 session still serving, the upper house ratified the other eleven amendments. The first two amendments never received the approval of enough legislatures to become part of the Constitution, but the remaining ten, upon ratification by the Virginia Senate on 15

---

17. James Curtis Ballagh, ed., *Letters of Richard Henry Lee* (New York, 1911–1914), 2:507–509.

18. *Journal of the House of Delegates, of the Commonwealth of Virginia . . . 1789* (Richmond, [1790]), 3, 79; *Madison Papers*, 12:454–455, 456, 460.

19. *Journal of the Senate of the Commonwealth of Virginia . . . 1789* (Richmond, 1828), 51–52, 58–59, 61–66; *Journal of the House of Delegates of the Commonwealth of Virginia . . . 1789*, 104, 105, 106, 107; *Madison Papers*, 12:454–455, 460, 464.

December 1791, became the Bill of Rights. Virginia had begun the process in the spring of 1776 and concluded it more than fifteen years later.[20]

•

Questions remained. Except that Congress is particularly mentioned in the First Amendment, the Bill of Rights does not name any agencies of government. Did the other amendments' restrictions apply only to Congress?

James Madison had always feared that the state governments rather than the national government posed the more serious threats to liberty. In Madison's day the United States was a predominantly agricultural nation of some 4 million people, and the scope of actions expected from the national government was narrow. The potential for invasion of liberties by Congress or the federal executive seemed slim compared to the potential misconduct of the state legislatures, which enacted laws that governed many facets of people's lives. Madison initially suggested that the Bill of Rights restrict the powers of *all* governments in the United States, but Congress was not inclined to restrain the state governments more than the Constitution already had, and ratification of a bill of rights that threatened the states with so explicit a statement of national superiority would have been impossible. Madison dropped the idea.

In 1833 a case reached the Supreme Court of the United States that presented this question clearly: did the Bill of Rights apply to the actions of state and local governments? The chief justice and author of the unanimous opinion of the court was John Marshall, who as a member of Virginia's Convention of 1788 had argued strongly for the Constitution. From his own knowledge Marshall explained that the men who adopted the Bill of Rights intended it as a restriction upon the national government only:

> the great revolution which established the constitution of the United States, was not effected without immense opposition. Serious fears were extensively entertained that those powers ... deemed essential to union ... might be exercised in a manner dangerous to liberty. In almost every convention by which the constitution was adopted, amendments to guard against the abuse of power were recommended. These amendments demanded security against the apprehended encroachments of the general government—not against those of the local governments.[21]

---

20. *Journal of the House of Delegates of the Commonwealth of Virginia ... 1791* (Richmond, 1791), 14, 103; *Journal of the Senate of Virginia, October Session, Anno Dom. 1791* (Richmond, 1791), 9, 60; *Madison Papers*, 14:85, 140–141.

21. *Barron* v. *Baltimore, U.S. Reports*, 32:250 (1833).

Between 1776 and 1833 Virginians such as Mason, Madison, and Marshall had taken the lead in the composition, adoption, and explanation of the Bill of Rights. After the Civil War, to protect the rights of former slaves, Congress proposed the Fourteenth Amendment, which prohibited state governments from depriving any person of "life, liberty, or property without due process of law." Ratified on 9 July 1868, the amendment soon gained broader significance: since the 1870s Congress and the federal courts have repeatedly declared that the liberty protected by the Fourteenth Amendment includes most of the fundamental guarantees embodied in the first ten amendments. In effect, the Fourteenth Amendment overturned John Marshall's decision and restored James Madison's original design to protect all the people from all abuses of government—federal, state, or local—with the Bill of Rights.

The fifteen years between the composition of the Virginia Declaration of Rights in Williamsburg and the final ratification of the Bill of Rights in Richmond transformed the relationship between citizens and their governments. By 1791 the basic structure of American government had been settled and the rights of the citizens protected by the Bill of Rights. Thomas Jefferson's hope, expressed in the spring of 1776, that his fellow Virginians would create a government better than that which they had known as subjects of the kings of England, was being realized. When President Jefferson read his inaugural address in 1801, the Bill of Rights was already a vital part of our American heritage. Among the principles by which Jefferson hoped to guide his administration, and by which he hoped the nation would guide its political future, were the cardinal provisions of the Bill of Rights:

> freedom of religion; freedom of the press, and freedom of person under the protection of the habeas corpus, and trial by juries impartially selected. These principles form the bright constellation which has gone before us and guided our steps through an age of revolution and reformation. The wisdom of our sages and blood of our heroes have been devoted to their attainment. They should be the creed of our political faith, the text of civic instruction, the touchstone by which to try the services of those we trust; and should we wander from them in moments of error or of alarm, let us hasten to retrace our steps and to regain the road which alone leads to peace, liberty, and safety.[22]

---

22. James D. Richardson, ed., *A Compilation of the Messages and Papers of the Presidents, 1789–1897* (Washington, D.C., 1896–1899), 1:323–324.

Jefferson's words embodied America's revolutionary faith that free people could govern themselves and that enlightened citizens, tolerant of diversity, would make a better world for themselves under the protections of the Bill of Rights than if individuals persecuted one another or employed the power of government to enforce conformity and crush freedom.

Congress shall make no law respecting an establishment of religion, or prohibiting the free exercise thereof; or abridging the freedom of speech, or of the press; or the right of the people peaceably to assemble, and to petition the government for a redress of grievances.
—First Amendment to the United States Constitution, *1791*

•

That Religion, or the duty which we owe to our Creator, and the manner of discharging it, can be directed only by reason and conviction, not by force or violence; and, therefore, all men are equally entitled to the free exercise of religion, according to the dictates of conscience; and that it is the mutual duty of all to practice Christian forbearance, love, and charity, towards each other.
—Article 16, Virginia Declaration of Rights, *1776*

The Bill of Rights

Chapter Two

Freedom of Religion and the First Amendment

MARTIN E. MARTY

MOST PEOPLE in all times and all places have been religious, ordering their lives in reference to that which they call sacred and sensing that life has purpose even if they cannot fully comprehend it. Whether or not they believed in God or the gods, they have found it important to engage themselves with some transcendent order of meaning, acknowledging, in George Mason's tolerant phrase, "the duty which we owe to our Creator." Most societies have set aside individuals and institutions to help people discharge this duty, and in Western society these individuals have charge of the institution we call the church.[1]

Most people in history have also been citizens, ordering their lives in reference to that which they call civil. Even anarchists, opponents of order, know that someone will force order upon them. Most people are not anarchists. They sense that order, as George Mason put it, "is, or ought to be, instituted for the common benefit, protection, and security of the people, nation, or community." In Western society this order is usually instituted as the state.[2]

In some societies the state is officially atheistic. Among these today the largest are in China and the Soviet Union. Such societies can easily define church-state relations. The all-powerful state seeks to do away with the church. Its leadership does not want competition from the church, does not want people to respond to any symbols or institutions except those of the state. Although in some such societies (including the Soviet Union) religion is so important to citizens that governments have had to allow them to worship, nevertheless laws closely regulate church affairs, and, in any competition between church and state, the state wins.[3]

---

1. Virginia Declaration of Rights, in *Mason Papers*, 1:289.

2. Ibid., 1:287.

3. For an account of the decisive early years of the Soviet Union, *see* N. S. Timasheff, *Religion in Soviet Russia, 1917–1942* (London, 1943); an author who consistently chronicles religion in Russia, any of whose works are commendable on this topic, is Michael Bordeaux.

In other societies the state is officially religious. The modern state of Iran, for example, is a theocracy (a word that literally means government by God). Religious leaders—in Iran the Shi'ite Muslim ayatollahs—have authority to make the laws of society correspond with the religious teachings of the official faith, as prescribed in the Koran and other sacred writings. Church prevails over state in public policy, and the state enforces the church's edicts.[4]

In the societies that are free or pluralistic—societies in which many religious views are openly represented—things are more complicated. Individual citizens may order their lives in reference both to the sacred and to the civil. The state cannot easily or permanently prevail over the church, because its policy of religious freedom allows citizens to resist its intrusions. Nor can the church prevail over the state, for not all citizens are members of the various denominations, and even if there were a single church the society would not permit it to decide secular matters.[5]

•

The society that first developed this modern concept of freedom of church and state was the United States. Beginning in the years just before the nation was formed in 1776 and continuing for several decades thereafter, Americans struggled—most dramatically in Virginia—to separate the civil and religious realms, church and state. The policy of separation developed for a number of reasons. The new nation was made up of thirteen colonies, in many of which an officially established religious denomination was given privileges and tax support while others were merely tolerated. Yet these colonies had different established churches, Congregationalism in the North, Anglicanism in the South, and no state-supported denominations in most middle colonies. The founders of the nation discovered that they could not possibly agree about which denomination should continue to be privileged.

What is more, most of these founders—notably Virginians such as Thomas Jefferson, James Madison, and even George Washington—did not believe that any church should be supported by people who did not want to support it. These men were members and often officers of the established Anglican church. But they were also influenced by the Enlightenment, an eighteenth-century network of ideas that promoted religious tolerance.

---

4. R. Hrair Dekmejian, *Islam in Revolution: Fundamentalism in the Arab World* (Syracuse, N.Y., 1985), surveys the entire Islamic militant scene.

5. For discussions of theoretical bases of church-state relations on an international basis, *see* A. F. Carrillo de Albornoz, *The Basis of Religious Liberty* (New York, 1963).

Enlightenment thinkers respected the Bible, Jesus, and Christianity; they generally believed in God. But they believed that human reason was able to reach God without miracles or divine revelation. Religion, they said, was a matter of opinion. You cannot force people to have an opinion, so you cannot force them to support an opinion they disagree with or find unimportant. Therefore they should not be forced to support or be members of any church.[6]

Some of these founders, in Virginia notably Patrick Henry with some support from George Washington, could approve what we call a "multiple establishment." That is an arrangement in which the state taxed people and then apportioned funds to the churches depending upon their size and other factors. Today such a position may seem foolish (especially when one considers that the *Yearbook of American and Canadian Churches* lists more than two hundred denominations and encyclopedias cite many more), but the view did not seem foolish then, when there were fewer churches. These founders could not imagine the state prospering without religion, without the church. For fourteen centuries the church in the Western world had always been supported by law. Take law, tax, and privilege away, and the churches might die—and morality or virtue would die with them.[7]

During the struggle for religious liberty in Virginia, Thomas Jefferson and James Madison took turns arguing the case for religious freedom. In 1784 Madison helped work for Patrick Henry's election to the governorship. This took Henry out of the legislature and made possible the passage, on 16 January 1786, of the Bill for Establishing Religious Freedom. With this act Virginia led the other states from the policy of religious toleration in Mason's Declaration of Rights ("the free exercise of religion, according to the dictates of conscience") toward the position that established churches contradicted "the plan of the holy author of our religion, who being lord both of body and mind, yet chose not to propagate [the church] by coercions on either . . . but to extend its influence by reason alone." New England was slower to make the change. Not until 1818 in Connecticut and 1833 in Massachusetts did establishment end. By that time most citizens of the United States had found that churches that were on their own—supported

---

6. Thomas J. Curry, *The First Freedoms: Church and State in America to the Passage of the First Amendment* (New York, 1986), traces the Virginian and other resolutions.

7. Henry F. May, *The Enlightenment in America* (New York, 1976), describes the Enlightenment background; *see* particularly "The Stoical South," 133–149.

by the donations of members—were healthier than state-subsidized religion had come to be.[8]

So decisive was the victory for separation of church and state that most latter-day Americans cannot imagine the day when their union had been taken for granted. Americans do not often think that they disrupted a fourteen-hundred-year-old pattern, that their founders pioneered a highly risky policy, one that they often called an experiment. Virtually all Americans today prefer things the way the founders arranged them and are strongly opposed both to the atheistic state and to the churchly state, and that is that.[9]

•

Or, that should be that, for it happens that the state struggles in Virginia, Connecticut, and Massachusetts did not settle, could not settle, everything. Two hundred years after those major battles, Americans still have not settled everything. As individuals most of them still live in church as well as state. Sometimes the claim of one competes with the other. Clearly, doing away with established churches did not mean the end of controversy.[10]

People still accuse others of trying to establish religion, to give the church privilege. Some see this happening when their fellow citizens propose that public funds even indirectly support parochial school education. Others complain that public support for chaplains in Congress or the military is a form of establishment. Just as frequently the controversy comes from another side: individuals or churches feel that the state forces its claims on their opinions, their consciences. Seldom does a month pass without newspaper headlines describing such conflicts.

• The religious beliefs of a sick child's parents do not permit blood transfusions, but a court steps in, takes the child into its custody, and orders a transfusion that saves its life.

• A denominational school in Nebraska will not allow the state to certify its teachers, and the minister goes to jail.

• Members of a religious group who resist sending their children to a "worldly" public high school run into laws requiring education until the age of sixteen.

---

8. Virginia Declaration of Rights, in *Mason Papers*, 1:289; A Bill for Establishing Religious Freedom, in *Jefferson Papers*, 2:545.

9. On "taken for grantedness" and radical change, *see* Winthrop S. Hudson, *The Great Tradition of the American Churches* (New York, 1953), chap. 2, "An Axiom of All Americans," 27–41.

10. An elaborate tracing of the consequential history is condensed from a three-volume work in Anson Phelps Stokes and Leo Pfeffer, *Church and State in the United States*, rev. ed. (New York, 1964); *see* especially 173–198.

• A church goes to court claiming that some of its commercial activities are religious and thus exempt from taxation. The courts find otherwise.

• Citizens fight over a constitutional amendment that would authorize prayer in public schools. Some say the founding fathers wanted religion, though not the church, to be part of the state. Others say such a policy violates the founders' intentions and is a form of privilege granted religion and thus, indirectly, the church.

When citizens cannot settle issues of this sort at the local level, they may press their cases until finally they reach the Supreme Court of the United States. Such cases are then decided on the basis of the Court's interpretation of the First Amendment, especially its religion clause.[11]

The First Amendment was the great federal constitutional effort to consolidate the states' various positions regarding religious freedom. At the same time it was designed to anticipate life in the new republic and set the guidelines and limits of federal involvement in religion. The religion clause of the amendment has only sixteen words, yet whole shelves of books, especially books of legal decisions, have been written on the basis of those words. Recent debates on the subject have also impelled scholars to learn more about the background of the First Amendment.[12]

Curiously, the religion clause reflects back on the Constitution itself and highlights one of that document's peculiarities. Until 1787, most societies assumed that their covenants and constituting documents had to mention God and define society's relationship to the deity. Not so in America, where the Constitution is almost silent about things religious. The Continental Congress often took up subjects relating to religion and in the Declaration of Independence forthrightly appealed to "nature's God," "their Creator," "the Supreme Judge of the world," and "Divine Providence," so we cannot say that the founders simply forgot about the subject.[13]

When they wrote the Constitution, however, the founders came up with a document in which one needs a microscope to find the religious traces, or

---

11. For contemporary debate, *see* Dean M. Kelley, ed., *Government Intervention in Religious Affairs* (New York, 1982).

12. Much of the debate over the First Amendment came from moderate and liberal sources until recently; for two differing neo-conservative approaches, *see* Robert L. Cord, *Separation of Church and State: Historical Fact and Current Fiction* (New York, 1982), and Walter Berns, *The First Amendment and the Future of American Democracy* (New York, 1976), chaps. 1 and 2, "Religion and the Founding Principle" and "Religion and the Supreme Court," 1–79.

13. On the constitutional process, *see* Curry, *The First Freedoms*, chap. 8, "Congress Shall Make No Law," 193–222.

at least a periscope to search for them around corners. The document is dated "in the year of our Lord," but that may have been habit. It excludes the Christian holy day, Sunday, from the days counted before a president must exercise his power of veto. The only important mention of religion is in article 6, which ruled out religious tests for officeholders.[14]

Had the founders foreseen our debates over church and state, some people argue today, they would have done something about the religious theme in the Constitution. Not likely. They not only seem to have anticipated "our" debates; they were already having them. In their day critics complained that their religious views were not surfacing in the charter documents of the republic. In the Philadelphia meetings of the Convention of 1787 the founders did not pray, and on 28 June 1787 the convention defeated a resolution by Benjamin Franklin who thought a prayer would be in order.[15]

When citizens in the states agitated for a bill of rights to limit the federal government, the issue of religion had to be faced. James Madison wrote the first draft of a religion clause, a committee argued over his wording and refined it, a conference committee worked out differences between House and Senate versions, and the result was the all-important final text:

> Congress shall make no law respecting an establishment of religion, or prohibiting the free exercise thereof.

People have argued over almost every one of these sixteen words, beginning with the first, which many regard as most important. The measure limited only the Congress. Since many states had religious establishments and wanted to keep them, the framers denied Congress any powers over state establishments.[16]

Both sides in the religion debates liked this clause. People such as Thomas Jefferson could use it to say that citizens had freedom *from* religion. Religious people who had known persecution or who were members of minority denominations that resented establishments could say that they had freedom *for* religion. This double-edged assurance was protected by the negative wording of the second phrase: Congress shall make no law "prohibiting the free exercise" of religion. In neither phrase of the religion

---

14. On the omission of *God* from the Constitution, *see* Stokes and Pfeffer, *Church and State*, 90–92.

15. An account of Franklin's call for prayer is in Esmond Wright, *Franklin of Philadelphia* (Cambridge, Mass., 1986), 340–344.

16. A lively and informed account of Madison's role is in William Lee Miller, *The First Liberty: Religion and the American Republic* (New York, 1986); *see* especially 124–126.

clause did the founders seek to summarize human history or write a book of philosophy. They were both people of conscience and politicians, which means that they had both to represent and protect the interests of their constituents and to be aware of what agreements could be struck with the other states and what practices of other states had to be avoided.[17]

•

For seventy years the story ended here. On 17 December 1791 the Bill of Rights went into effect. Congress was out of the picture in matters of religion, which were left exclusively to the states, where patterns and policies varied. Some states had established denominations. Some had constitutional limits on the free exercise of religion—including, for a time, some "Christian" clauses that made Judaism and other faiths technically illegal.[18]

The issue grew more complicated seventy years later. During Reconstruction, in an effort to assure rights to black Americans in all states, the nation adopted the Fourteenth Amendment to the Constitution in 1868. This amendment does not mention religion, and its framers probably would have been surprised to learn that their amendment ever touched on the subject. However, the Fourteenth Amendment provides that "No state shall abridge the privileges or immunities of citizens of the United States" and assures due process and equal protection of the law to residents of every state.[19]

Between 1900 and 1939 the Supreme Court began to view the First Amendment in light of the Fourteenth. In a famous case in 1940, *Cantwell v. Connecticut*, the Court ruled that the state of Connecticut had violated the rights of Jehovah's Witnesses. The Fourteenth Amendment was seventy years old before it was used to settle a case involving religious freedom, but it has been so used ever since, and today no one can look at the First Amendment except through Fourteenth Amendment spectacles.[20]

In recent controversies some Americans have argued that we should go back to the original notion. Those who advocate a state's rights approach believe that we would have very different rulings on church and state and

---

17. *See* ibid., 125–132, on "free exercise."

18. For continuing constitutional struggles respecting, especially, Jews, *see* Morton Borden, *Jews, Turks, and Infidels* (Chapel Hill, 1984), 11–15, 28–52.

19. The assault on application of the Fourteenth Amendment to church-state cases is a political issue in recent years; typical of the attacks is Cord, *Separation of Church and State*, chap. 4, "Extending the Covenant: The Establishment Clause and the Fourteenth Amendment," 84–101.

20. On "Cantwell," *see* Richard E. Morgan, *The Supreme Court and Religion* (New York, 1972), 60–67.

religious freedom if the states were free to determine policy. Many state legislatures and courts might allow public schools to have devotions and to teach the truth of religion in "values" courses. The Supreme Court, with its eye on the greater national variety and interests, limits such practices, and so far no one has successfully challenged its application of the Fourteenth Amendment in First Amendment cases.[21]

Today's citizens take for granted two very broad and general ideas. Congress will not do anything overt to set up what in colonial America looked like an establishment of religion. Congress will pass laws assuring great measures of free exercise of religion. Americans also assume that there are certain limits to free exercise. If someone advocated infant sacrifice in the name of religion, the law would prohibit this. Most of the time, however, citizens boast of the fact that America assures a freer exercise of faith than has any other complex society in history.[22]

These broad outlines, however, are far removed from the way life is lived. Since about 1940 the nation has witnessed a constant testing of the First Amendment, an unending sequence of debates about its meaning. Anyone who thought religion was a quiet, settled, or dead issue would quickly revise his or her opinion simply by watching the Court's experience with religion. To make sense, then, of the First Amendment, we do well to note some of the ways it has come up in modern Supreme Court cases, both with respect to establishment and to the free exercise of religion.

•

The issues of religious freedom, church establishment, and free exercise have come a long way since the Virginia debates of the 1780s and the First Amendment of 1791. No one then pictured a nation with freed slaves, people of Oriental faiths, and thriving churches with billions of dollars worth of real estate and programs that touch the lives of people throughout the country and the world. The cozy world of established and dissenting Protestant churches is gone, and a wild pluralism of religious options has replaced it. Decades of court decisions have extended the boundaries of permissible and defensible free exercise.[23]

This is not the place to review all the possible situations. So far as free exercise of religion is concerned, the most interesting First Amendment

---

21. For conservative evangelical and fundamentalist Protestant arguments, *see* Lynn R. Buzzard and Samuel Ericsson, *The Battle for Religious Liberty* (Elgin, Ill., 1982).

22. On the limits of sectarian appreciation, *see* Kelley, *Government Intervention in Religious Affairs.*

23. A convenient excerpting of and introduction to "free exercise" cases is Leo Pfeffer, *Religious Freedom* (Lincolnwood, Ill., 1977), pt. 3, "Free Exercise," 105–174.

tests concern conscientious objection to military service. A nation that considers its defense important cannot lightly permit religiously based claims to prevent conscription for military service, but some faiths anchor their pacifist beliefs so deeply that the draft would limit their free exercise. Some of the smaller religious groups pose the most difficult cases. The Jehovah's Witnesses, for example, refuse to salute the flag or engage in patriotic exercises, since they consider these to be idolatrous. The courts have interpreted the free exercise clause to extend the widest possible liberties to the Witnesses.

While free exercise cases usually engage the interest of small minorities or individuals, such as conscientious objectors, the establishment cases involve large portions of the electorate and more complex social issues. The best illustration of this is found in the cases of *Engel* v. *Vitale* (1962) and *School District of Abington Township, Pennsylvania* v. *Schempp* (1963). The first prohibited a state-prescribed prayer in public schools, and the second any devotional exercises in public school classrooms. The Supreme Court ruled that such exercises, even if they appeared to be voluntary, discriminated against children whose families were opposed to devotion and prayer or whose religious convictions did not permit them to participate in such prayer in pluralist settings.[24]

The rulings were unpopular. Almost 80 percent of the American people had no objection to the hint of religious establishment that goes with a public school setting up religious exercises. Therefore, there have been efforts to ignore the Court rulings, to restrict the Court's jurisdiction in such cases, or to amend the Constitution in order to allow for such public religious exercises. Only slightly less emotionally charged have been cases involving transporting children to parochial schools on public school buses, providing lunches or textbooks for parochial school children, or offering "released time" for religious education. The courts have seen most of these practices as subtle forms of religious establishment, and have tended to rule against them on the basis of the First Amendment.[25]

Such controversy has led students of the First Amendment and advocates of differing policies into several camps. One camp maintains a "secular" reading. Its critics say that in this reading the First Amendment itself becomes an idol, an icon, an article of faith used by the Court to elevate a godless religion to a privileged position. A second camp would recede from

---

24. On establishment clauses, *see* ibid., pt. 2, "Establishment," 37–104.

25. Conservative Protestant complaint on these decisions is discussed in Lynn R. Buzzard, *Schools: They Haven't Got a Prayer* (Elgin, Ill., 1982).

the Fourteenth Amendment readings and go back to the First Amendment as originally fashioned. This would simply take the federal government entirely out of establishment and free exercise cases and throw them into the politics of the states. A third camp says that the founders were religious people who could not have meant the First Amendment to prevent either religious exercises in public schools or the state subsidy of some parochial school activities. They say that since the founders were deists or theists, people who believed in religion or God, we must assume that they did not intend the First Amendment to rule out a religious interpretation of American life. They assert that religion, though not the churches, should be privileged.[26]

Through the years, as the texture of American life becomes ever more diverse with the contributions of Oriental, black, Hispanic, and other groups, we can probably expect Court decisions to shift interpretations to some extent. Whatever may be ahead, we can also expect that Americans will not agree on all details of First Amendment debates and resolutions. They have the right to disagree, to state their cases, to try to win approval for them in state legislatures, Congress, the court of public opinion, or the courts. They have these rights because "it's a free country." It's a free country because the founders, in drafting our Constitution and Bill of Rights, helped assure that it would be free—if later generations cared to keep it so.

---

26. An excellent Madisonian outline for background to these debates is Paul J. Weber, "James Madison and Religious Equality," in *Review of Politics* 44 (1982): 163–186.

Congress shall make no law respecting an establishment of religion, or prohibiting the free exercise thereof; or abridging the freedom of speech, or of the press; or the right of the people peaceably to assemble, and to petition the government for a redress of grievances.
—First Amendment to the United States Constitution, *1791*

•

That the freedom of the Press is one of the great Bulwarks of liberty and can never be restrained but by despotic Government.
—Article 12, Virginia Declaration of Rights, *1776*

The
Bill of
Rights

Chapter Three

Freedom of the Press

ROBERT A. RUTLAND

THE CONCEPT OF FREEDOM OF THE PRESS, unique to Western civilization, first took root in England and was transplanted to the North American seaboard colonies early in the eighteenth century. Not all the thirteen colonies had been established when the idea gained currency, but by 1765 all of them defended it vigorously. Few ideas have permeated a society so quickly as this notion. Children born during the Stamp Act crisis were just entering adulthood when the abstract theory became part of the Constitution of the United States in 1791. Considering mankind's aversion to the alteration of fundamental ideas, this rapid commitment to a free press as a bedrock of democratic societies is almost without precedent.

The use of movable type began in northern Europe in the middle of the fifteenth century. A century later, the technique had spread and was used for purposes far beyond the original scheme of biblical copywork. Printing made freedom of expression possible, but the controls on printing and ideas were part of a churchly apparatus that absolute monarchs soon adapted to their own purposes. As the Vatican and secular rulers perceived dangers in an uncontrolled press they devised forms of censorship to prevent the publication of heretical or treasonous works. By the 1660s, after challenges to authority had brought civil war in England, centuries of suppression had created a long list of martyrs. Less than two decades after the poet John Milton's defense of freedom of thought in *Areopagitica* (London, 1644), Parliament passed the Licensing Act of 1662, which empowered royal officials to investigate and suppress unauthorized pamphlets, books, or broadsides.[1]

When the explosion of commercial activity in England, Holland, Venice, and other seafaring states demanded the easy exchange of information, enterprising printers developed newspapers to serve merchants, shipowners, insurance brokers, and investors. Such late-seventeenth-century courants

---

1. Carl Stephenson and Frederick G. Marcham, eds., *Sources of English Constitutional History* (New York, 1937), 387; Fredrick Seaton Siebert, *Freedom of the Press in England, 1476–1776* (Urbana, Ill., 1952), 48–260.

and gazettes were often semiofficial, but others quickly turned this newly created medium, the newspaper, into a vehicle for expressing ideas concerning more than sea voyages, cargoes, and maritime risks.

One of the earliest libertarian heroes was John Lilburne, an English political agitator who was charged before the Star Chamber in 1637 with printing seditious books. In his classic defense, Lilburne told his judges they could not force him to give incriminating evidence against himself. "I think by the law of the land, that I may stand upon my just defence, and not answer to your interrogatories," the printer insisted. Lilburne's stand was justified, and it became part of English law by an act of Parliament in 1641, but it took another fifty years before Parliament surrendered the right of government surveillance over the printing houses of England.[2]

•

Meanwhile, a printing press had been brought to the Massachusetts Bay Colony in 1638, although as much as a century later ink-stained colonial journeymen labored only in Boston, Philadelphia, New York, Williamsburg, Charleston, and a few other seaports. Both overbearing royal appointees and colonial legislatures kept the spirit of the Licensing Act alive in America long after its formal death in 1695, so that printers who defied local authorities still risked fines, imprisonment, and the ruin of their trade. The 1735 trial of John Peter Zenger, a German immigrant who printed the *New York Weekly Journal*, lit a beacon for Americans who resisted authoritarianism in any form.[3]

Zenger was charged with printing seditious libel, and his conviction was almost a certainty, for by common law the jury was expected to ascertain only one fact: had Zenger printed the material in question? By means still not perfectly clear, however, the jury brushed aside the matter of publication and acquitted Zenger, holding both that truth was a defense and that juries could determine the validity of the evidence and thus reach verdicts based on common sense rather than common law. The lesson was not lost on Americans as tension built between the colonies and the mother country.[4]

In England the rigorous rules of law had been challenged by courageous essayists such as Thomas Gordon and John Trenchard, whose *Cato's Letters* (newspaper essays first printed in England between November 1720 and

---

2. Siebert, *Freedom of the Press in England*, 260–263.

3. Livingston Rutherfurd, *John Peter Zenger, His Press, His Trial and A Bibliography of Zenger Imprints* (New York, 1904); Leonard W. Levy, *Emergence of a Free Press* (New York, 1985), 38–45.

4. James Alexander, *A Brief Account of the Case and Trial of John Peter Zenger*, ed. Stanley N. Katz, 2d. ed. (Cambridge, Mass., 1972); Levy, *Emergence of a Free Press*, 128–134.

December 1723 and reprinted throughout the colonies by Zenger and others) helped promote the notion that freedom of expression was an Englishman's birthright. Their "Letter No. 32," first published in 1721, struck one of the earliest blows on behalf of a free press, for it attacked the prevailing concept that criticism of government officials was libelous per se: "The exposing therefore of public Wickedness, as it is a Duty which every Man owes to Truth and his Country, can never be a Libel in the Nature of Things." The Zenger ruling was in this spirit, and although English lawyers and jurists decried the decision it was a warning for all to heed.[5]

In 1765 the first major break between colonists and the British administration tested American printers and their readers. Searching for new revenues, Parliament had imposed a relatively light tax on colonial newspapers that was similar to the levy already imposed on English newspapers. When Parliament passed the Stamp Act in 1764 the American newspapers were few—twenty-three in all the colonies—but their reach was long and powerful. Literate British Americans read attacks on the obnoxious law from the Maine district to Georgia as printers reacted to the Stamp Act with widespread unanimity. Most proprietors of presses vowed that they would not buy stamped paper, and the Sons of Liberty menaced those who dared accept the new law without protest. Ultimately, not a single American newspaper appeared on stamped paper, and mob action made the law a dead letter in all the colonies. Indeed, so prevalent was the American public's acceptance of the free press as a "Palladium of English liberty" that the contemporary London cause célèbre stirred by government actions against John Wilkes and his *North Briton* extended across the Atlantic. Wilkes became a popular hero to newspaper readers in Boston, Philadelphia, and Williamsburg.[6]

During the eighteenth century, nothing akin to the proliferation of newspapers in Great Britain and America was going on elsewhere. Absolutism still reigned over most of the world, and the clash of political or religious ideas was suppressed by censorship, royal edict, and imprisonment. Throughout British North America, literacy, distaste for royal authority, bustling energy, and the population's antipathy toward governmental regulation or interference gave the term *New World* far more than just a

---

5. John Trenchard and Thomas Gordon, *Cato's Letters: Or, Essays on Liberty, Civil and Religious, and Other Important Subjects*, 6th ed. (London, 1755), 1:246–247.

6. Robert Allen Rutland, *The Birth of the Bill of Rights, 1776–1791* (Chapel Hill, 1955; reprint, Boston, 1983), 4–11; Edmund S. Morgan and Helen M. Morgan, *The Stamp Act Crisis: Prologue to Revolution* (Chapel Hill, 1953), 240–242; Bernard Bailyn, *The Ideological Origins of the American Revolution* (Cambridge, Mass., 1967), 110–111.

geographical meaning. Englishmen began to prize their political freedom
and to exalt its value beyond life itself. British Americans of the 1770s
considered the English heritage theirs, too, but their vision was of a future
with greater opportunities, a more abundant life, and a wider variety of
freedoms than even contemporary Britons enjoyed. This message was
implicit in the propaganda barrage mounted when the Intolerable Acts of
1774 began to force Americans to decide whether the old ties with England
were worth retaining. Samuel Adams, John Dickinson, James Otis, Jr., and
Thomas Jefferson were foremost among the essayists who exhorted American readers in pamphlets and newspaper columns.[7]

The Continental Congress itself resorted to the press in 1774, establishing
a committee that "superintend[ed] the translating, printing, publishing &
dispersing" of an inflammatory *Letter to the Inhabitants of the ·Province of
Quebec.* In this instructive propaganda piece the Congress set forth a list of
liberties, including freedom of the press, that British Americans possessed
from birth. The importance of a free press consisted

> besides the advance of truth, science, morality, and arts in general, in its
> diffusion of liberal sentiments on the administration of government, its ready
> communication of thoughts between subjects, and its consequential promo-
> tion of union among them, whereby oppressive officers are shamed or
> intimidated, into more honourable and just modes of conducting affairs.

A better definition of what the Founding Fathers meant by a free press
cannot be found. Clearly, freedom of the press—that shibboleth of American revolutionary propaganda—was a right exercised in order to maintain
political liberty. Accordingly, tory printers, by their pro-British stance,
rendered themselves unfit custodians of this birthright. After blood was shed
at Lexington and Concord, they were often forced to flee patriot mobs. The
tory's right to freedom of the press extended only the length of British
bayonets: tory presses operated openly only where the British army was in
control.[8]

---

7. Samuel Adams to Richard Henry Lee, 15 July 1774, in *Writings of Samuel Adams*, ed.
Harry Alonzo Cushing (New York, 1904–1908), 3:139; Benjamin Fletcher Wright, Jr.,
American Interpretations of Natural Law (Cambridge, Mass., 1931), 64–71; Thomas Jefferson,
A Summary View of the Rights of British America, in *Writings*, ed. Merrill D. Peterson (New
York, 1984), 120–122.

8. *Proceedings of the Continental Congress* (Philadelphia, 1774), 3; Worthington Chauncey
Ford et al., eds., *Journals of the Continental Congress, 1774–1789* (Washington, D.C.,

•

By 1776 the movement for independence had raised questions about the kind of government that would best preserve the liberty that colonists believed Great Britain denied them. Virginia, the largest and most populous state, supplied not only a commander in chief for the Continental army but also a stock of popular political ideas that were grafted onto local political procedures throughout the country. Abstract notions of legislative supremacy or of checks and balances within a republican framework were heard everywhere in America early in 1776, but the main business of constitution making required a sturdier base. John Adams, combining flattery with truth, said "We all look up to Virginia for examples."[9]

The political leadership of the Old Dominion responded, first by calling on the Continental Congress to declare that the colonies "were, and of right ought to be, free and independent states." Then, before Congress was able to act, the Virginians themselves held a convention (which succeeded the defunct House of Burgesses) and drafted both the Constitution of 1776 and the Declaration of Rights, documents that became bellwethers for other colonies. Written chiefly by George Mason, both documents were adopted in Virginia before Congress cut the imperial knot in July.[10]

Mason's elegantly worded list of the elements of a British American's birthright included life, liberty, and "the Means of acquiring and possessing Property, and pursueing and obtaining Happiness and Safety," as well as provisions for religious toleration and jury trials. Someone on the drafting committee—probably Thomas Ludwell Lee—added a few significant clauses, including the one declaring "that the freedom of the press, being the great bulwark of Liberty, can never be restrained but in a despotic government."[11]

Four states adopted a similar proposition during the constitution-drafting decade that followed Virginia's exemplary action. Nor was this clause considered a mere abstraction, for the men who served on drafting committees had lived through the Stamp Act crisis, read of Wilkes's ordeal, and watched the path to independence charted in newspaper columns by the

---

1904–1937), 1:63n, 113; Robert A. Rutland, *The Newsmongers: Journalism in the Life of the Nation, 1690–1972* (New York, 1973), 50–51.

9. John Adams to Patrick Henry, 3 June 1776, in *Papers of John Adams*, ed. Robert J. Taylor et al. (Cambridge, Mass., 1977–), 4:234–235.

10. David John Mays, *Edmund Pendleton, 1721–1803* (Cambridge, Mass., 1952; reprint, Richmond, 1984), 2:108–109; Samuel Eliot Morison, ed., *Sources and Documents Illustrating the American Revolution, 1764–1768, and the Formation of the Federal Constitution*, 2d. ed. (Oxford, 1929), 149.

11. *Mason Papers*, 1:274–291.

"Pennsylvania Farmer," John Dickinson, and other critics of royal colonial policy after 1764. Even where the states made no provision for a free press (or, as in Connecticut and Rhode Island, kept going with old charters tacitly amended), the idea that Americans possessed something unique in their freedom of expression took root at once. In 1787 a Harvard senior finished reading Montesquieu's *Spirit of the Laws* and observed: "I think he says not all he would have said, had he lived in a Country where a man might with impunity publish his sentiments." Within little more than a decade the linkage between general political liberty and freedom of the press had become commonplace.[12]

In 1787, when sporadic problems of credit, commerce, unpaid taxes, and other financial ills seemed beyond solution under the Articles of Confederation, the convention in Philadelphia proved strikingly successful. Not only did the best minds in the young republic gather in one hall but a sense of urgency pushed them to create, within a matter of months, a whole new system of national government. The business was far advanced when George Mason, a member of the five-man Virginia delegation, sounded the alarm over the convention's failure to include a bill of rights in the draft constitution. Content with the counterargument that most states already had formal documents guaranteeing personal freedom, Mason's colleagues in Philadelphia shouted him down, finished the Constitution, and in September 1787 dispatched it to the thirteen states for their approval.[13]

Those who opposed an unqualified ratification of the Constitution quickly seized upon this misjudgment by the majority at the Convention of 1787: "There is no declaration of rights," Mason wrote in his critical pamphlet, which became a chief weapon in the hands of the Antifederalists.[14] Even as perceptive a political leader as James Madison, who had worked with Mason in Virginia's convention of 1776, had misread the people's attachment to the principles embodied in written bills of rights.

Madison, serving in the last sessions of the Continental Congress in New York, made his desk a clearinghouse for allies committed to ratifying the Constitution. Early in 1788 it was apparent that compromises might be necessary to get the plan ratified and keep the Constitution intact until the new government could have a few years' trial. Starting with the Massachu-

---

12. David Grayson Allen et al, eds., *Diary of John Quincy Adams* (Cambridge, Mass., 1981–), 2:146.

13. Rutland, *Birth of the Bill of Rights*, 116–125.

14. Max Farrand, ed., *Records of the Federal Convention of 1787* (New Haven, 1911–1937), 2:637–640.

setts convention in February, Federalists conceded that once the Constitution was in operation some kind of bill of rights would be considered by the new federal Congress.[15]

Madison soon realized that, even in his home state, an unconditional ratification could not be achieved without some compromise on this glaring omission. During one of the greatest political debates in American history, Madison took on Mason and Patrick Henry in the Virginia Convention of 1788. He directed the Federalists to a narrow victory only after conceding a lengthy list of recommended amendments to the opposition. Then Madison ran for a seat in the newly created House of Representatives against his old friend, James Monroe, who had voted against ratification. He defeated Monroe, but only after assuring voters in his piedmont district that he would put the adoption of a bill of rights among the first orders of business in 1789.[16]

Campaign promises are never easily filled. Madison scoured the bills of rights and recommended amendments passed by the state conventions, searching for a consensus about the essence of American freedom. Undeterred by the apathy of his colleagues in the House of Representatives, Madison introduced a set of amendments in June 1789 that included a clause holding that freedom of the press "shall be inviolable." When the House and Senate committees went over Madison's list, the now-famous First Amendment emerged with its explicit prohibition: "Congress shall make no law . . . abridging freedom of speech, or of the press."[17]

The proposed amendment was third in the list of twelve sent from Congress to the states for ratification. The first and second proposals on that list failed to win sufficient support from the states and were dropped, so that on 15 December 1791, when Virginia ratified the surviving ten amendments, the Bill of Rights as we know it at last became the law of the land.[18] Virginians like to point out that many of George Mason's phrases from Virginia's 1776 Declaration of Rights were proposed to the whole nation in

---

15. Samuel Bannister Harding, *The Contest Over the Ratification of the Federal Constitution in the State of Massachusetts* (New York, 1896), 24; Rutland, *Birth of the Bill of Rights*, 146–150.

16. James Madison to George Eve, 2 Jan. 1789, in *Madison Papers*, 11:404–405; Lyman H. Butterfield, "Elder John Leland, Jeffersonian Itinerant," *American Antiquarian Society Proceedings*, new ser., 62, pt. 2 (1952): 164.

17. Hugh Williamson to James Madison, 24 May 1789, and James Madison to Thomas Jefferson, 27 May 1789, *Madison Papers*, 12:183–186.

18. *Annals of Congress*, 1:440–467. Madison's manuscript outline is reprinted in *Madison Papers*, 12:193–195; Rutland, *Birth of the Bill of Rights*, 217.

1789 by James Madison and declared ratified in 1791 by Secretary of State Thomas Jefferson.

Whatever its antecedents, the Bill of Rights promised the blessings of liberty to all Americans. More state bills of rights guaranteed a free press as Vermont, Kentucky, and Tennessee came into the Union, but a serious challenge to an untrammeled press came in 1798 when Congress passed the Alien and Sedition Acts. Signed by President John Adams, the sedition law imposed heavy penalties on any person who "with intent to defame" the federal government, the Congress, or the president spoke, wrote, or printed words judged to be "false, scandalous and malicious." The law was full of words like "sedition," "unlawful combinations," and "hostile designs," but in practice its intent was to gag Republican newspapers and orators who were trying to vote the Federalists out of office.[19] The short-lived legislation expired in 1800, but some editors were jailed and fined, and critics who claimed that the law violated the First Amendment never tested its constitutionality.

•

Through technological improvements, the press grew at a remarkable pace during the nineteenth century without concern for censorship of the sort attempted between 1798 and 1800. When an antebellum newspaper editor was threatened, it was by an offended citizen with a bullwhip or by a mob angry about an antislavery editorial or the spread of unorthodox religious sects. During the Mexican War, when some northern editors opposed to the war recommended that American soldiers find "hospitable Mexican graves," no censor's lash prevented their outbursts. In the Civil War, however, a combination of federal marshals and furious mobs intimidated Northern critics of the Union war effort while Confederate editors exasperated Southern generals and civilian officials alike with outspoken criticism of their conduct.[20]

War tests the limits of free expression. During World War I public opinion and legislation dried up the nation's major foreign-language newspapers and severely crimped the Socialist party press. The wave of state sedition and antisyndicalism laws after 1917 tested the nation's will and elicited Justice Oliver Wendell Holmes's view (which the Supreme Court

19. James Morton Smith, "The Enforcement of the Alien Friends Act of 1798," *Mississippi Valley Historical Review* 41 (1954–1955): 86; John C. Miller, *Crisis in Freedom: The Alien and Sedition Acts* (Boston, 1951), 138–139; James Morton Smith, *Freedom's Fetters: The Alien and Sedition Laws and American Civil Liberties* (Ithaca, N.Y., 1956), 179–187.

20. Rutland, *Birth of the Bill of Rights*, 219–228.

endorsed twenty years later) that freedom of expression could only be abridged when

> words are used in such circumstances and are of such a nature as to create a clear and present danger that they will bring about the substantive evils that Congress has a right to prevent.

Then, in its *Gitlow* v. *New York* decision of 1925, the high court held that freedom of the press was a right protected from state interference under the due process clause of the Fourteenth Amendment.[21]

The breakthrough decision came in 1931, when the Court declared that a Minnesota "gag" law permitting injunctions to prevent newspapers from printing scandalous, defamatory, or obscene material violated the constitutional guarantee of a free press. Citing Blackstone's position that "the liberty of the press . . . consists in laying no *previous* restraints upon publication," the Court went on to say that while this old concept was too narrow, "liberty of speech, and of the press, is . . . not an absolute right." After this *Near* v. *Minnesota* decision, federal and state officials were wary of any attempt to bridle the press so long as the published matter was subject to the usual restraints of libel and defamation laws. In such cases, proof that the published statements were true and published without malice made a perfect defense.[22]

With the exception of wartime censorship and the occasional restrictions imposed by vociferous public opinion, the freedom of the press (including radio, television, and motion pictures) has been constantly expanding since the *Near* decision. The common intent of 1791 that freedom of the press should allow unlimited discussion of public issues came into historic focus in 1964 when the Supreme Court ruled in *New York Times Co.* v. *Sullivan* that criticism of public officials could go beyond the ordinary rules of restraint and still not constitute a violation of the First Amendment. The key legal words—*defamatory* and *malicious*—applied in the cases of private citizens, the Court decided, but did not shield elected or appointed public officials from the media.[23] In the 1979 *Richmond Newspapers, Inc.* case the Court decided in favor of media access to criminal trials regardless of circumstances. Only

---

21. *Schenck* v. *United States, U.S. Reports*, 249:52 (1919); Edward S. Corwin, *The Constitution and What It Means Today*, 11th ed. (Princeton, 1954), 196–198; *Gitlow* v. *New York, U.S. Reports*, 268:666 (1925).

22. Rutland, *Birth of the Bill of Rights*, 229–230.

23. Ibid., 230–238; Robert J. Steamer, *The Supreme Court in Crisis: A History of Conflict* (Amherst, Mass., 1971), 193–194; Robert G. McCloskey, *The Modern Supreme Court* (Cambridge, Mass., 1972), 338.

inside courtrooms—where most judges forbid cameras as impediments to justice—are reporters subject to some control.

The few curbs on the press in the early 1980s related to local obscenity laws, still a murky area, and the authority of judges to call reporters to testify about their sources in connection with criminal prosecutions or civil litigation. Although some reporters and editors have been found guilty of an invasion of "the right of privacy," the courts have been lenient in most cases involving public figures. The Supreme Court noted in 1931 that freedom of the press is not an absolute right, but Americans fifty years later still seem to believe that the risks of a free press are less onerous than the dangers known to exist where the press is shackled. To distinguish between liberty and licentiousness has always been difficult, and what can be safely predicted is that the distinction will continue to vex us, despite our Bill of Rights.

Congress shall make no law respecting an establishment of religion, or prohibiting the free exercise thereof; or abridging the freedom of speech, or of the press; or the right of the people peaceably to assemble, and to petition the government for a redress of grievances.
—First Amendment to the United States Constitution, *1791*

The Bill of Rights

Chapter Four

Freedom of Speech and Free Government

The First Amendment, the Supreme Court, and the Polity

DAVID M. O'BRIEN

THE AUTHORS of the United States Constitution saw an intimate connection between free speech and free government. Their eighteenth-century understanding of freedom of speech reflected a protracted struggle that dated to the Middle Ages in England, however, and thus it was considerably more circumscribed than our contemporary understanding of this essential freedom.

The practice of governmental censorship in England stemmed from the 1275 enactment of a law, *De Scandalis Magnatum*, that imposed criminal penalties for false and "seditious words" about the king or his officials. During the sixteenth and seventeenth centuries, the king's council, which met in the "starred chambre" at Westminster and became infamously known as the Court of Star Chamber, extended the application of *Scandalis Magnatum* against seditious libel, or defamation of the government, to support an expanded use of censorship. Even after the Star Chamber was abolished in 1641, the principles it had articulated were applied by common-law courts, which gradually became guardians of the morals of the realm. Criminal liability for libel remained a question of law, not of fact—the truth or falsehood of a spoken or published statement was immaterial. Star Chamber abuses left both an immediate legacy of human tragedy and an indelible imprint on that English heritage from which the authors of the United States Constitution and Bill of Rights drew their principles of free government.[1]

---

1. *De Scandalis Magnatum*, 3 Edward I, chap. 34 (1274). *See also* Sir Thomas Erskine May, *Treatise on the Law, Privilege, Proceedings, and Usage of Parliament*, 16th ed. (London, 1957); Fredrick Seaton Siebert, *Freedom of the Press in England, 1476–1776* (Urbana, Ill., 1952).

At the onset of the American Revolution, the men who were beginning to shoot at one another generally agreed that speech and the press should be free, but not unconditionally free. In England the freedom of speech and press was restricted by the law of seditious libel and the irrelevance of truth as a defense. Colonial governments were no less given to suppression than the Crown and Parliament, indeed the restrictions of English common law were generally enforced in colonial common law by both Puritan and royalist judges. Freedom of speech and press basically meant freedom from *prior* censorship: "Every freeman has an undoubted right to lay what sentiments he pleases before the public," Sir William Blackstone observed, "but if he publishes what is improper, mischievous, or illegal, he must take the consequences of his own temerity."[2]

The struggle for freedom of speech during the colonial and revolutionary periods was over the application of traditional principles. Libertarians accepted the common-law principle of punishment for seditious and licentious communications, but they also accepted truth as a defense. They quarreled about what statements were licentious. Seventeenth- and eighteenth-century libertarians, in other words, differentiated between critical political comment, a natural and political right that benefited the polity, and seditious or licentious speech, which they agreed was pernicious and punishable.[3]

•

After the Philadelphia convention sent the proposed constitution to the states in autumn 1787, the focal points of political intrigue became the state ratifying conventions. In the Virginia and New York conventions, where the controversy over the absence of a declaration of rights was heated, the debates in the state conventions and the local press reveal the prevailing understanding of freedom of speech at the time the First Amendment was written. The debates were between those who embraced Blackstone's common-law understanding of freedom of speech and more libertarian thinkers, such as James Madison and Thomas Jefferson. The prevalent understanding was neo-Blackstonian. This is evident from Alexander

---

2. *State Trials*, 3:561; Thomas B. Macaulay, *History of England* (London, 1906), 4:248; Sir William Blackstone, *Commentaries on the Laws of England* (Oxford, 1765–1769), 4:151–152.

3. *State Trials*, 17:675; Leonard W. Levy, ed., *Freedom of the Press from Zenger to Jefferson* (New York, 1966).

Hamilton's eloquent defense, in the New York convention and in the essays of Publius, both of the Constitution and of the absence of a bill of rights. It is evident, too, in the pro-Constitution arguments of James Wilson in the Pennsylvania convention and the Antifederalist arguments of Richard Henry Lee in Virginia.

Adoption of a bill of rights, Alexander Hamilton argued in his celebrated essay number eighty-four of *The Federalist*, would be "not only unnecessary . . . but would even be dangerous." Any enumeration of rights was unnecessary because "the Constitution is itself, in every rational sence, and to every useful purpose, a bill of rights." Parchment guarantees would also prove dangerous, Hamilton thought. By prohibiting the exercise of powers for which the Constitution granted no authority, a bill of rights would invite an expansion of the powers of the state.[4]

"Why," Hamilton asked, "should it be said that the liberty of the press shall not be restrained, when no power is given by which restrictions may be imposed?" And what would it mean, he asked (posing a persistently vexatious definitional question), to declare "that the liberty of the press shall be inviolably preserved? What is the liberty of the press? Who can give it any definition which would not leave the utmost latitude for evasion?" It was "impracticable" to define freedom of speech, Hamilton concluded, and from this he inferred that the security of this freedom, "whatever fine declarations may be inserted in any constitution respecting it, must altogether depend on public opinion, and on the general spirit of the people and of the government."[5]

James Madison and Thomas Jefferson advanced powerful libertarian arguments for the adoption of a bill of rights, but they failed to supplant the widely accepted Blackstonian understanding of freedom of speech. Madison was far too libertarian for his contemporaries. Jefferson's position, while congenial to the common-law approach, foreshadowed later constitutional developments. Jefferson, unlike Madison, did not question the propriety of punishing licentious speech. He objected to the national government's exercise of the power. Jefferson made clear in his letters and in the Kentucky Resolutions, passed in 1799 in opposition to the Alien and Sedition Acts, that the states might properly punish seditious and licentious words. More tolerant of the abuses of speech and press than his contemporaries, Jefferson

---

4. *The Federalist*, No. 84, in *The Federalist Papers: Alexander Hamilton, James Madison, John Jay*, ed. Clinton Rossiter (New York, 1961), 510–520.

5. Ibid.

generally accepted common-law doctrines but advocated that only the states constrain licentious excesses of speech or press.[6]

In 1789, when the first federal Congress entertained amendments to the Constitution, Madison endeavored to reject Blackstonian common-law principles for freedom of speech. Madison advanced the broadest possible view of freedom of speech and press with his proposed constitutional amendment that "No State shall violate the equal rights of conscience, or the freedom of the press." Madison's absolute freedom of speech, however, simply did not represent his generation's or even subsequent generations' interpretation of that freedom. But the colonial experiences of censorship by the Crown and legislative assemblies nevertheless had fostered general agreement among the nation's first congressmen that rights of free speech and press, if not Madison's "rights of conscience," should be guaranteed. Indeed, there was little debate in Congress on adopting what became the First Amendment to the Constitution. Those who feared the abuse of freedom of speech expected the states to continue common-law restrictions on libel and other licentious speech.[7]

When ratified by the commonwealth of Virginia on 15 December 1791, the First Amendment gave a constitutional basis to the Blackstonian, common-law view of freedom of speech and press. The amendment was thought to protect only against prior restraint by the national government, not to provide absolute immunity for what speakers or publishers might utter or print. In historical perspective, the First Amendment was to Hamilton superfluous, to Madison an insufficient safeguard for individual freedom, and to Jefferson a reaffirmation both of the limits of the national government's power and of the reserved powers of the states.

The Blackstonian view of free speech served as the touchstone for understanding the First Amendment for more than a century. Freedom of speech and press meant the absence of prior restraint but also the permissibility of subsequent punishment for speech or writing that was "improper, mischievous or illegal." The line between liberty and licentiousness, between protected and unprotected speech, fluctuated with public opinion.

---

6. James Madison to Edward Everett, 28 Aug. 1830, *Writings of James Madison*, ed. Gaillard Hunt (New York, 1900–1910), 9:383; Thomas Jefferson to Thomas McKean, 19 Feb. 1803, in *Writings of Thomas Jefferson*, ed. Paul Leicester Ford (New York, 1892–1899), 8:218–219; and "Kentucky Resolutions of 1798 and 1799" in Elliot, *Debates*, 4:540–544.

7. *Annals of Congress*, 1:766. *See also* James Madison's "Report on the Virginia Resolutions" in Elliot, *Debates*, 4:569–570.

Not surprisingly, shifting tides of opinion frequently deprived individuals of the right to express unpopular ideas.[8]

After the public outcry against the Alien and Sedition Acts and a subsequent ruling that there was no common law of seditious libel, the national government during the first half of the nineteenth century left the punishment of licentious speech largely to the states and public opinion. Beginning in the 1830s and throughout the Civil War, the dissemination of information about slavery, for example, was punished in the North and South by enthusiasts both of abolition and of the institution of slavery.[9]

Where abolitionist tracts were deemed to be against the public good in the early nineteenth century, lewd and obscene materials became the object of condemnation later. Along with a mounting number of obscenity prosecutions, actions for criminal libel increased in the last quarter of the nineteenth century. Wary of socialism, anarchism, and syndicalism, and fearful of violent revolution as espoused by radical political groups such as Communists, Congress passed the Espionage Act of 1917. By the end of World War I no fewer than thirty-two states enacted laws against criminal syndicalism or sedition. The Supreme Court was drawn into these political questions about free speech and forced to define the scope of First Amendment protection. Throughout the nineteenth century the Court had repeatedly ruled that the states, but not the national government, could permissibly restrict the exercise of speech and press in accordance with traditional common-law proscriptions.[10]

The rush of wartime convictions brought the twentieth-century Court into direct confrontation with two long-avoided but inevitable tasks. First, the Court had to decide whether the basic First Amendment guarantee protected individuals against state restrictions on their free speech claims. In 1833, in one of Chief Justice John Marshall's last major decisions, the Court had ruled that the Bill of Rights applied solely to the federal government and

---

8. Joseph Story, *Commentaries on the Constitution of the United States* (Boston, 1833), 735; Thomas Cobley, *Treatise on Constitutional Limitations* (Boston, 1868), 2:886, 931–940; *Barron* v. *Mayor and City Council of Baltimore*, U.S. *Reports*, 32:243 (1833); and *Robertson* v. *Baldwin*, U.S. *Reports*, 165:275, 281 (1897).

9. Harold L. Nelson, ed., *Freedom of the Press from Hamilton to the Warren Court* (New York, 1967); John Lofton, *The Press as Guardian of the First Amendment* (Columbia, S.C., 1980), 79–102; and Russell B. Nye, *Fettered Freedom: Civil Liberties and the Slavery Controversy, 1830–1860*, 2d ed. (Urbana, Ill., 1972).

10. James C. N. Paul and Murray L. Schwartz, *Federal Censorship: Obscenity in the Mail* (New York, 1961); Zechariah Chafee, Jr., *Free Speech in the United States* (Cambridge, Mass., 1941), 100–102, 298–305; *Barron* v. *Baltimore*, U.S. *Reports*, 32:243 (1833); and *Robertson* v. *Baldwin*, U.S. *Reports*, 165:275 (1897).

had partially justified its ruling with language from the First Amendment: "Congress shall make no law." Almost one hundred years later, however, the Court ruled that the Fourteenth Amendment's due process clause extended First Amendment provisions to the states. This nationalization of the amendment's protection partially affirmed Madison's broader view of freedom of speech. It also permitted lower federal courts to accept jurisdiction in cases challenging state legislation that allegedly infringed on an individual's freedom of speech.[11]

The second and more difficult task of defining, to paraphrase Hamilton, the virtually indefinable sphere of First Amendment protection has proved to be a major preoccupation of the Court in the twentieth century. Indeed, the unenviable judicial task of articulating constitutional principles for the protection of speech and press has engendered bitter controversy among members of the Court. Yet, the broad freedom of speech that Americans presently enjoy is less an achievement of the founders than a tribute to the Supreme Court's actions in the twentieth century.

•

When reviewing cases of wartime prosecutions, the Court initially drew on common-law doctrines and was reluctant to formulate its own standard for freedom of speech. Majorities of the justices presumed the "reasonableness of legislation" to draw the boundary between liberty and licentiousness based on the "bad tendency" of subversive speech. Thus, in 1925, when upholding the conviction of Benjamin Gitlow for writing a socialist pamphlet, Justice Edward Sanford wrote that no First Amendment right was absolute and that states may punish "utterances inimical to the public welfare, tending to corrupt public morals, incite to crime, or disturb the public peace."[12]

When the first of the Espionage Act cases reached the Court, however, Justice Oliver Wendell Holmes voiced a more libertarian standard for protected expression. "The most stringent protection of free speech, would not protect a man falsely shouting fire in a theater and causing a panic," Holmes wrote in his classic 1919 opinion in *Schenck* v. *United States*. "The question in every case is whether the words are used in circumstances and are of such a nature as to create a clear and present danger that they bring about the substantive evils that Congress has a right to prevent. It is a question of proximity and degree." During the next two decades, Holmes

---

11. *Barron* v. *Baltimore, U.S. Reports*, 32:243 (1833); *Gilbert* v. *State of Minnesota, U.S. Reports*, 254:325, 333 (1920); and *Gitlow* v. *People of New York, U.S. Reports*, 268:652 (1925).
12. *Gitlow* v. *New York, U.S. Reports*, 268:652, 669 (1925).

and Louis Brandeis sought to persuade their fellow justices of the propriety of the "clear and present danger" test—perhaps the most famous of all judicial approaches to the First Amendment. In only one case, however, during the 1920s did a majority opinion discuss (and then reject) the "clear and present danger" standard. In the 1930s the standard was once again raised (and again rejected) in a majority opinion, and it was defended in a sole dissenting opinion. At the same time Chief Justice Charles Evans Hughes's decisions in the 1930s enlarged the scope of the First Amendment by resurrecting the doctrine of no prior restraint.[13]

Not until the 1940s did the "clear and present danger" standard become ascendant with the general elevation of the First Amendment rights to a preferred position among other liberties. But the concept of "clear and present danger" itself profoundly changed, too. The original Holmes-Brandeis formulation had focused only on matters of evidence or the circumstances giving rise to particular cases. In a broad range of cases involving religious speech and peaceful picketing in the 1940s, however, the Court began using the "clear and present danger" test as a standard for judging the constitutionality of legislation per se.[14]

This incremental recasting of the "clear and present danger" test pro-voked disagreements among the justices. Felix Frankfurter, during his years on the bench from 1939 to 1962, was especially critical of his colleagues for their "idle play on words" and their "perversion" of Holmes and Brandeis's doctrine. And the justices' disagreements about the First Amendment were exacerbated by political passions during the World War II era. Amid dire warnings about the dangers of fascism and communism, on 28 June 1940 Congress had enacted the Alien Registration Act, or Smith Act, the first federal sedition act in peacetime since the Alien and Sedition Acts of 1798. Fear of the Communist party continued into the next decade, and Congress overrode President Harry Truman's veto to pass on 23 September 1950 the Internal Security Act, or McCarran Act, which required all members of the party to register with the attorney general of the United States. Bitterly

---

13. *Schenck* v. *United States*, U.S. *Reports*, 249:47, 52 (1919); *Gitlow* v. *New York*, U.S. *Reports*, 268:652 (1925); *Herndon* v. *Lowry*, U.S. *Reports*, 301:242 (1937); *Herndon* v. *Georgia*, U.S. *Reports*, 295:441 (1935); *Lovell* v. *City of Griffin*, U.S. *Reports*, 303:444 (1938); *Grosjean* v. *American Press Co., Inc.*, U.S. *Reports*, 297:233 (1936); and *Near* v. *State of Minnesota*, U.S. *Reports*, 283:697 (1931).

14. *Murdock* v. *Pennsylvania*, U.S. *Reports*, 319:105 (1943); and *Marsh* v. *Alabama*, U.S. *Reports*, 326:501 (1946); *Thornhill* v. *Alabama*, U.S. *Reports*, 310:88 (1940); *Cantwell* v. *Connecticut*, U.S. *Reports*, 310:296 (1940); and *Pennekamp* v. *Florida*, U.S. *Reports*, 328:331 (1946).

divided over the interpretation of the First Amendment, the Supreme Court affirmed the constitutionality of the Smith Act in its 1951 ruling in *Dennis* v. *United States* and of the McCarran Act in the 1961 decision in *Communist Party* v. *Subversive Activities Control Board*.[15]

Dennis v. *United States* remains the watershed case, for the Court's attempt to apply the "clear and present danger" test to this case demonstrated the futility of future reliance on the standard for ad hoc balancing of individual and societal interests. Writing a dissenting opinion in the *Dennis* case, however, Justice Hugo Black presaged his and Justice William O. Douglas's "absolutist-literalist" interpretation of the First Amendment.[16]

To Black and Douglas, the history of the writing and passage of the Bill of Rights justified their Madisonian reading of the First Amendment. They asserted that no judicial creativity was necessary to explain that "'Congress shall make no law' means Congress shall make no law." Black, unblushingly denying Frankfurter's deference to federalism, supported the application of the Bill of Rights to the states: neither legislatures nor courts should pass judgment on an individual's exercise of free speech or limit the public's free flow of information. Unlike his colleagues, Black also embraced Jefferson's distinction between speech and overt action, and in cases arising from incidents of picketing and demonstrations he attempted to make the distinction support reasonable regulations governing the time, place, and manner of expressions of speech-plus-conduct. "While the First Amendment guarantees freedom to write and speak," Black argued, "it does not guarantee that the people can, wholly regardless of the rights of others, go where they please and when they please to argue for their views."[17]

The Supreme Court's abandonment of the "clear and present danger" test during Earl Warren's years as chief justice, from 1953 to 1969, is the measure of Justice Black's contribution. The fifty-year-old standard was laid to rest by the 1969 decision in *Brandenburg* v. *Ohio*. Only once in the 1960s had it surfaced, and during the 1970s the phrase "clear and present danger" had only rhetorical use. The Warren Court abandoned an ad hoc approach to First Amendment cases. Most of the justices recognized that ad hoc balancing failed to provide predictable and unambiguous standards for lower tribunals; nevertheless, they could not embrace the naked absolutist-

15. *Bridges* v. *California, U.S. Reports*, 314:252, 295 (1941); and *Craig* v. *Harney, U.S. Reports*, 331:367, 391 (1947); *Dennis* v. *United States, U.S. Reports*, 341:494 (1951); and *Communist Party* v. *Subversive Activities Control Board, U.S. Reports*, 367:1 (1961).

16. *Dennis* v. *United States, U.S. Reports*, 341:580 (1951).

17. Hugo LaFayette Black, *A Constitutional Faith* (New York, 1968), 45.

literalist interpretation advocated by Black and Douglas. Instead, they sought to establish principles by which categories of speech could be defined as protected or unprotected under the First Amendment.[18]

As early as 1942 Justice Frank Murphy's opinion for the Court's unanimous decision in *Chaplinsky* v. *New Hampshire* had suggested just such an approach to the First Amendment. Murphy had ruled that the amendment provided no protection for "utterances [that] are no essential part of any exposition of ideas." Certain categories of speech—such as insulting or fighting words, obscenity, or libel—had minimal social value, if any, and therefore were not worthy of constitutional protection. Consequently, Murphy had asserted, the First Amendment fell short of protecting categories of speech that were "no essential part of any exposition of ideas" and that were "clearly outweighed by the social interest in order and morality."[19]

The Supreme Court's preoccupation with cases of alleged subversive political speech during the early part of the twentieth century, and its deference toward state legislative and common-law proscriptions, had the effect of postponing the definition of these categories of unprotected expression until the era of the Warren Court. Not until 24 June 1957 did the Supreme Court rule directly on the constitutionality of century-old federal and state obscenity laws. In *Roth* v. *United States* the Court declared that obscenity was not a constitutionally protected form of expression. The First Amendment, Justice William Brennan wrote, "was fashioned to assure unfettered interchange of ideas for the bringing about of political and social changes desired by the people. . . . But implicit in the history of the First Amendment is the rejection of obscenity as utterly without redeeming social importance."[20]

By 1970, definitions were also firmly established for libel. As in the *Roth* case, Justice Brennan wrote the Court's 1964 decision in *New York Times Co.* v. *Sullivan*. Unlike prosecutions for obscenity, he said, civil libel suits brought by government officials against private citizens had to be considered "against the background of a profound national commitment to the principle that debate on public issues should be uninhibited, robust and wide-open, and that it may well include vehement, caustic, and sometimes unpleasantly sharp attacks on government and public officials." But the protection for free

---

18. *Brandenburg* v. *Ohio*, U.S. *Reports*, 395:444, 445 (1969); David M. O'Brien, *The Public's Right to Know: The Supreme Court and the First Amendment* (New York, 1981), 87; *United States* v. *Robel*, U.S. *Reports*, 389:258, 268 n. 20 (1967).

19. *Chaplinsky* v. *New Hampshire*, U.S. *Reports*, 315:568 (1942).

20. *Roth* v. *United States*, U.S. *Reports*, 354:476 (1957).

expression of political views was not unlimited. Brennan ruled that public officials might recover damages for libel if they proved that a statement was "made with 'actual malice'—that is, with knowledge that it was false or with reckless disregard of whether it was false or not." This "actual malice" rule thus drew a line "between speech unconditionally guaranteed [by the First Amendment] and speech which may legitimately be regulated."[21]

In the 1970s and 1980s the Supreme Court has continued to grapple with the vexing problems of defining *fighting words*, *obscenity*, *libel*, and *commercial speech*. Generally during the tenure of Chief Justice Warren Burger the Court continually broadened the scope of First Amendment protection. For example, while not abandoning the unprotected category of fighting words, the Court has applied the category so narrowly as virtually to eliminate it. The Burger Court sharpened its definitional balancing approach to libel involving either public or private individuals. By contrast, its revisions of obscenity law have been more extensive. In *Miller* v. *California*, the Burger Court's 1973 obscenity decision, the chief justice set forth clear rules for obscenity prosecutions and gave greater flexibility to states and localities. The founders probably would have agreed with Justice John Paul Stevens's observation that "there is surely less vital interest in the uninhibited exhibition of material that is on the borderline between pornography and artistic expression than in the free dissemination of ideas of social and political significance." In recent years, the Court has asserted that the First Amendment guarantee of freedom of speech is "primarily an instrument to enlighten public decision-making in a democracy."[22]

●

In historical perspective, the two hundred years of struggle for freedom of speech and of the press have seen a constant expansion of the scope of the First Amendment, extending its protection to more kinds of expression than political debate, and applying its principles to new communications technologies. Despite the dramatic changes in America's political, social, and economic life since the Republic was founded, the central meaning of the First Amendment remains intact. The freedom of speech and of the press remains crucial for the individual citizen's self-determination and the

---

21. *New York Times Co.* v. *Sullivan*, *U.S. Reports*, 376:254 (1964).

22. *Gooding* v. *Wilson*, *U.S. Reports*, 405:518 (1972); *Gertz* v. *Robert Welch, Inc.*, *U.S. Reports*, 418:323 (1974); *Miller* v. *California*, *U.S. Reports*, 413:15 (1973); *Young* v. *American Mini Theatres, Inc.*, *U.S. Reports*, 427:50, 63–73 (1976); *Virginia State Board of Pharmacy* v. *Virginia Citizens Consumer Council*, *U.S. Reports*, 425:748, 765 (1976). *See also First National Bank of Boston* v. *Bellotti*, *U.S. Reports*, 435:765 (1978).

nation's capacity for self-government. By broadening the protections offered by the First Amendment, the Supreme Court has affirmed the daring vision of the Americans who wrote and ratified the Bill of Rights: free speech concerning public affairs, the Court stated in 1964, "is the essence of self-government."[23]

23. *Lovell* v. *City of Griffin*, U.S. Reports, 303:444 (1938) (pamphlets); *Schneider* v. *State (Town of Irvington)*, U.S. Reports, 308:147 (1939) (leaflets); *Thornhill* v. *Alabama*, U.S. Reports, 310:88 (1940) (signs); *Roth* v. *United States*, U.S. Reports, 354:476, 488 (1957) (dicta) (books); *Joseph Burstyn, Inc.* v. *Wilson*, U.S. Reports, 343:502 (1952) (motion pictures); *New York Times Co.* v. *Sullivan*, U.S. Reports, 376:254, 266 (1964) (noncommercial advertisements); *Red Lion Broadcasting Co.* v. *Federal Communications Commission*, U.S. Reports, 395:367 (1969) (radio); and *Estes* v. *Texas*, U.S. Reports, 381:532 (1965) (dicta) (television). *See also* O'Brien, *The Public's Right to Know*, 61–66, 102–108; *Garrison* v. *Louisiana*, U.S. Reports, 379:64, 74–75 (1964).

A well-regulated militia being necessary to the security of a free State, the right of the people to keep and bear arms shall not be infringed.
—Second Amendment to the United States Constitution, *1791*

•

That a well regulated Militia, composed of the Body of the People, trained to Arms, is the proper, natural, and safe Defence of a free State; that standing Armies, in Time of Peace, should be avoided, as dangerous to Liberty; and that, in all Cases, the Military should be under strict Subordination to, and governed by, the Civil Power.
—Article 13, Virginia Declaration of Rights, *1776*

The
Bill of
Rights

Chapter Five

A Well-Regulated Militia

The Origins and Meaning of the Second Amendment

LAWRENCE DELBERT CRESS

UNLIKE PROVISIONS of the Bill of Rights that guaranteed such individual rights as freedom of speech, due process, and religious choice, the Second Amendment to the United States Constitution was not written to assure private citizens the prerogative of carrying weapons. To the leaders of the American Revolution it meant something very different. The Second Amendment was intended to guarantee that the sovereign citizenry of the republic (armed, propertied, and able to vote) would always remain a vital force in America's constitutional order.[1] Despite the militia's poor showing

---

1. The Second Amendment has been the object of scholarly inquiry before. Most recently Robert E. Shalhope, "The Ideological Origins of the Second Amendment," *Journal of American History* 69 (1982–1983): 599–614, has argued that Americans of the revolutionary generation understood the Second Amendment to guarantee a personal right to bear arms. Robert A. Sprecher, "The Lost Amendment," *American Bar Association Journal* 51 (1965): 554–557, 665–669; and Stuart R. Hays, "The Right to Bear Arms, A Study in Judicial Misinterpretation," *William and Mary Law Review* 2 (1959–1960): 381–406, take a similar stand. Shalhope, consciously responding to the modern debate over gun control, has founded his argument in what he believes was the ideological context of late-eighteenth-century America. Sprecher and Hays focus more narrowly on the legal and legislative history of the amendment. Peter Buck Feller and Karl L. Gotting, "The Second Amendment: A Second Look," *Northwestern University Law Review* 61 (1966–1967): 46–70; Lucilius A. Emery, "The Constitutional Right to Keep and Bear Arms," *Harvard Law Review* 28 (1914–1915): 473–477; George I. Haight, "The Right to Keep and Bear Arms," *Bill of Rights Review* 2 (1941): 31–42; and Ralph J. Rohner, "The Right to Bear Arms: A Phenomenon of Constitutional History," *Catholic University of America Law Review* 16 (1966–1967): 53–84, argue that the amendment supports the collective right of state militias to bear arms. Feller and Gotting, Emery, Haight, and Rohner also focus their analysis in legal and constitutional issues. What follows here places the legal and constitutional antecedents of the Second Amendment in America and England into an ideological context that differs fundamentally from that described by Shalhope.

during the revolutionary war, Americans remained convinced that republican government would fail without a "well-regulated militia."

The lessons of history, they believed, were clear. Only a citizenry organized into local militia companies could deter ambitious tyrants or foreign invaders. Republics, whether ancient or modern, thrived only when their citizens were willing and able to leave the plow for the field of battle. When a professional army usurped the citizenry's role in national defense, especially as a consequence of political intrigue or moral decadence, republics withered and liberty fell victim to tyranny and oppression.

A well-regulated militia not only protected citizens against the intrigues of ambitious rulers, it also protected the body politic against civil disorder. Daniel Shays's Rebellion, an armed insurrection in western Massachusetts in 1786, had sent tremors through the nation. And, history suggested that republican governments were especially vulnerable to domestic turmoil. To the generation that wrote it, the Second Amendment was at once a declaration of a fundamental principle of good government and a means to protect the stability of republican institutions. It did not guarantee individuals, such as Daniel Shays and his followers, the right to stockpile armaments.

•

The Second Amendment had roots deep in Anglo-American political and constitutional theory. Since the mid-seventeenth century, English political theorists had linked the militia to the maintenance of a balanced, stable, and free constitution. James Harrington, whose *Commonwealth of Oceana* (London, 1656) was widely read by Americans of the revolutionary generation, recommended the militia both for national defense and to deter the misuse of political power. Political writers at the time of the Glorious Revolution of 1689 emphasized the militia's importance for constitutional stability. Algernon Sidney warned that tyranny arose whenever the militia was allowed to decay. John Trenchard, later popular in the colonies as the author with Thomas Gordon of *Cato's Letters*, began his career as a pamphleteer by chiding Parliament for providing William III with a standing army after the Treaty of Ryswick in 1697. Standing armies, he wrote, were the agents of political intrigue and corruption. Only a militia could be counted upon to protect both the territory and the liberties of free people.[2]

---

2. For a detailed analysis of the debate over the militia and standing army in eighteenth-century thought, *see* Lawrence Delbert Cress, *Citizens in Arms: The Army and the Militia in American Society to the War of 1812* (Chapel Hill, 1982). J. G. A. Pocock, *The Machiavellian Moment: Florentine Political Thought and the Atlantic Republican Tradition* (Princeton, 1975), offers a penetrating analysis of classical republican theory from the sixteenth through the eighteenth century.

Between 1763 and 1776, Americans felt the truth of Trenchard's indictment. The occupation of Boston by British soldiers in 1768 and again in 1774, to say nothing of the Boston Massacre of 1770, confirmed the belief that hired soldiers were agents of political oppression. Although America did resort to professional soldiers in the revolutionary war, the country emerged from the Revolution no less persuaded by Trenchard's condemnation of standing armies. When they framed the Bill of Rights with an eye to preserving the republican gains of the Revolution, both the danger of standing armies and the militia's positive role as the armed manifestation of the sovereign people were important considerations.

The statutory antecedents of the Second Amendment reached far into the Anglo-American past. Magna Carta, a feudal compact accepted by King John at Runnymede in 1215 in exchange for renewed pledges of loyalty from his rebellious nobles, outlined the prerogatives of the nobility and the limits of royal authority. As an agreement between the king and the politically articulate community of the realm, Magna Carta served as an important touchstone for the development of Anglo-American law. Chapter 29 guaranteed every knight the right to serve in the castle-guard or to send someone of his own choosing to perform that duty and prohibited the king from forcing noblemen to pay taxes in lieu of personal service. The nobles in effect prevented King John from creating an army supported by their taxes but independent of their control. Magna Carta was the first step toward insuring the citizenry (then narrowly defined as the nobility) a role in the realm's defense.

Parliament grappled with similar matters during the Glorious Revolution. In the 1680s James II increased the number of Roman Catholic military officers and excluded Protestant officers in violation of the 1673 Test Act, and he imported Irish Catholics to fill the army's expanding ranks. Thus, as the English Bill of Rights phrased it, he "did endeavor to subvert and extirpate the Protestant religion, and the laws and liberties of this kingdom" by "raising and keeping a standing army . . . without consent of parliament" and by "causing several good subjects, being Protestants, to be disarmed, at the same time when papists were both armed and employed." To correct this, the Bill of Rights of 1689 prohibited the English monarchy from raising an army during peacetime without Parliament's consent and guaranteed that "subjects which are Protestants, may have arms for their defence suitable to their conditions, and as allowed by law." The English Bill of Rights did not create an unlimited right to bear arms, however, for Protestants were to "have arms for their defence" only as was "suitable to their conditions and as allowed by law." Arms were denied to men who did not own lands worth at least £100, unless they were the sons or heirs of an esquire, knight, or nobleman. Parliament also reserved the future option of restricting "by law" access to arms. These provisions were intended to ensure a stable government free from the threat of disruptions by Catholic Jacobites and the intrigues of future monarchs.[3]

•

A century later, the framers of the American states' declarations of rights also sought to lay the foundations for constitutional stability. When Thomas Jefferson indicted George III in the Declaration of Independence for keeping "among us in time of peace, standing armies without the consent of our legislatures," he underscored the American concern about the relationship between liberty and citizen soldiers, but the militia tradition had more than just rhetorical significance. Patriot leaders in the colonies during the winter and spring of 1774–1775 adopted resolutions declaring "that a well-regulated Militia, composed of the gentlemen, freeholders, and other freemen, is the natural strength and only stable security of free Government."[4] With independence at hand, the states' declarations of rights identified the militia as an institution necessary for the preservation of liberty.

Virginia's Declaration of Rights—adopted on 12 June 1776, nearly a month before the American colonies officially announced their independence—set the pattern. Article 13, drafted by George Mason and approved by a committee that included James Madison, declared "that a well regulated Militia, composed of the Body of the People, trained to Arms, is the proper, natural, and safe Defence of a free State." Two months later, Pennsylvania adopted in article 13 of its own declaration of rights the proposition that "the people have a right to bear arms for the defence of themselves and the state." The language was slightly different, but the meaning was the same. Only the trained, armed, and organized citizen militia could be depended upon to preserve republican liberties for "themselves" and to ensure the constitutional stability of the "state." Both Virginians and Pennsylvanians warned that standing armies were "dangerous to liberty" and stipulated that

---

3. Schwartz, *Roots*, 1:42–43.

4. Thomas Jefferson, "A Summary View," [July 1774], *Jefferson Papers*, 1:133. The resolution cited here is from the Maryland convention, 8 Dec. 1774, in *American Archives*, ed. Peter Force, 4th ser. (Washington, 1837–1846), 1:1032.

the military be kept "under strict subordination" to the civil government. Without a strong, popularly based militia, liberty would succumb to the dictates of tyrants.[5]

Delaware, Maryland, and North Carolina adopted similar declarations during the first year of independence, the first two states by borrowing language from Virginia's article 13, and North Carolina following Pennsylvania's lead by declaring that "the people have a right to bear arms, for the defence of the state." Vermont, though not formally a state until 1792, quoted Pennsylvania's article 13 in its 1777 declaration of rights. In the same year, New York incorporated an equally clear statement in the body of its constitution. Announcing it to be "the duty of every man who enjoys the protection of society to be prepared and willing to defend it," New Yorkers proclaimed that the "militia . . . at all times . . . shall be armed and disciplined."[6]

In Massachusetts, John Adams drafted the bill of rights that was ratified with the 1780 constitution. "The people," he wrote, "have a right to keep and bear arms for the common defence." New Hampshire's 1783 bill of rights made the same point, declaring "A well regulated militia is the proper, natural, and sure defence of a state." Both documents condemned standing armies and subordinated the military to civil authority, while affirming the citizen militia's collective role as the protector of personal liberty and constitutional stability against ambitious tyrants and uncontrolled mobs.[7]

Several states put limits on citizens' militia obligation. Pennsylvania, Delaware, and Vermont provided that no "man who is conscientiously scrupulous of bearing arms" could be "compeled" to serve in the militia, but they required that conscientious objectors meet their obligations with "equivalents," payments equal to the cost of their militia service. These clauses permitting conscientious objection to military service demonstrate yet again that for eighteenth-century Americans "to bear arms" meant militia service. State after state guaranteed a role in the common defense collectively to the "people" or the "militia." On the other hand, when describing individual rights such as freedom of conscience they used the terms "man" or "person." New Hampshire's bill of rights—the last written during the Confederation period and, as such, a compendium of previous thinking on the matter—is a case in point. It declared the importance of "a well regulated

---

5. Schwartz, *Roots*, 2:235, 266.

6. Ibid., 2:278, 282–287, 312, 324. For a summary of state constitutional provisions bearing on the militia and its relationship to civil authority, *see* Cress, *Citizens in Arms*, 60–62.

7. Schwartz, *Roots*, 2:342, 378.

militia" to the defense of the state and exempted from service any "person
. . . conscientiously scrupulous about the lawfulness of bearing arms." The
individual right of conscience was asserted against the collective responsibility for the common defense. These same concerns surfaced in the debate
about the Constitution.[8]

During the last days of the Philadelphia convention, Virginia delegate
George Mason, having failed to secure a separate bill of rights, sought an
explicit statement of the militia's place in republican government. He
wanted a clause explaining that the congressional power to arm, organize,
and discipline the militia was intended to secure "the Liberties of the People
. . . against the Dangers of regular Troops or standing Armies in time of
Peace." When the Convention failed to agree, Mason refused to sign the
Constitution. As he explained in his widely read "Objections to the
Constitution of Government formed by the Convention," the document
contained "no Declaration of Rights" and specifically lacked a "declaration of
any kind . . . against the danger of standing armies." To correct this
omission, Mason backed an amendment, drafted on the eve of Virginia's
ratification convention, declaring that the "People have a Right to keep &
bear Arms" because "a well regulated Militia [is] the proper natural and safe
Defence of a free State." Mason's proposal also rehearsed the dangers of
standing armies and the need for the "strict Subordination" of military to
civil authority. A separate amendment would have provided that a person
"religiously scrupulous of bearing Arms" be allowed "to employ another to
bear Arms in his Stead." Never did Mason challenge the Constitution's
failure to guarantee individual access to weapons.[9]

During the debates over the Constitution, many critics worried that the
proposed government threatened the militia's important role in the republic.
Maryland Antifederalist Luther Martin challenged the proposed government's military prerogatives: "Instead of guarding against a standing army,
. . . which has so often and so successfully been used for the subversion of
freedom," Martin argued, the Constitution gave "it an express and constitutional sanction." Congress's authority over the state militias, he warned,
could be used "even to disarm" them. Worse, the militia might be needlessly
mobilized and sent marching to the far reaches of the Union so that the
people would be glad to see a standing army raised in its stead. "When a
government wishes to deprive its citizens of freedom," Martin noted, "it

---

8. Ibid., 2:265, 277, 312, 323, 377.

9. *Notes of Debates in the Federal Convention of 1787, Reported by James Madison* (Athens, Ohio, 1966), 630, 639–640; *Mason Papers*, 3:991–993.

generally makes use of a standing army [while leaving] the militia in a situation as contemptible as possible, lest they might oppose its arbitrary designs."[10] Pennsylvania's Antifederalists demanded that the states be given a veto over any call for militia service outside a state's borders.

Concern arose too over the Constitution's failure to protect conscientious objectors. Antifederalist candidates for the New York convention charged that the Constitution left "men conscientiously scrupulous of bearing arms . . . liable to perform military duty."[11] Reflecting the sentiments of the state declarations of rights, the Antifederalists were determined to preserve the militia as a bulwark of republican government but also anxious to protect the individual's free exercise of conscience.

•

The notion that individual citizens should be guaranteed access to weapons surfaced several times during the debate over the Constitution. A minority report from the Pennsylvania ratifying convention borrowed language from the state's own declaration of rights to declare not only the people's right "to bear arms for the defence of themselves and their own State or the United States" but also the right to bear arms "for the purpose of killing game," while adding the proviso that "no law shall be passed for disarming the people or any of them." Samuel Adams, of Massachusetts, argued that the Constitution should never be construed "to authorize Congress to . . . prevent the people of the United States, who are peaceable citizens from keeping their own arms" but then renounced that position after reflecting on Shays's Rebellion in western Massachusetts. Finally, among a series of amendments recommended for consideration by the First Congress, New Hampshire proposed that "Congress shall never disarm any citizen unless such as are or have been in Actual Rebellion."[12]

The principles of these resolutions were close to the classical republican understanding of the armed citizenry. In each case, bearing arms was linked

10. Luther Martin, *Genuine Information* (delivered to the Maryland legislature, 29 Nov. 1787), in *Records of the Federal Convention of 1787*, ed. Max Farrand (New Haven, 1911–1937), 3:207–208; Luther Martin, "Letter on the Federal Convention of 1787," 27 Jan. 1788, Elliot, *Debates*, 1:371–372.

11. *Mason Papers*, 3:1070–1071. Concern over the Constitution's failure to protect conscientious objectors was commonplace in Antifederalist tracts. "A Manifesto . . . from Albany County," in Kenyon, *Antifederalists*, 362, was typical in charging that "Men conscienciously scrupulous of bearing arms [were] made liable to perform military duty." *See also* note 10.

12. "Pennsylvania Minority Report," Kenyon, *Antifederalists*, 36; William V. Wells, *Life and Public Service of Samuel Adams* (Boston, 1865), 3:267; Elliot, *Debates*, 2:162; "New Hampshire Ratifying Convention to Congress," 21 June 1788, Elliot, *Debates*, 1:326.

to the citizenry's collective responsibility for defense, familiar warnings about the danger of standing armies, and affirmations of the need to subordinate military to civil authority. Neither Pennsylvania's critics nor New Hampshire's cautious supporters of the Constitution had moved far, if at all, beyond the eighteenth-century notion that bearing arms meant militia service, and no other state followed their lead. Pennsylvania's Antifederalists provided for the disarming of criminals and conceded that further action would be appropriate if society faced "real danger of public injury from individuals." The order and safety of society always took precedence over the individual's claim to possess weapons, and constitutional stability remained the preeminent consideration. The only other hint that Americans may have viewed bearing arms as an individual right occurs in one of Thomas Jefferson's early draft proposals for Virginia's new state constitution. Jefferson's draft had a clause guaranteeing every freeman the use of arms "within his own lands or tenements," but this provision was not incorporated in the Constitution of 1776. Virginia's statesmen were satisfied that George Mason's thirteenth article of the Declaration of Rights protected the "Militia, composed of the body of the people, trained to arms" and accurately stated the armed citizenry's proper role in a republic.[13]

The amendments proposed in the state ratifying conventions reflected the concerns about national military power and the republican principles embodied in the states' declarations of rights. New York and North Carolina wanted to limit congressional power to raise a peacetime army by requiring "the consent of two thirds" of the House and Senate. Maryland suggested limiting a soldier's enlistment to four years to prevent Congress from creating a permanent military force. More than half of the states advocated strong state militias to counter the tyrannical potential of the Constitution. Fearing that the militia would be purposely neglected, some states proposed guarantees that the states could organize, arm, and discipline their citizens if Congress failed to fulfill its responsibilities. Against the more common fear that Congress's right to call out the militia would prove detrimental to republican liberties, New Yorkers recommended that a state's militia not be allowed to serve outside its borders longer than six weeks "without the consent of the legislature thereof." Others worried that the subjection of the militia to martial law might lead to abuses. The Maryland and North Carolina conventions asked Congress to amend the Constitution so that the militia could be placed under martial law only "in time of war, invasion, or

---

13. "Pennsylvania Minority Report," Kenyon, *Antifederalists*, 36; *Jefferson Papers*, 1:344, 353, 363.

rebellion." Finally, several state conventions stated firmly that no person "religiously scrupulous of bearing arms" should be compelled to serve in the military.[14]

•

Virginia's proposed amendments, which directly influenced Madison's draft of the Bill of Rights, bring into focus the concerns that ultimately produced the Second Amendment. Indeed, the changes proposed by the commonwealth's ratifying convention neatly defined the issues raised during later congressional debates. Declaring that "the people have a right to keep and bear arms," Virginians asked for constitutional recognition of the principle that "a well regulated Militia, composed of the Body of the People trained to Arms, is the proper, natural, and safe Defence of a free State." This proposition addressed the fear that the new government might disarm the citizenry while raising an oppressive standing army. To reinforce the point, the convention urged a constitutional declaration that standing armies "are dangerous to liberty, and therefore ought to be avoided, as far as the circumstances and protection of the community will admit." The Constitution was also found wanting for failing to pronounce the military "in all cases" subordinate to "civil power." The Virginia convention prepared a separate amendment "That any person religiously scrupulous of bearing arms ought to be exempted, upon payment of an equivalent to employ another to bear arms in his stead." No one expressed concern about an individual citizen's access to weapons.[15]

Madison had Virginia's recommendations in mind when, on 8 June 1789, he proposed to Congress that the Constitution be amended to provide that "The right of the people to keep and bear arms shall not be infringed; a well armed and well regulated militia being the best security of a free country: but no person religiously scrupulous of bearing arms shall be compelled to render military service in person." Six weeks later, a committee composed of Madison and ten representatives (one from each of the other states that had ratified the Constitution), began preparing a formal slate of amendments, using as a guide both Madison's recommendations and those proposed by the states. The committee revised Madison's original recommendation and

---

14. "Pennsylvania Minority Report," Kenyon, *Antifederalists*, 36–37; Elliot, *Debates*, for New York, 1:328, 330–331; for Rhode Island, 1:334–336; for Maryland, 2:550–552; for Virginia, 3:659–660; for North Carolina, 4:244–247. For the amendments proposed by New Hampshire, *see*, Schwartz, *Bill of Rights*, 2:760–761.

15. Elliot, *Debates*, 3:659–660.

stated more explicitly the armed citizenry's importance to the constitutional order.[16]

Such doubts as were raised remind us of the militia's importance in the political theory of the day. The failure to link freedom of conscience with the obligation to find a substitute or pay an "equivalent" troubled many members of the House. Requiring one part of the population to provide for the defense of the other was simply "unjust," argued James Jackson, of Georgia. Others believed that matters of "religious persuasion" had no place in an amendment designed to guarantee a fundamental principle of republican government. "It is extremely injudicious," warned one congressman, "to intermix matters of doubt with fundamentals." Such concerns brought the House of Representatives within two votes of striking the conscientious objection clause from the proposed amendment.[17]

Congressman Ædanus Burke, of South Carolina, proposed a clause declaring that a "standing army . . . in time of peace is dangerous to public liberty, and such shall not be raised . . . without the consent of two-thirds of the members present of both Houses" and an explicit statement of the subordination of military to civil authority. Burke's motion was defeated because some congressmen thought a simple majority vote was sufficient and other congressmen complained that the debate had already been closed. Nevertheless, Burke's amendment again demonstrates what Congress meant by the Second Amendment. The aim was to confirm a fundamental principle of republican government, that a well-regulated militia was "the best security of a free State."[18]

Little is known about the Senate debate on the Second Amendment; it seems to have been similar to that in the House. The Senate joined the House in rejecting the proposal to restrict Congress's power to raise armies during peacetime but denied approval to the controversial conscientious objection clause. The Senate's changes were accepted by a joint conference committee of both houses, and on 24 and 25 September 1789, the House and Senate respectively voted their approval.

We also know little about debate on the Second Amendment in the states. No state legislature rejected it. As a statement of republican principles already commonplace in state declarations of rights, it probably evoked little

---

16. *Annals of Congress*, 1:451 (8 June 1789); 1:685–691 (21 July 1789); 1:778 (17 Aug. 1789); "Committee of Eleven Report on Proposed Amendments," 28 July 1789, in Schwartz, *Roots*, 5: illustration following 1014.

17. *Annals of Congress*, 1:778–780 (17 Aug 1789).

18. Ibid., 780.

discussion. If any doubts were raised, they might have focused on the amendment's failure explicitly to describe the dangers of a standing army.

•

When Virginia ratified the Second Amendment on 15 December 1791 the statement that "A well regulated militia, being necessary to the security of a free State, the right of the people to keep and bear arms, shall not be infringed," became a part of the United States Constitution. The militia had played an important role in stemming the tide of oppression that necessitated independence from Great Britain, and it alone offered a republican remedy to domestic disorders such as Shays's Rebellion. The Second Amendment gave constitutional sanction to the idea that the militia was the institutional expression of the citizenry's collective obligation to bear arms against the internal and external enemies of the state—"a well regulated militia" to defend the liberties of the people against a demagogue's armed mob or a tyrant's standing army.

No Soldier shall, in time of peace, be quartered in any house, without the consent of the Owner, nor in time of war, but in a manner to be prescribed by law.
—Third Amendment to the United States Constitution, *1791*

The
Bill of
Rights

Chapter Six

A Free People's Intolerable Grievance

The Quartering of Troops and the Third Amendment

B. CARMON HARDY

IF THERE IS A POOR COUSIN among the articles of the Bill of Rights, surely it is the Third Amendment. Commentary about every other guarantee in the national charter of liberties is extensive, but this declaration against the arbitrary quartering of troops has passed comparatively unnoticed both by history and the law. No case based on the Third Amendment has ever been tried before the United States Supreme Court. Students of American constitutional history dismiss the amendment as an insignificant legal fossil. But for the revolutionary generation, its solution to the problem of quartering soldiers was both the capstone to an ancient and troubled bit of legal history and a protection against abuses that Americans themselves had felt.[1]

At issue in the Third Amendment is the relationship between civilians and the warriors who protect them, a problem as old as any other addressed in the Bill of Rights. As long as there have been soldiers, they have needed food and shelter. Reflecting the rough pragmatism of their occupation,

---

1. The article has often been mentioned in the court's published opinions, but only with cursory notice. Neither of the two modern examinations of the Third Amendment at the state level raised the civil-military conflicts that the amendment was meant to obviate (*Lord & Burnham Company* v. *City of New York* [1928] in *Miscellaneous Reports*, ed. F. B. Delehanty et al. [Albany, N.Y., 1893–1955], 132:64; *New York Supplement*, 1st ser. [Saint Paul, Minn., 1888–1938], 229:598, 604; *State ex rel. Charlton, Adjutant General* v. *French, State Treasurer* [1940] in *Report of Cases Determined in the Supreme Court of the State of New Mexico*, ed. Charles H. Gildersleeve et al. [San Francisco; Chicago; Columbia, Mo.; Santa Fe, N.M.; and Saint Paul, Minn., 1881–], 44:169). Typical is Justice Samuel F. Miller's comment that "this Amendment seems to have been thought necessary . . . [but] is so thoroughly in accord with all our ideas that further comment is unnecessary" (Edward S. Corwin, ed., *Constitution of the United States of America* [Washington, D.C., 1953], 817).

soldiers were notorious for abusing civilians when it was a matter of need—and often when it was not.

•

During the Middle Ages, practices associated with the quartering of soldiers were often brutal, subjecting to peril a householder's beds and goods on the approach of any army, friend or foe. Circumstances in England did not change much before or after the Norman Conquest. Nevertheless, in Magna Carta there is no explicit mention of the problem of quartering troops.[2]

The fourteenth-century atrocities chronicled by Jean Froissart were not confined to campaigns in France. Soldiers on their way to and from the Continental wars often demanded free quarter from English householders along their way. Englishmen repeatedly complained to Parliament of abuses such as those described in Piers Plowman where a man complained of losing his wife, his barn, his livestock, his home, and the maidenhood of his daughter Margaret, not even "minding her kicks."[3]

Efforts to regulate the quartering of troops first appeared in town and borough charters. These documents, which sometimes predated Magna Carta itself, are the major legal antecedents of the Third Amendment. London's charter of 1131, for example, required that quarters within the city walls, whether for the royal family or others, be given voluntarily. The Norwich charter of 1199 prohibited the taking of any lodgings or provisions by force. Three important charter provisions relating to quartered men retained their identity throughout the entire period of Anglo-American concern with the problem: quartering in accordance with established legal procedures, civilian allocation of facilities, and voluntarism. The obligation to billet, or immunity from it, was established in the charters. Town marshals or constables alone had authority to admit soldiers through the city gate. In company with an appropriate military officer, the town officer selected

---

2. Austin Lane Poole, ed., *Medieval England*, rev. ed. (Oxford, 1958), 132; Charles Warren Hollister, *Anglo-Saxon Military Institutions on the Eve of the Norman Conquest* (Oxford, 1962), 25–28, 125–131, 137, 142–144; Herbert James Hewitt, *Organization of War under Edward III, 1338–62* (Manchester, Eng., and New York, 1966), 43, 45; Michael Powicke, *Military Obligation in Medieval England: A Study in Liberty and Duty* (London and New York, 1962), 123–133; J. F. Verbruggen, *De Krijgskunst in West-Europa in de Middeleeuwen, IXe tot Besin XIVe Eeuw* (Brussels, 1954), 148–194, 197, 246–297; William Sharp McKechnie, *Magna Carta: A Commentary on the Great Charter of King John*, rev. ed. (New York, 1958), 332–333; F. M. Stenton, *First Century of English Feudalism, 1066–1166* (Oxford, 1932), 233.

3. Sir John Froissart, *Chronicles of England, France, Spain, and the Adjoining Countries*, rev. ed. (New York, 1901), 1: chap. 12; Hewitt, *Organization of War*, 84, 175; William Langland, *Vision of William Concerning Piers the Plowman*, ed. Walter W. Skeet, 10th ed., rev. (Oxford, 1945), Passus 4, lines 49 to 62.

buildings to be marked with chalk indicating where the troops should lodge and how many in each dwelling. But even then, quartering was forbidden by the requirements of the charter if quartering ran contrary to the will of the property owners concerned.

Once soldiers were admitted to civilian homes, anything they took was supposed to be paid for with tallies, chits, or billets redeemable by the government or applied against one's taxes, but frequently a soldier's receipts proved worthless, and "billeting" came to be synonymous with free room and board. From the thirteenth through the sixteenth centuries the manner of lodging and feeding troops changed little, and the restraints provided by town and borough charters were violated again and again. Tudor attempts at more centralized control through the appointment of lords lieutenant and the appropriation of "coat and conduct money" met with only moderate success.[4]

•

Under the Stuarts, quartered troops became one of the problems that led the nation into civil war. Expeditions intended to advance Charles I's interests on the Continent mistreated English citizens as they traveled to

4. Adolphus Ballard, ed., *British Borough Charters, 1042–1216* (Cambridge, 1913), 86–87; Edward Arthur Lewis, *Mediaeval Boroughs of Snowdonia* (London, 1912), 37–38, 173–174; Carl Stephenson, *Borough and Town: A Study of Urban Origins in England* (Cambridge, Mass., 1933), 139–140; Adolphus Ballard and James Tait, eds., *British Borough Charters, 1216–1307* (Cambridge, 1923), 110–111; Michael Powicke, *Military Obligation in Medieval England*, 189; Sir William Holdsworth, *History of English Law*, 7th ed., rev. (London, 1956–1972), 4:76–78, 134; William Stubbs, *Constitutional History of England in Its Origins and Development* (Oxford, 1874–1878), 2:402, 423, 435, 453, 564–568; Charles Austin Beard, *Office of Justice of the Peace in England in Its Origin and Development* (New York, 1904), 29–30, 65; William Alfred Morris, *Medieval English Sheriff to 1300* (Manchester, Eng., and New York, 1927), 171, 266–271, 278; Bertie Wilkinson, *Studies in the Constitutional History of the Thirteenth and Fourteenth Centuries* (Manchester, Eng., 1937), 231–233; Bryce Lyon, *Constitutional and Legal History of Medieval England* (New York, 1960), 379–380, 394–395; Hewitt, *Organization of War*, 58–59; William Stubbs, *Select Charters*, 9th ed., rev. (Oxford, 1962), 392; Thomas Rymer, *Foedera* (London, 1704–1735), 7:480–481 (1385); Lewis, *Medieval Boroughs of Snowdonia*, 173–174; May McKisack, *Fourteenth Century, 1307–1399* (Oxford, 1959), 241–242; J. R. Tanner, *Tudor Constitutional Documents, A.D. 1485–1603, with an Historical Commentary*, 2d ed. (Cambridge, 1951), 598–599; and Charles G. Cruickshank, *Elizabeth's Army*, 2nd ed. (Oxford, 1966), 18–21, 77; Geoffrey Parker, *The Army of Flanders and the Spanish Road, 1567–1659: The Logistics of Spanish Victory and Defeat in the Low Countries' Wars* (Cambridge, 1972), 89; Gladys Scott Thomson, *Lords Lieutenants in the Sixteenth Century: A Study in Tudor Local Administration* (New York, 1923), 80–81; G. W. Prothero, ed., *Select Statutes and Other Constitutional Documents Illustrative of the Reigns of Elizabeth and James I*, 2d ed. (Oxford, l898), cxix–cxx, 154–156; Barnabe Rich, *A Right Exelent and Pleasaunt Dialogue, Between Mercury and an English Souldier* (London, 1574?).

their passages across the channel. Large military forces needing year-round facilities and support were a recent development inspired by rivalries between emerging nation states. Charles I and his army were part of this military innovation, but logistics were not keeping pace with the development of armies themselves. Barracks, in particular, were almost nonexistent. Charles attempted to maintain a modern, mobile army, but the House of Commons was unwilling to provide revenue to support it. Warships sat idle in English harbors while soldiers languished ashore. Without barracks or money to pay their keep at the inns, the men had no choice but to billet themselves in private homes.[5]

Such were the circumstances attending Parliament's famous Petition of Right. "Great companies of soldiers and mariners have been dispersed into divers counties of the realm, and the inhabitants against their wills have been compelled to receive them into their houses," the 1628 document complained, "against the laws and customs of this realm and to the great grievance and vexation of the people." The Petition of Right was the first important definition of the problem of quartered troops as a grievance with a legal identity of its own, and it made some minimal guarantee about the lodging of soldiers an enduring part of the English constitution.[6]

---

5. Samuel R. Gardiner, *History of England from the Accession of James I to the Outbreak of the Civil War, 1603–1642* (London, 1899–1901), 6:247–248; Arthur Wilson, *History of Great Britain* (London, 1653), 283–294; John Rushworth, *Historical Collections of Private Passages of State* (London, 1682–1701), 1:56, 419–420; John Forster, *Sir John Eliot: A Biography, 1590–1632* (London, 1864), 2:56–57n; Lindsay Boynton, "Billeting: The Example of the Isle of Wight," *English Historical Review* 74 (1959): 23–40; Edward Hyde, earl of Clarendon, *History of the Rebellion and Civil Wars in England* (Oxford, 1849), 1:56; Michael Roberts, *Military Revolution, 1560–1660* (Belfast, 1956), 12–15; Sir George Norman Clark, *Seventeenth Century*, 2d ed. (New York, 1961), 101–104, 108–109, 112; Correlli Barnett, *Britain and Her Army, 1509–1970: A Military, Political and Social Survey* (London, 1970), 17–19, 126–127; Eugene Heishmann, *Die Anfänge des Stehenden Heeres in Osterreich* (Vienna, 1925), 9–55, 223; Hans Delbrück, *Geschichte der Kriegskunst im Rahmen der Politischen Geschichte* (Berlin, 1907–1936), 4:1–25, 255–332; Francis Grose, *Military Antiquities Respecting a History of the English Army from the Conquest to the Present Time* (London, 1786–1788), 2:233; Sir Sibbald David Scott, *British Army: Its Origin, Progress, and Equipment* (London and New York, 1868–1880), 3:399.

6. Gardiner, *History of England*, 6:236; Paul de Rapin de Thoyras, *History of England* (London, 1732–1747), 2:265–266; J. R. Tanner, *English Constitutional Conflicts of the Seventeenth Century, 1603–1689* (Cambridge, 1962), 61–67; Frances Helen Relf, *Petition of Right* (Minneapolis, Minn., 1917). The Grand Remonstrance of 1641 decreed an end to "Coat and Conduct" money (Samuel Rawson Gardiner, ed., *Constitutional Documents of the Puritan Revolution, 1625–1660*, 3d ed., rev. [Oxford, 1906], 221).

During the English Civil War, Royalist and Roundhead armies used tents extensively but often demanded free quarter from rich and poor alike. Parliament abolished the much-abused system of military purveyance but grievances about billeting continued. The king resorted to "maintenance" and the Roundheads to "contributions" in their efforts to supply their troops and repay those who lodged them. Neither system worked.[7]

The Restoration of 1660 did not bring much improvement. Trouble between soldiers and civilians broke out during the Third Anglo-Dutch War of 1672–1674. Before Parliament finally consented to erect a few barracks, it passed the Anti-quartering Act of 1679. More than just a protest about the billeting of soldiers, this law reached a new level of principle by challenging the traditional notion that although a homeowner was immune from forced quartering, inns and public houses were not. As far as the rights of homeowners were concerned, the 1679 law made no exceptions and no distinction between war and peace: "Noe officer military or civill nor any other person whatever shall from henceforth presume to place quarter or billet any souldier or souldiers upon any subject or inhabitant of this realme of any degree quality or profession whatever without his consent and that it shall and may be lawful for every such subject and inhabitant to refuse to sojourne or quarter any souldier or souldiers." In practice under James II it was as if the law had never passed. Barracks remained few in number, and complaints about soldiers continued to be heard in London and especially in the coastal towns.[8]

---

7. C. H. Firth and R. S. Rait, eds., *Acts and Ordinances of the Interregnum, 1642–1660* (London, 1911), 1:945, 1017, 1048–1049; 2:110–118, 1057; C. H. Firth, *Cromwell's Army: A History of the English Soldier During the Civil Wars, the Commonwealth and the Protectorate*, 3d ed. (London, 1921), 395–398; J. H. P. Pafford, ed., *Accounts of the Parliamentary Garrisons of Great Chalfield and Malmesbury, 1645–1646* (Devizes, Wiltshire, Eng., 1940); Herman de Watteville, *British Soldier: His Daily Life from Tudor to Modern Times* (New York, [1955]), 41–44; Scott, *British Army*, 399–401, 466–489; C. A. Holmes, "The Eastern Association" (Ph.D. diss., Cambridge University, 1969), 359–365; Edgar L. Erickson, ed., *Journals of the House of Commons, 1547–1900* (London, 1902), 9:246 (1672), 286–287 (1673); Charles M. Clode, *Military Forces of the Crown: Their Administration and Government* (London, 1869), 1:61, 452–454.

8. 31 Charles II, chap. 1, sec. 54 (1679); C. M. Iles, "Early States of English Public House Regulation," *Economic Journal* 13 (1903): 251–262. Soldiers were among the travelers that inns were expected to lodge throughout Europe (Jean Chaubert, *La Responsabilité Civile de l'hôtelier à raison des Effets Apportés par le Voyageur, Droits Français, Anglais, Allemand et Suisse* [Lausanne, 1914], 33, 47–48). Parliamentary debate over the Petition of Right and billeting of soldiers recognized inns could be required to accommodate soldiers, and in 1647 the Puritan regime continued this requirement ("Proceedings in Parliament Relating to the Liberty of The Subject," *State Trials*, 3: chap. 66; Firth and Rait, *Acts and Ordinances*, 1:1049;

•

These and other grievances precipitated the Glorious Revolution of 1689. James II fled to France and was replaced by his nephew and son-in-law, William of Orange. "The Billeting of a large Standing Army," concludes one authority, "was probably the greatest social evil endured by the people when William III reached England." The 1689 Bill of Rights listed the "keeping [of] a standing army within this kingdom in time of peace without consent of parliament and quartering soldiers contrary to law" among its indictments of James II, but made no corresponding statement in its declaration of the rights of Englishmen. For the second time in a century, abuses associated with quartered troops contributed to the dethroning of an English king.[9]

Immediately after the Glorious Revolution, Parliament enacted a revised mutiny law directing local civilian magistrates to quarter soldiers only in alehouses, inns, stables, and the like, and forbidding the placement of soldiers in private domiciles against the wills of their owners. The Mutiny Act failed to provide state-financed barracks. The military, it assumed, was less likely to challenge civilian government if soldiers lived among the people. Barracks were a symbol of a dangerous, independent military establishment—a standing army.[10]

Narcissus Luttrell, *Brief Historical Relation of State Affairs from September 1678 to April 1714* [Oxford, 1857], 1:456–459, 467; Clode, *Military Forces of the Crown,* 2:81; Scott, *British Army,* 3:537, 564).

9. Clode, *Military Forces of the Crown,* 1:229. The omission in the Declaration of Rights of a statement about quartering troops, Lois G. Schwoerer observed, "may well be laid both to haste, for opposition to quartering soldiers was a feature of the anti–standing army attitude, and perhaps to reluctance to blame James for something that could also be charged against William" (Schwoerer, *Declaration of Rights, 1689* [Baltimore, 1981], 71).

10. J. R. Western, *English Militia in the Eighteenth Century: The Story of a Political Issue, 1660–1802* (London, 1965); Frederick Bernays Wiener, *Civilians under Military Justice: The British Practice since 1689 Especially in North America* (Chicago, 1967); Clode, *Military Forces of the Crown,* 1:568–575. In Scotland and Europe, quartering of troops by civilians was practiced long after it was forbidden in England (Henry Home, Lord Kames, *Statute Law of Scotland Abridged* [Edinburgh, 1757], 104; Parker, *Army of Flanders,* 87–90); Sir William Blackstone, *Commentaries on the Laws of England* (Oxford, 1765–1769), 1:13; Edgard Boutaric, *Institutions Militaires de la France avant les Armées Permanentes* (Paris, 1863), 311–312; André Crovisier, *L'armée Française de la Fin du XVIIe Siècle au Ministère de Choiseul: Le Soldat* (Paris, 1964), 2:703–728; Thomas C. Hansard, comp., *Parliamentary History of England from the Earliest Period to the Year 1803* (London, 1806–1820), 7:510 (1717); 8:914–918 (1732); *Collection of the Parliamentary Debates in England from the Year 1668 to the Present Time* (London, 1741–1742), 20:278–279 (1741); Robert Chambers, *History of the Rebellion of 1745–6,* 7th ed. (London and Edinburgh, 1869), 270, 276; *Journals of the House of Commons,* 28:73, 75 (1758); 33:716, 783 (1772). Arguments against the upkeep of regular

The Mutiny Act did not extend to the North American colonies, where circumstances were such that for a century and a half it had no application. The colonists built their defenses around an adapted militia system. Virtually all men over sixteen years of age were required to bear arms in response to public danger, but the need for provisions or lodging outside one's own county was rare. This is not to say there was no conflict between early colonists and quartered soldiers. In 1677 the Dutch inhabitants of Wiltwyck, New York, lost property to garrisoned English soldiers who beat the citizens in their houses and thrust a sword "threww Dirck the sd Hendrixes Breeches." Crowding and the use of private homes to quarter troops during King Philip's War raised complaints in Massachusetts and Connecticut. Allegations of forced billeting were heard again in New York under Governor Edmund Andros at the time of the Dominion of New England, and more troubles connected with quartered troops occurred in the West Indies, Virginia, South Carolina, and Nova Scotia.[11]

---

armed forces paralleled the general emergence of such armies in Europe (Lois G. Schwoerer, *"No Standing Armies!" The Antiarmy Idealogy in Seventeenth-Century England* [Baltimore, 1974]; William Shippen, *Four Speeches against Continuing the Army, &c., as They Were Spoken in the House of Commons on Several Occasions* [London, 1732]).

11. Leonard Woods Labaree, ed., *Royal Instructions to British Colonial Governors, 1670–1776* (New York, 1935), 1:562–563; Joseph Henry Smith, *Appeals to the Privy Council from the American Plantations* (New York, 1950), 464–522; "The Papers That Concerne ye Esopus Mutineys with ye Death of Henrick Cornelius," in *Documents Relative to the Colonial History of the State of New-York*, ed. Edmund B. O'Callaghan and Berthold Fernow (Albany, N.Y., 1853–1887), 13:406; Military Documents, 67:271–272, 279a (1675), Massachusetts State Archives, Boston; James Hammond Trumbull, ed., *Public Records of the Colony of Connecticut, {1636–1776}* (Hartford, Conn., 1850–1890; reprint, New York, 1968), 2:394–396; 3:94, 583–584; 4:770; 6:397–398, 409; Michael G. Hall, Lawrence H. Leder, and Michael G. Kammen, eds., *The Glorious Revolution in America: Documents on the Colonial Crisis of 1689* (Chapel Hill, 1964), 174; George Madison Bodge, *Soldiers in King Philip's War*, 3d ed., rev. (Baltimore, 1967), 57, 210–212; CO 137/5/pts. 4–6, and Bollan to Newcastle, 19 Aug. 1747, CO 5/13; W. L. Grant and James Munro, eds., *Acts of the Privy Council of England, Colonial Series* (London, 1908–1912), 3: nos. 68, 303, 400; William Noel Sainsbury et al., eds., *Calendar of State Papers, Colonial Series, America and West Indies* (London, 1860–), *1708–1709*: no. 116, and *1726–1727*: no. 524; Wilcomb E. Washburn, *The Governor and the Rebel: A History of Bacon's Rebellion in Virginia* (Chapel Hill, 1957), 99–105; Trevor Richard Reese, *Colonial Georgia: A Study in British Imperial Policy in the Eighteenth Century* (Athens, Ga., 1963), 89–95; Verner W. Crane, *The Southern Frontier, 1670–1732* (Durham, N.C., 1928; reprint, Ann Arbor, Mich., 1956), 235, 245–246; Stephen Saunders Webb, *The Governors-General: The English Army and the Definition of the Empire, 1569–1681* (Chapel Hill, 1979). Helpful studies of the colonial militia include George E. Howard, *Introduction to the Local Constitutional History of the United States* (Baltimore, 1889), 1:60, 278–280, 345–351, 364, 400–404; Herbert L. Osgood, *American Colonies in the Seventeenth Century*

The first colonial statement of a legal right to be protected from billeted soldiers appeared in the New York Assembly's 1683 Charter of Libertyes and Priviledges: "Noe Freeman shall be compelled to receive any Marriners or Souldiers into his house and there suffer them to Sojourne, against their willes provided Always it be not in time of Actuall Warr within this province." Similar enactments passed by other colonies made the traditional exceptions of "innholders or other houses of entertainment."

Quartered soldiers became a major problem in the colonies with the arrival of thousands of British regulars during the Seven Years' War and an increasingly acute issue after 1763. When the British decided to maintain a military force in North America during peacetime, and especially after 1768 when they began using soldiers for law enforcement and stationing them near seaboard cities, quartered troops became the object of colonial hostility. The colonial assemblies were jealous of Parliament's prerogatives, and, conversely, the British military commanders were anxious to bring the quartering requirements of the Mutiny Act to bear wherever possible. General Edward Braddock's requests for quarters and other provisions during the French and Indian War met with rebuffs. His successor, John Campbell, earl of Loudoun, reported in 1756 that Americans cited "Rights and Privileges" to oppose him at nearly every turn.[12]

(New York, 1904–1907), 1:497–499; 2:375, 385, 399–400; Osgood, *American Colonies in the Eighteenth Century* (New York, 1924), 1:32–33; Allen French, "Arms and Military Training of Our Colonizing Ancestors," *Proceedings of the Massachusetts Historical Society* 67 (1945): 3–21; Louis Morton, "Origins of American Military Policy," *Military Affairs* 22 (1958): 75–82; John W. Shy, "A New Look at Colonial Militia," *WMQ*, 3d ser., 20 (1963): 175–185; Howard H. Peckham, *Colonial Wars, 1689–1762* (Chicago and London, 1964); Douglas Edward Leach, "Military System of Plymouth Colony," *New England Quarterly* 24 (1951): 342–364; Leach, *Arms For Empire: A Military History of the British Colonies in North America, 1607–1763* (New York, 1973); and John Kenneth Rowland, "Origins of the Second Amendment: The Creation of the Constitutional Rights of Militia and of Keeping and Bearing Arms" (Ph.D. diss., Ohio State University, 1978).

12. *Colonial Laws Of New York from the Year 1664 to the Revolution* (Albany, 1894), 1:114; Leon de Valinger, Jr., *Colonial Military Organization in Delaware, 1638–1776* (Wilmington, Del., 1938), 32–33; *Acts and Resolves, Public and Private, of the Province of the Massachusetts Bay* (Boston, 1869–1922), 1:133; Aaron Leaming and Jacob Spicer, *Grants, Concessions, and Original Constitutions of the Province Of New Jersey (1664–1702)* (Philadelphia, 1752; reprint, Somerville, N.J., 1881), 371; *Acts And Laws of His Majesty's Province of New-Hampshire in New England* (Portsmouth, 1771), 99; John Shy, *Toward Lexington: The Role of the British Army in the Coming of the American Revolution* (Princeton, 1965), 45–83; Peter D. G. Thomas, "New Light on the Commons Debate of 1763 on the American Army," *WMQ*, 3d ser., 38 (1981): 110–112; John F. Burns, *Controversies between Royal Governors and Their Assemblies in the Northern American Colonies* (New York, 1923; reprint, New York, 1969), 415; Jack P.

In 1756 when Loudoun marched three hundred men into New York City for the winter, he was denied quarters. After quarrels, delay, and the threat of bringing in several more battalions, the city raised a fund to pay for their billets. In Pennsylvania, the army requested lodging in autumn 1756 but the legislature stalled for weeks. When Colonel Henry Bouquet and his men arrived in Philadelphia, as many as possible were crowded into a few buildings, but more than a hundred slept without shelter in the snow. Scores of Bouquet's soldiers fell victim to small pox. In the end, Bouquet's men were accepted under roof only after the commanders threatened to bring more soldiers to town and fill the homes of inhabitants. Similar disputes occurred in Massachusetts, New Jersey, Nova Scotia, and South Carolina.[13]

After the Treaty of Paris in 1763, General Thomas Gage told officials in London that the Mutiny Act was generally ignored in America and recommended that its terms be explicitly extended to the colonies. Parliament

Greene, *The Quest for Power: The Lower Houses of Assembly in the Southern Royal Colonies, 1689–1776* (Chapel Hill, 1963); Stanley Pargellis, ed., *Military Affairs in North America, 1748–1765* (New York, 1936), 81–92, 273; Winthrop Sargent, *History of an Expedition Against Fort Du Quesne, in 1755* (Philadelphia, 1855), 148, 266. For the services available from early American inns, *see* Elise Lathrop, *Early American Inns and Taverns* (New York, 1926), 31, 41–42.

13. Loudoun to Sir Charles Hardy, Albany, 1 Sept. 1756, Loudoun Papers, Huntington Library; PRO, Law Officers' Department 38/1669 (hereafter cited as LO); Pargellis, *Military Affairs*, 231, 272–273; Loudoun to Sir Charles Hardy, 1 Sept. 1756, LO 38/1669; "Conduct of a Noble Commander in America, Impartially Reviewed, Etc.," *London Magazine* 27 (1758): 267; Stanley McCrory Pargellis, *Lord Loudoun in North America* (New Haven, 1933), 194–206; entry for 8 Apr. 1757 in CO 5/18; Loudoun's messages in LO 38/1673, 54/2342, 56/2419; S. K. Stevens, Donald H. Kent, and Autumn L. Leonard, eds., *Papers of Henry Bouquet* (Harrisburg, Pa., 1951–), 1:30–31, 35–36, 38–39, 42; Leonard W. Labaree et al., eds., *Papers of Benjamin Franklin* (New Haven, 1959–), 7:38–49, 53–66; and John J. Zimmerman, "Governor Denny and the Quartering Act of 1756," *Pennsylvania Magazine of History and Biography* 91 (1967): 266–281; Thomas Pownall to Loudoun, 4 Nov. 1757, PRO, War Office 34/25/43 (hereafter cited as WO); Gertrude Selwyn Kimball, ed., *Correspondence of William Pitt when Secretary of State with Colonial Governors and Military and Naval Commissioners in America* (New York, 1906), 1:186; Thomas Gage to Lt. Gov. Wilmot, 21 Dec. 1764, Gage MSS, University of Michigan; Edgar Jacob Fisher, *New Jersey as a Royal Province, 1738 to 1776* (New York, 1911), 347; Lawrence Henry Gipson, *British Empire before the American Revolution* (New York, 1936–1970), 7:308, 446; John Shy, "Quartering His Majesty's Forces in New Jersey," *Proceedings of the New Jersey Historical Society* 78 (1960): 84–87; Henry Bouquet to Gov. William H. Lyttleton, 28 Feb. 1758, AB 1/25; Lyttleton to the South Carolina Assembly, 15 Mar. 1758, AB 1/42; and Lyttleton to Loudoun, 21 Mar. 1758, AB 2/59, Abercromby Papers, Huntington Library; *Papers of Henry Bouquet*, 1:212–231, 248–260, 265–269; Jack P. Greene, "South Carolina Quartering Dispute, 1757–1758," *South Carolina Historical Magazine* 60 (1959): 193–204.

responded in 1765 with a law providing that when barracks were inadequate in America, alehouses, inns, stables, and victualing houses were to be hired for the soldiers. If these could not be had, uninhabited structures, barns, and outhouses might be used. Fire, candles, vinegar, salt, and small beer or cider were to be furnished to the men at provincial expense. This parliamentary enactment succeeded only in raising the more compelling constitutional question: who had authority over the property and homes of the colonists, Parliament or the provincial assemblies?[14]

The New York legislature promptly answered Gage's request to quarter and provision his men according to the new law by resisting throughout the harsh winter. Parliament responded with a special law suspending the New York Assembly until the soldiers were cared for. By June, the assembly gave in. Parliament got its way because, as one New Yorker put it, "people . . . had rather part with their Money, tho' rather unconstitutionally, than to have a parcel of Military Masters put by Act of Parliament abed to their Wives and Daughters." Ugly encounters between soldiers and civilians in New York City continued for years.[15]

•

Yet another kind of jurisdictional dispute over quartered troops arose in clashes between civilian and military authorities. In West Florida during the mid-1760s, Governor George Johnstone fought over the scope of his authority with every military commander sent to the provincial capital at Pensacola. A disagreement over some bark huts passing for barracks and the use of a civilian's home by one of the soldiers led to open conflict between

---

14. *Gage Correspondence*, 1:49, 2:24, 262–266; Shy, *Toward Lexington*, 176–185; 5 George III, chap. 33 (1765).

15. O'Callaghan and Fernow, *Documents Relative to New-York*, 7:845–846, 867–868; *Gage Correspondence*, 1:76–77, 2:328–329; 7 George III, chap. 59 (1766); Joseph Redington, ed., *Calendar of Home Office Papers of the Reign of George III, 1760–{1775}* (London, 1878–1899; reprint, Nendeln, Liechtenstein, 1967), 2:12; "Trumbull Papers," in *Collections of the Massachusetts Historical Society*, 5th ser., 9 (1885): 230; Dorothy C. Barck, ed., "Letter Book of John Watts, Merchant and Councillor Of New York, January 1, 1762–December 22, 1765," in *New-York Historical Society Collections* 61 (1928): 354; Lee E. Olm, "The Mutiny Act for America: New York's Noncompliance," *New-York Historical Society Quarterly* 58 (1974): 188–214; Frederic Shonnard and W. W. Sponner, *History of Westchester County, New York, from Its Earliest Settlement to the Year 1900* (New York, 1900), 280–281; Nicholas Varga, "New York Restraining Act: Its Passage and Some Effects, 1766–1768," *New York History* 37 (1956): 233–258; Lee R. Boyer, "Lobster Backs, Liberty Boys, and Laborers in the Streets: New York's Golden Hill and Nassau Street Riots," *New-York Historical Society Quarterly* 57 (1973): 281–308; Philip Lawson, "George Grenville and America: The Years of Opposition, 1765 to 1770," *WMQ*, 3d ser., 37 (1980): 565–566.

the irascible governor and the ranking military officer at the fortress. Johnstone arrested the officer, placed him under guard, and went for a walk. Soon the governor found himself locked outside the gates. Undaunted, he shinnied over the stockade and retook the garrison with oaths and fists.[16]

Large numbers of British troops also were stationed in Canada for fear of insurrection by the French inhabitants. Quebec and Montreal witnessed a continuing competition between civilian and military personnel over winter shelter. On one occasion a group of evicted soldiers avenged themselves on a city magistrate by cutting off his ear. The cause of these problems and similar ones in Connecticut, Georgia, Maryland, and East Florida, was the lack of barracks.[17]

The problem of barracks took on its largest proportions in Boston, when opposition to British trade and revenue regulations such as the Stamp Act led in 1768 to the redeployment of military units from the North American interior to urban centers to assist with law enforcement. Four regiments—one soldier for every five citizens—were posted to Boston, igniting a clash

---

16. Robert Farmer to Gage, 21 and 24 Dec. 1764, 5 Jan. 1765, 2 Feb. 1765, 21 and 24 Mar. 1765, 13 Apr. 1765; Gov. Johnstone to Gage, 2 Jan. 1765, Gage MSS, University of Michigan; *Gage Correspondence*, 1:87–89, 112–113; Gage to Barrington, 23 Dec. 1766, CO 5/84; David Wedderburn to Alexander Wedderburn, 14 Apr. 1765, Wedderburn Papers, 1:6, University of Michigan; Chester to Frederick Haldimand, 23 and 29 Aug. 1771, and Hillsborough to Gage, 11 Jan. 1772, BL, Add. MSS 21665. Good secondary accounts are Cecil Johnson, *British West Florida, 1763–1783* (New Haven, 1943), 49–60; and Clinton N. Howard, *British Development of West Florida, 1763–1769* (Berkeley and Los Angeles, 1947), 20–25.

17. Gov. James Murray to Amhurst, 27 Aug. 1763, WO 34/2/203–204; Murray to Gage, 1 Aug. 1765, Guy Carleton to Gage, 8 Mar. 1767, Gage MSS, University of Michigan; *Gage Correspondence*, 1:74–75, 133; 2:412; Arthur G. Doughty and Adam Shortt, eds., *Documents Relating to the Constitutional History of Canada, 1759–1791* (Ottawa, 1907), 93–116; A. L. Burt, "Mystery Of Walker's Ear," *Canadian Historical Review* 3 (1922): 233–255; S. Morley Scott, "Civil and Military Authority in Canada, 1764–1766," *Canadian Historical Review* 9 (1928): 117–136; Edward H. Tatum, Jr., ed., *American Journal of Ambrose Serle, Secretary to Lord Howe, 1776–1778* (San Marino, Calif., 1940), 138; Abercromby to Ebenezer Silliman, 3 May 1758, AB 5/228; Silliman to Abercromby, 30 Oct. 1758, AB 15/792, Huntington Library; Webster, *Journal of Amherst*, 104; *Gage Correspondence*, 1:120–121, 126, 134, 170–171; 2:409; address of the Maryland Assembly and Sharpe to Loudoun, 17 Dec. 1757, WO 34/34/14–18 and 34/34/21; William Hand Browne et al., eds., *Archives of Maryland* (Baltimore, 1883–1972), 6:509, 521–522; Gov. James Wright to Gage, 25 Feb. 1767, Gage MSS, University of Michigan; Wright to Shelburne, 6 Apr. 1767, Shelburne MSS, 58:192–194; Gage to Conway, 28 Mar. 1766, Shelburne MSS, 51:6–7, University of Michigan; Gage to Shelburne, 7 Apr. 1767, CO 5/85; Charles L. Mowat, *East Florida as a British Province, 1763–1784* (Berkeley and Los Angeles, Calif., 1943; reprint, Gainesville, Fla., 1964), 27, 30–31.

between Governor Francis Bernard and the Massachusetts Assembly over housing for so large a force. Existing facilities, which were inadequate, were three miles offshore on Castle Island in the harbor. Boston leaders used every means possible to avoid quartering the men. Some did find warehouses and stores near the customs house, and others rented accommodations from private homeowners.[18]

Living in the midst of the people, however, soldiers began deserting by the score. Military guards responded by challenging civilians and soldiers alike in Boston's dark streets. Fistfights and riots followed, until summer 1769 when the army decided to withdraw two regiments. Still, matters became worse. A year after the regiments had landed, their commanding officer informed General Gage in New York that all authority had passed to the hands of the mob. Simultaneously, the Bostonians pleaded their rights as Englishmen: "The quartering of troops upon British Americans, in time of peace, is quite repugnant to the Bill of Rights, and a measure that always has been considered as an intolerable grievance, by a free people."[19]

The confrontation of 5 March 1770—the Boston Massacre—could have happened on any number of occasions during the previous year and a half. As it was, by firing into a threatening crowd a small guard seemed to confirm all the revolutionaries' allegations about a conspiracy at Whitehall to enslave Americans. With five Bostonians dead, city and military leaders agreed that all soldiers should leave Boston for Castle Island. There they whiled their time singing:

> Our fleet and our army, they soon will arrive,
> Then to a bleak island, you shall not us drive.
> In every house, you shall have three or four,

---

18. *Gage Correspondence*, 2:61–66, 68–69, 72–74; Gov. Bernard to Shelburne, 24 Dec. 1766, Shelburne MSS, 58:174–176, and Bernard to Gage, 24 Sept. 1768, Gage MSS, University of Michigan; Edward Channing and Archibald Cary Coolidge, eds., *Barrington-Bernard Correspondence and Illustrative Matter, 1760–1770* (Cambridge, Mass., 1912), 171–207; Oliver Morton Dickerson, comp., *Boston under Military Rule (1768–1769), as Revealed in a Journal of the Times* (Boston, 1936), 3, 11; and Thomas Hutchinson, *History of the Colony and Province of Massachusetts Bay*, ed. Lawrence Shaw Mayo (Cambridge, Mass., 1936), 3:122–178.

19. Dickerson, *Journal of the Times*, 9, 15–19, 21–22, 26, 28–31, 34, 38–39, 42, 51, 74; Lt. Col. Carr to Gage, 6 Mar. 1769, Gage to Maj. Gen. McKay, 4 June 1769, and Col. Dalrymple to Gage, 28 and 29 Oct., 3 and 12 Nov. 1768, 29 Oct. 1769, Gage MSS, University of Michigan; Whitmore, *Reports*, 16:286; depositions by soldiers of the 14th and 29th regiments, CO 5/88; *Gage Correspondence*, 1:227; John Phillip Reid, *In Defiance of the Law: The Standing-Army Controversy, the Two Constitutions, and the Coming of the American Revolution* (Chapel Hill, 1981), 193–228.

And if that will not please you, you shall have half a score.

Derry down, down, hey derry down.[20]

Boston had directly challenged the prerogative claimed by Parliament. Further aggravated by the Boston Tea Party, Parliament passed a new quartering act in 1774, stipulating that troops be quartered in or near cities if military authorities wished and empowering governors to provide housing for soldiers without the concurrence of colonial councils or assemblies. Colonists promptly revived the connection between the grievance against billeted troops and the ancient English opposition to standing armies in peacetime.[21]

In the mid-1770s the American revolutionaries found it advantageous to link together a variety of grievances, but the issue of quartered troops always retained an integrity of its own. It was memorialized annually in liturgical-like orations about the Boston Massacre; Samuel Adams cited it in his 1772 "List of Infringements and Violations of Rights"; the First Continental Congress complained about it in the Declaration and Resolves of 1774, and when the break came, the issue found a place among the usurpations cited in the Declaration of Independence.[22]

On the eve of the revolutionary war, moderate Joseph Galloway, of Pennsylvania, attempted to dissuade Americans from rebellion by insisting that an American army too would be undisciplined, "travelling over your estates, entering your houses—your castles, . . . seizing your property, . . . ravishing your wives and daughters, and afterwards plunging the dagger into their tender bosoms." Both British and American soldiers *were* quartered by civilians during the war, often at great inconvenience to the inhabitants, despite the wartime efforts of the newly independent states to regulate the

---

20. Frank Moore, comp., *Songs and Ballads of the American Revolution* (New York, 1855; reprint, Port Washington, N.Y., 1964), 51–52.

21. Hiller B. Zobel, *The Boston Massacre* (New York, 1970); *Short Narrative of the Horrid Massacre in Boston, Perpetrated in the Evening of the Fifth Day of March, 1770, By Soldiers of the 29th Regiment, Which with the 14th Regiment Were Then Quartered There* (Boston, 1770; reprint, New York, 1971); Donald R. Gerlach, "A Note on the Quartering Act of 1774," *New England Quarterly* 39 (1966): 80–88; Reid, *In Defiance Of The Law,* 148–156.

22. Gipson, *British Empire Before the American Revolution,* 9:15; Harry Alonzo Cushing, ed., *Writings Of Samuel Adams* (New York, 1904–1908), 2:362; Worthington Chauncey Ford et al., eds., *Journals of the Continental Congress, 1774–1789* (Washington, D.C., 1904–1937), 1:64, 69. Orations commemorating the Boston Massacre were delivered on its anniversary until 1784 when Bostonians began celebrating the occasion along with the Fourth of July: *Orations Delivered at the Request of the Inhabitants of the Town of Boston* (Boston, [1785]); James Spear Loring, *The Hundred Boston Orations Appointed by the Municipal Authorities and Other Public Bodies, From 1770 to 1852,* 2d ed. (Boston, 1853).

quartering of American armies. More importantly, at this same time the states were writing their own declarations of rights, which sometimes included prohibitions against billeting soldiers in private households.[23]

The American concern for protecting the rights of private homeowners against quartered troops was the product both of direct experience and their English political heritage. As such, it was sure to survive the revolutionary war. Those who wrote a new constitution, and especially the statesmen who prepared the Bill of Rights, did not overlook the ancient problem of armies

----

23. Merrill Jensen, comp., *Tracts of the American Revolution 1763–1776* (Indianapolis, 1967), 375–376; Ewald Gustav Schaukirk, *Occupation of New York City by the British* (New York, 1969), 5, 10, 11, 19, 22, 23, 24; Charles Stedman, *History of the Origin, Progress, and Termination of the American War* (London, 1794), 1:309; Patrick J. Furlong, "Civilian-Military Conflict and the Restoration of the Royal Province of Georgia, 1778–1782," *Journal of Southern History* 38 (1972): 415–442; Varnum Lansing Collins, ed., *Brief Narrative of the Ravages of the British and Hessians at Princeton in 1776–77* (Princeton, 1906), 30; James Thacher, *Military Journal of the American Revolution* (Hartford, Conn., 1862), 34; Franklin Bowditch Dexter, ed., *Literary Diary of Ezra Stiles* (New York, 1901), 2:96, 104; David Duncan Wallace, *South Carolina: A Short History, 1520–1948* (Chapel Hill, 1951; reprint, Columbia, S.C., 1961), 238; Israel Pemberton to his father, 19 Dec. 1777, Pemberton Papers, 31:73, Historical Society of Pennsylvania, Philadelphia; Samuel Seabury to [S.P.G.], 29 Dec. 1776, Society for the Propagation of the Gospel, MSS B, 2:658, Library of Congress, Washington, D.C.; Shonnard and Sponner, *History of Westchester County*, 318–319; Richard Frothingham, Jr., *History of the Siege of Boston, and of the Battles of Lexington, Concord, and Bunker Hill*, 2d ed. (Boston, 1851), 282; Margaret Wheeler Willard, ed., *Letters on the American Revolution, 1774–1776* (Boston and New York, 1925), 241, 255; E. Alfred Jones, *The Loyalists of New Jersey: Their Memorials, Petitions, Claims, Etc. from English Records* in *Collections of the New Jersey Historical Society* 10 (Newark, 1927): 122, 202; Stephen Bonsal, *When the French Were Here* (Garden City, N.Y., 1945), 55; Adelaide L. Fries et al., eds., *Records of the Moravians in North Carolina* (Raleigh, N.C., 1922–1969), 4:1775, 1777, 1906; *Archives of Maryland*, 11:463–464, 16:195, 21:240; Henry C. Van Schaack, *Life of Peter Van Schaack* (New York, 1842), 54; John C. Fitzpatrick, ed., *Writings of George Washington* (Washington, D.C., 1931–1944), 4:485–486, 8:465, 20:76; *Journals of the Continental Congress*, 10:44, 184; John Russell Bartlett, ed., *Records of the State of Rhode Island and Providence Plantations in New England* (Providence, R.I., 1856–1865), 7:295, 472–473; *Laws of the State of New-York* (New York, 1789), 1:28, 36, 54; *Minutes of the Provincial Congress and the Council of Safety of the State of New Jersey* (Trenton, N.J., 1879), 330; Samuel Hazard, ed., *Minutes of the Provincial Council of Pennsylvania . . . 1683–1776 {and} of the Supreme Executive Council of Pennsylvania . . . 1776–1790* (Harrisburg, Pa., 1851–1853), 11:144; *Proceedings of the Convention of Delegates from the Counties and Corporations in the Colony of Virginia* (Richmond, [1775]; reprint, 1816), 35–36; Francis Newton Thorpe, ed., *Federal and State Constitutions, Colonial Charters, and Other Organic Laws of the States, Territories, and Colonies* (Washington, D.C., 1909), 3:16, 88; *Journal of the Convention for Framing a Constitution of Government for the State of Massachusetts Bay . . . September 1, 1779 to . . . June 16, 1780* (Boston, 1832), 227.

and householders. Before the Philadelphia Convention of 1787 adjourned, Charles Pinckney, of South Carolina, proposed guarantees of personal liberty that included freedom from forced billeting. Weary of debate, however, the delegates submitted the document to the states for ratification without a bill of rights. Prominent among Antifederalist arguments against the plan was the dangerous absence of provisions to protect against abuses in the quartering of soldiers. During the ratification contest, of the eight states recommending specific articles for a national declaration of rights, five included a prohibition of the arbitrary billeting of troops. The provision was part of every draft of the Bill of Rights considered by Congress in 1789, and it was ratified by the requisite number of states, along with the rest of the first ten amendments, in December 1791.[24]

After centuries of dispute, a formal statement prohibiting the forced quartering of soldiers in peacetime, a legal right that stood beyond discretionary repeal, had been written. The product of trials in both the Old and New Worlds, the Third Amendment reflected a special regard for the sanctity of the home. It bespoke ancient commitments to legally established procedures and to the subordination of the military to civilian authority. It protected all property holders without exception, including innkeepers and tavern owners. It insisted on appropriate laws to govern the housing of soldiers in time of war. All this in the simple statement: "No Soldier shall, in time of peace be quartered in any house, without the consent of the Owner, nor in time of war, but in a manner to be prescribed by law."

•

The Third Amendment is the only passage in the Constitution that speaks directly to the issue of civil-military relations in both war and peace, and the amendment secured for Americans a right exceeding that in Great Britain even to the present day. As it expressed itself through state declarations of rights and the federal Bill of Rights, the American Revolution did more than just restore traditional English liberties.

Compared with the centuries of abuse that men and women suffered from billeted armies in the past and all the failed attempts at relief, two hundred years are a brief deliverance. In an era of military ascendancy, we do well to recall Patrick Henry's words in the Virginia Convention of 1788. Without

---

24. Max Farrand, ed., *Records of the Federal Convention of 1787* (New Haven, 1911–1937), 2:341; Richard Henry Lee, *An Additional Number of Letters from the Federal Farmer to the Republican* ([New York], 1788; reprint, Chicago, 1962), 151; Herbert J. Storing, ed., *Complete Anti-Federalist* (Chicago, 1981), 2:262, 329; 5:26, 97; Elliot, *Debates*, 1:326, 328, 338–340; 2:552; 3:659; 4:244; Schwartz, *Bill of Rights*, 2:983–1204; *Bill of Rights: A Reprint of the Twelve Proposed Amendments to the Federal Constitution* (San Marino, Calif., 1943).

protection against the arbitrary billeting of troops, Henry argued, American homes were helpless and vulnerable to domestic military invasion. "This," he said, had been "one of the principle reasons for dissolving the connection with Great Britain." Having provided for a powerful national government, the need for a bill of rights was "greater in this government than ever it was in any government before."[25]

---

25. Clode, *Military Forces of the Crown*, 1:240–243; Watteville, *British Soldiers*, 90; 44 and 45 Victoria, chap. 58, sec. 102 et seq. (1881); 3 and 4 Elizabeth II, Chap. 18, secs. 154–176 (1955); *Manual of Military Law* (London, 1956), 1:368–374; Elliot, *Debates*, 3:410–413, 445.

The right of the people to be secure in their persons, houses, papers, and effects, against unreasonable searches and seizures, shall not be violated, and no warrants shall issue but upon probable cause, supported by oath or affirmation, and particularly describing the place to be searched, and the persons or things to be seized.
—Fourth Amendment to the United States Constitution, *1791*

•

That General Warrants whereby any Officer or Messenger may be commanded to search suspected places without evidence of a fact committed Or to seize any Person or Persons not named or whose Offence is not particularly described and supported by evidence are grievous and oppressive and ought not to be granted.
—Article 10, Virginia Declaration of Rights, *1776*

From General to Specific Warrants

The Origins of the Fourth Amendment

WILLIAM CUDDIHY

BEWILDERING AT FIRST GLANCE, the Fourth Amendment implies that the people must be secured against several kinds of unreasonable searches and seizures, but it focuses only on general warrants. To prevent the abuse of general warrants, which allowed officials to arrest, search, and seize any person or thing they found, the Fourth Amendment confines the scope of searches and seizures to particular places, persons, and objects. However, the Fourth Amendment does not define "probable cause" or explain when searches and seizures might be conducted either without a warrant or with an arrest warrant.[1]

The history of the Fourth Amendment clarifies these matters and shows some, but not all, of the searches and seizures that it calls unreasonable. At the time Virginia was first settled, English common law admonished officials to announce their purpose to the inhabitants of a dwelling and enter by force only if resistance was offered. In the period between American independence and the ratification of the Fourth Amendment, law and practice in most states prohibited searches at night. Furthermore, according to custom and the common law, only the person who personally witnessed a crime

---

1. Joint Congressional Resolution, 25 Sept. 1789, Bill of Rights and Ratifications, 1789–1985, Constitutional Papers, 1789–1985, General Records of the United States Government, Record Group 11, National Archives, Washington, D.C. The Fourth Amendment as sent to the states by Congress was the sixth of twelve proposed amendments; only the last ten were ratified, and the numbering of articles of the Bill of Rights changed accordingly. Important studies of the origin of the Fourth Amendment are Nelson B. Lasson, *History and Development of the Fourth Amendment to the United States Constitution* (Baltimore, 1937); Joseph J. Stengel, "Background of the Fourth Amendment to the Constitution of the United States," *University of Richmond Law Review* 3 (1968–1969): 278–298, 4 (1969–1970): 60–75; and William Cuddihy and B. Carmon Hardy, "A Man's House Was Not His Castle: Origins of the Fourth Amendment to the United States Constitution," *WMQ*, 3d ser., 37 (1980): 371–400.

could immediately seize and search the perpetrators without a warrant. A citizen who witnessed a murder could, without a warrant, arrest and search the perpetrator or even break into a house into which the citizen saw him flee. If the murderer escaped, however, and later was suspected of hiding in a house, a search warrant became necessary.[2]

The Fourth Amendment's restrictions about general searches have a long history, for general warrants were a major tool of British law enforcement. At least one form of general search was used in the thirteenth century, and each succeeding era saw new applications devised. Taxation was probably the first issue addressed by the general search. From about 1290 Parliament gave royal officials virtually unlimited power to search persons, houses, and ships in connection with the imposition of customs taxes on imports and exports. Typical proclamations forbade the importation of certain goods and empowered Crown agents "to enter into all, and all manner of shoppes, Cellers, Workhouses, Warehouses, Storehouses or other Rooms or places whatsoever by them suspected within Our Realme."[3]

Parliament formalized the procedures for customs searches in 1662 by codifying writs of assistance, which empowered customs officers to demand

---

2. *Semayne's Case* (King's Bench, 1604), *The Fifth Part of the Reports of Sir Edward Coke*, 91 at 91b, in *English Reports*, 77:194 at 195–196; *Acts and Laws of the Commonwealth of Massachusetts* (Boston, 1890–), *1782–1783*: 131–132; A. S. Batchellor and Henry H. Metcalf, eds., *Laws of New Hampshire* (Manchester, Bristol, and Concord, N.H., 1869–1922), 4:98; *Acts and Laws . . . of the State of Connecticut* (New London, 1783), 622; *{Acts Passed} at the General Assembly . . . {October 1785}* (Providence, [1785]), 43; *Laws of the State of New York . . . {1777–1801}* (Albany, 1886–1887), 1:480, 2:17; James T. Mitchell and Henry Flanders, eds., *Statutes at Large of Pennsylvania* (Harrisburg, Pa., 1896–1919), 11:577, 12:421; *{Laws of Maryland} . . . 1784* (Annapolis, Md., 1785), n.p.; *Acts of the Sixth General Assembly, of . . . New Jersey, . . . the Second Sitting* (Trenton, N.J., 1782), 101; Hening, *Statutes*, 12:308; Walter Clark, ed., *State Records of North Carolina* (Raleigh, N.C., 1895–1905), 24:550; Thomas Cooper and David J. McCord, eds., *Statutes at Large of South Carolina* (Charleston, S.C., 1836–1841), 4:581–582; Allen D. Chandler and Lucian LaMar Knight, eds., *Colonial Records of the State of Georgia* (Atlanta, 1904–1916), vol. 19, pt. 2, pp. 507–508; *Conductor Generalis* (New York, 1788), Gaine, 12, 25–27, 130, Patterson, 25, 159; John Faucheraud George Grimké, *South Carolina Justice of Peace* (Philadelphia, 1788), 20–21; François-Xavier Martin, *Office and Authority of a Justice of Peace* (New Bern, N.C., 1791), 38, 46.

3. A. Luders et al., eds., *Statutes of the Realm* (London, 1810–1822), 1:219a; 9 Edward III, stat. 2, chaps. 9, 10 (1335); 9 Edward III, 273–274. (While English and British statutes are cited by regnal year, chapter, and section, texts of pre-1713 statutes are quoted from the cited volumes and of post-1713 statues from Danby Pickering, ed., *Statutes at Large from the Magna Carta* [London, 1762–1807].) James F. Larkin and Paul L. Hughes, eds., *Royal Proclamations of King James I, 1603–1625* (Oxford, 1973), 445; *see also* 448, 604–605, 628–631.

assistance from other officials and from bystanders. Writs of assistance are still in use today in Great Britain and many Commonwealth countries. Between 1467 and 1700 the king and parliament granted many of England's craft guilds similar powers of search to protect monopolies that they enjoyed.[4] A 1548 statute concerning London leatherworkers instructed official searchers to

> make true searche and view in all and everie house and houses, place and places as well within the saide Cittie and suburbes thereof, as in everie other place within thre myles compasse of the saide Cittie where any Tanner . . . Shomaker, or Cobler dothe or shall dwell.[5]

The English Reformation caused a massive escalation in general searches and seizures. From 1535 onward, the government sought to police both English Catholics and extreme Protestants, to suppress books critical of the Crown and the established official church, and to intercept Jesuit missionaries. By Elizabeth I's death in 1603, Crown and church authorities could rely on a complex but effective network of parliamentary legislation, executive agencies such as the Privy Council, courts such as Star Chamber and High Commission, local justices of the peace, and even the London Company of Stationers to suppress religious dissent. Vast and terrifying searches became commonplace. Royal agents invaded houses by the score, bursting doors in the dead of night, brandishing swords and pistols before astonished householders, and in some cases literally terrifying sick and aged Britons to death. By 1695, however, when the last statutory authorization for such behavior expired, England had experienced a great transformation. The Stuart kings, who had been dethroned in 1649 and reinstated in 1660, were expelled forever in the Glorious Revolution of 1688–1689.[6]

---

4. 13 and 14 Charles II, chap. 11, sec. 4 (1662); 7 Edward IV, chap. 1 (1467); 11 Henry VII, chap. 27, sec. 2 (1494); 3 Henry VIII, chap. 14 (1512). Modern sequels include *The Public General Acts and General Synod Measures, 1979* (London, [1979]), 27 and 28 Elizabeth II, chap. 2, "Customs and Excise Management Act, 1979," sec. 161, pp. 109–110; *Revised Statutes of Canada, 1970* (Ottawa, 1970), chap. 40, secs. 139, 145, pp. 63, 67; and *Acts of the Australian Parliament, 1901–1973* (Canberra, Austl., 1974–1975), 3:832–833, Customs Act, Schedule 3, The Commonwealth of Australia, Writ of Assistance.

5. 2 and 3 Edward VI, chap. 9, sec. 5 (1548).

6. John Foxe, *Actes and Monuments* (London, 1563), 513a; Edward Cardwell, ed., *Documentary Annals of the Reformed Church of England*, new ed. (Oxford, 1839), 1:223–226; John Strype, *Life and Acts of Matthew Parker* (London, 1711), 3:221–222; G. W. Prothero, ed., *Select Statutes and Other Constitutional Documents Illustrative of the Reigns of Elizabeth and James I*, 4th ed. (Oxford, 1913), 170–172; John Roch Dasent, ed., *Acts of the Privy Council of England*, new ser. (London, 1890–), 21:392–393, 409; 24:221–222; 3 James I, chap. 4, sec.

•

Despite the advances of other civil liberties in seventeenth-century England, the use of general searches to suppress dissent continued; only its targets changed. Between 1629 and 1642 the Crown hounded its parliamentary opponents with searches, and between 1642 and 1660 Parliament turned the tables on its royalist adversaries. One royalist temporarily exiled in France lamented in 1649 that "not a presse dares wagge her tayl, but one of these [parliamentary] scumms of Raskallity comes with a warrant . . . stealing everything of value they can lay their theevish fingers on."[7]

Hundreds of houses throughout England were searched in 1605 after Catholic zealots botched the Gunpowder Plot to kill James I with a bomb planted in the Houses of Parliament. Similar invasions on a lesser scale were routine when officials sought fugitives or stolen property, or when they acted against vagrancy, prostitution, poaching, tax evasion, or smuggling. Any hint of a threat to the government could inspire officials to ransack half a village, but so could a stolen purse or the local manor lord's vague hunch that his neighbor's cellar held wines smuggled from France or deer poached from a private preserve. The upper levels of British society were least affected by the massive "privy searches" for vagrants that plagued the poor. The nobility enjoyed immunity from whole categories of searches, for parliamentary legislation ensured that the privileged classes were spared the inconvenience of rude searches.[8]

The general warrant was Britain's routine method of search, but the British also originated the ideas that culminated in our Fourth Amendment.

---

21 (1606); 3 James I, chap. 5, sec. 15 (1606). For examples of practice in 1591, *see* John Morris, ed., *Troubles of Our Catholic Forefathers* (London, 1872–1877), 3d ser., 16–18; Morris, ed., *Condition of Catholics under James I* (London, 1871), xxxix–xl; Anthony G. Petti, ed., *Letters and Dispatches of Richard Verstegen* (London, 1959), 7.

7. *Journals of the House of Commons* (London, 1803–), 3:200, 11:306; 3 Charles I, chap. 1 (1628); 1 William and Mary, chap. 18 (1688); John Rushworth, comp., *Historical Collections of Private Passages of State* (London, 1721–1722), 1:661, 4:34–35; *State Trials*, 3:293, 313; *An Exact Collection of All Remonstrances . . . Betweene the King's Most Excellent Majesty and . . . Parliament* (London, 1643), 197; C. H. Firth and R. S. Rait, eds., *Acts and Ordinances of the Interregnum, 1642–1660* (London, 1911), 1:185, 1022; 2:245–248, 251, 269, 696–698; *Mercurius Pragmaticus* (London), quoted 13–20 Feb. 1649, *see also* 27 Feb.–5 Mar. 1649.

8. Gunpowder Plot Book, 5 Nov.–12 Dec. 1605, pp. 10–154, PRO; Larkin and Hughes, *Royal Proclamations*, 123, 128–129, 445; 11 Henry VII, chap. 2, sec. 1 (1495); 7 James I, chap. 4, sec. 5 (1610); 7 James I, chap. 11, sec. 7 (1610); Michael Dalton, *Countrey Justice* (London, 1618), 314, 318–319; William Fleetwood to Lord Burghley, 14 Jan. 1582 and 7 July 1585, Lansdowne Manuscripts, 34:3, 7r–8r, and 44:38, 113r–115v, BL; 13 and 14 Charles II, chap. 3, sec. 13, and chap. 33, secs. 14, 18 (1662).

Although subject to abuse, there were formal restraints on the intended operation of British general search warrants: writs of assistance could not be used at night. Legislation giving search powers to guilds and excisemen confined general searches to the homes and shops of artisans or to distinct geographical boundaries. These measures could not prevent against abuse, but they were important legal precedents for limiting the search process.[9]

British legal thinkers made great contributions to the definition of the right against unreasonable search and seizure. As early as 1589, Robert Beale, a member of Queen Elizabeth's Privy Council, charged that the general search warrants used against Puritans violated Magna Carta, the charter of liberties extorted at sword's point from King John by the barons at Runnymede in 1215. In the seventeenth and eighteenth centuries such titans of English law as Sir Edward Coke, Sir Matthew Hale, and Sir William Blackstone embellished Beale's theme with erudite citations to English common law.[10]

Magna Carta, in fact, said nothing about searches, houses, and warrants. The charter forbade the illegal taking of life, liberty, or property, even by the king, but otherwise was more concerned with baronial privileges than with our modern provisions for the rights of the criminally accused. Indeed the common-law court case usually cited against the general warrant, *Semayne's Case* (of 1604 and 1606), exempted the Crown from its ruling that one could not force entry to the dwelling of another: a man's house was his castle only against intrusions by his fellow subjects, not by the Crown. When the public welfare was at stake, the king's key legally opened all doors.[11]

Critics of general searches did not propose the specific warrant as a remedy. Victims of searches execrated the experience itself, not the terms of the warrant used. The nobleman's indignation that a general search affronted his social station implied that searches were acceptable for commoners. A husband's outrage that his pregnant wife had miscarried during a violent

---

9. 13 and 14 Charles II, chap. 11, sec. 4 (1662); 2 and 3 Edward VI, chap. 9, sec. 5 (1548); 5 and 6 William and Mary, chap. 20, sec. 10 (1694).

10. Robert Beale, "A Collection Shewing What Jurisdiction the Clergie Hathe Heretofore Used," Cleopatra F.1, 40v, Cottonian Manuscripts, BL. (Of the surviving copies of Magna Carta, the example in the best condition is in the same collection: Augustus II, no. 106.) Sir Edward Coke, *Fourth Part of the Institutes of the Laws of England* (London, 1644), 176–177; Sir Matthew Hale, *Historia Placitorum Coronae* (London, 1736), 1:577–578; 2:110–112, 149–150; Sir William Blackstone, *Commentaries on the Laws of England* (Oxford, 1765–1769), 1:308, 4:287–288.

11. William Sharp McKechnie, *Magna Charta: A Commentary on the Great Charter of King John*, 2nd ed. (New York, 1914), 49, 84, 109–138, 375–395; *Semayne's Case* (K. B. 1604), 5 Coke 91a–93a, *English Reports*, 77:194–198.

search became an appeal for sympathy rather than a demand for legislation. Strictly speaking, before the American Revolution, denials of the legality of the general search were based on little more than myth.[12]

Still, these protests acquired legitimacy through repetition. The text of Magna Carta said nothing about search warrants, but by 1700 England's greatest and most influential legal theorists had taught generations of lawyers that it did. This belief became a formidable ideological weapon against the general search, and in time it was used by Parliament. In 1680 Parliament impeached Chief Justice William Scroggs for, among other things, issuing general warrants by which citizens were "vexed, their houses entered into, and they themselves grievously oppressed, contrary to law." Eight years later Parliament repealed a law that it described as a "badge of slavery on the whole people, exposing every man's house to be entered and searched by persons unknown to him."[13]

There was a gap, however, between these expressions of Parliament's sentiments about search and seizure and the terms of the legislation it enacted. The same Parliament that impeached Scroggs also wrote a censorship statute with provisions strongly resembling Scroggs's general warrants. This law and writs of assistance survived the Glorious Revolution, and two poaching statutes passed in the 1690s allowed the harshest use of general warrants in English legal history.[14]

Use of the general search expanded further in the first half of the eighteenth century. Legislation allowing general warrants against religious and political dissent expired in 1695, but the courts refused to intervene when Crown officials continued to use them, and between 1700 and 1763 more than a hundred were issued to suppress publications or persons offensive to the government. More legislation authorizing general searches surfaced between 1688 and 1713 than in any other period of English legal history. The earlier authorizations for general searches and warrants were renewed and new ones added for land taxes, recruitment of soldiers and sailors, and the suppression of counterfeiting.[15]

---

12. [Henry Barrow] to the Privy Council, [Jan. 1593], Lansdowne MSS, no. 109, art. 12, fol. 34, BL; Morris, *Troubles*, 3d ser. (1877): 17, 70; Petti, *Verstegen Letters*, 8.

13. *History and Proceedings of the House of Commons from the Restoration to the Present Time* (London, 1742–1744), 2:66; 1 William and Mary, chap. 10, sec. 1 (1688).

14. 1 James II, chap. 17, sec. 15 (1685); 2 William and Mary, chap. 4, sec. 2 (1689); 3 William and Mary, chap. 10, sec. 2 (1691); 4 William and Mary, chap. 23, sec. 2 (1692); 4 William and Mary, chap. 24, sec. 15 (1692).

15. *Journals of the House of Commons*, 11:306; Philip Carteret Webb, comp., *Copies Taken from the Records of the Court of King's Bench at Westminster . . . of Warrants* (London, 1763),

The most significant eighteenth-century development was the increased vulnerability of British and American houses to the excise. In the seventeenth century, the houses of persons who made, sold, or transported intoxicating beverages were subject to unwelcome and warrantless inspection by the excisemen. In the eighteenth century Parliament increased the number of excised commodities to include salt, soap, paper, candles, and glass. Consequently, the proportion of the population subject to search grew apace. When sugar and wine joined ale and beer on the excise list, a wit wrote:

> Grant these and the Glutton
> 	Will roar out for mutton,
> Your Beef, Bread, and Bacon to boot,
> 	He'll thrust down his Gullet,
> Whilst the Labourer munches a Root.
>
> . . . . .
>
> Your Cellars he'll range
> 	Your Pantry and Grange;
> No Bars can the monster restrain.

If an exciseman suspected clandestine operations by unlicensed persons, he could state his suspicion under oath before a magistrate and obtain a warrant to enter any premises concerned.[16]

•

The American colonies copied British practice and used general searches to collect taxes, discourage poaching, capture felons, and reclaim stolen merchandise. A typical Connecticut warrant of 1739 charged John Bellamy with counterfeiting and commanded the sheriff of New Haven to "make Dilligent and thorow Search" for Bellamy and his handiwork "in the hous where the s[ai]d Bellamy dwells and in all the other Neighboring houses buildings and places and any other places that you shall have reason to Suspect." Except for a few instances in Massachusetts and Pennsylvania, colonial officials never used general searches to harass religious minorities or

---

12–62; 1 William and Mary, sess. 2, chap. 1, sec. 10 (1688); 6 and 7 William III, chap. 17, sec. 8 (1695); 3 and 4 Anne, chap. 10, sec. 1 (1704); 3 and 4 Anne, chap. 11, sec. 3 (1704); 4 and 5 Anne, chap. 6, secs. 1, 2, 4 (1705); 4 and 5 Anne, chap. 21, secs. 1, 11 (1705); 13 George I, chap. 23, sec. 7 (1726).

16. *Britannia Excisa: Britain Excis'd* (London, 1733), 4–5. *See also* 1 Anne, stat. 1, chap. 15, sec. 2 (1702); 10 Anne, chap. 15, secs. 13, 22, 25, 52, 53, 59, 80 (1711); 6 George I, chap. 21, sec. 14 (1719); 19 George II, chap. 12, sec. 9 (1746); 10 Anne, chap. 18, sec. 103 (1711); 10 George I, chap. 10, sec. 13 (1723).

to censor the press. In the slaveholding southern colonies, on the other hand, general searches without warrant were a mainstay of social regulation by quasi-military slave patrols.[17]

Massachusetts was the first jurisdiction to make the specific, not general, search warrant the standard method of search and seizure. The Bay Colony's reform began in response to the abusive searches conducted by Edward Randolph, a royal customs officer, but the legislature imposed the same restraints on their own customs officer. General search warrants were already limited by legislation in Massachusetts, but between 1682 and 1699 the Massachusetts legislature created short-term warrants for customs searches and stipulated, first, that their issuance had to be based on a sworn complaint by an informant, and second, that informants were vulnerable to a civil suit if their information resulted in a needless search. Technically, the bearer of such a warrant could still enter every house in sight, but these legal encumbrances discouraged such capriciousness.[18]

After 1703 Massachusetts returned to general searches, for these limitations had fostered smuggling, but the earlier experiment was never forgotten. The memory fueled new protests both when the British used general searches to impress Boston seamen into the Royal Navy and when the colonial legislature adopted such searches for collecting taxes. A tide of protest greeted the Massachusetts General Court's enactment in 1754 of an excise that required every householder to reveal how much taxable liquor his family consumed each year. Two years later the colony switched to specific warrants, first to enforce the excise and the impost, then to combat military desertion, and finally, in 1764, to suppress poaching of game.[19]

---

17. James Whiteing to sheriff, New Haven, 27 Feb. 1739, "Crimes and Misdemeanors," 4:103, Connecticut State Library, Hartford. *See also* James Athearn to sheriff, 26 Oct. 1762, Court Files, Suffolk, vol. 492, no. 83,471, Office of the Supreme Court Clerk, Suffolk County Courthouse, Boston, Mass.; John Harvie Creecy, ed., *Princess Anne County Loose Papers, 1700–1789* (Richmond, 1954), 61–62; Cuddihy and Hardy, "A Man's House Was Not His Castle," 387 n. 79, 390 n. 5; Nathaniel B. Shurtleff, ed., *Records of the Governor and Company of the Massachusetts Bay* (Boston, 1853–1854), 5:134; Samuel Hazard et al., eds., *Pennsylvania Archives*, 1st ser. (Harrisburg, Pa., 1852–1949), 3:64; *Statutes at Large of South Carolina*, 2:254–255, 3:681–685; *Colonial Records of Georgia*, 18:389.

18. Acts of May 1646 and 26 May 1652, Shurtleff, *Records of . . . Massachusetts Bay*, 2:150, 4:82, 5:338; *Acts and Resolves, Public and Private, of the Province of Massachusetts Bay* (Boston, 1869–1922), 1:32–33, 119, 271–274, 371–374; Michael Garibaldi Hall, *Edward Randolph and the American Colonies, 1676–1703* (Chapel Hill, 1960), 46–78.

19. *Acts and Resolves of Massachusetts Bay*, 1:273, 502, 513; 2:39; 3:403–406, 787–788, 908, 911, 936–937; 4:156–157, 684; Boston Record Commissioners, *Report* 14 (1885): 85.

Relations between provincial merchants and British customs officers were poor, writs of assistance came to the attention of the Massachusetts Superior Court, for the merchants thought that customs regulations were being enforced unfairly. The death of King George II in 1760 meant that writs issued in his name expired six months later, but local merchants petitioned the court not to reissue them. The customs establishment argued that writs of assistance were general search warrants and that a Massachusetts statute empowered the court to issue them just as they were issued them in England. In rebuttal, James Otis, Jr., who represented the merchants and whose father was the family candidate for a seat on the superior court, inaccurately claimed that the provincial court had not recently exercised this authority.[20]

Dozens of British laws expressly authorized general searches, but Otis referred to an article in the *London Magazine*, cited Sir Edward Coke's exaggeration of Magna Carta, incorrectly asserted that Coke required all search warrants to be specific, and appealed to "higher law." General searches violated natural and common law, Otis reasoned, therefore writs of assistance were void if their wording followed the statute. He asked the court to regard them as specific search warrants. Persuaded by Otis's eloquence, the court delayed its decision.[21]

When the court learned that writs used in England *were* general, it approved the issuance of provincial writs of assistance over Otis's continued objections. The Massachusetts legislature responded by reducing the salaries of the judges and by passing a bill that defined the writs as specific warrants. Governor Francis Bernard, who had appointed Thomas Hutchinson to an office coveted by Otis's father, vetoed the bill, and later Hutchinson traced the beginning of his own political demise to his support for writs of assistance. *Paxton's Case*, as this episode is known, led to the rejection by other Massachusetts courts of customary general search warrants in *Bassett* v. *Mayhew* and other cases decided in the 1760s and became an important precedent for the Fourth Amendment.[22]

---

20. Josiah Quincy, *Reports of Cases . . . in the Superior Court of . . . Massachusetts Bay, Between 1761 and 1772* (Boston, 1865), 412–418; L. Kinvin Wroth and Hiller B. Zobel, eds., *Legal Papers of John Adams* (Cambridge, Mass., 1965), 2:123–144; Thomas Hutchinson, *History of the Colony of Massachusetts-Bay*, 2d ed. (London, 1765–1828), 3:86–88.

21. *London Magazine*, 29 (1760): 125–126; Wroth and Zobel, *Legal Papers of John Adams*, 2:125–129, 139–144.

22. Quincy, *Reports*, 57, 495–499; Wroth and Zobel, *Legal Papers of John Adams*, 1:91, 99, 102–105; 2:144–147; *Acts and Resolves of Massachusetts Bay*, 16:735. Thomas Hutchinson to

•

In Britain, the Wilkes cases, a cluster of forty cases between 1763 and 1769, paralleled *Paxton's Case*. At issue in these British trials were general warrants, based on custom rather than statute, used by the state to suppress pamphlets and authors who criticized the government. John Wilkes's *North Briton*, No. 45, triggered the warrant and search. The British secretary of state commanded "diligent search" for the author, printer, and publisher of a satirical journal, *North Briton*, No. 45, and the seizure of their papers. Under the power of this document, Crown officers searched at least five houses, arrested forty-nine (mostly innocent) persons, and confiscated thousands of books and papers. Wilkes, a member of Parliament and principal author of *North Briton*, sued every official connected with the warrant and inspired many of the others who had been arrested to do the same.[23]

In the first trial, on 6 July 1763, the chief justice of the Court of Common Pleas criticized the *North Briton* warrant because it had specified no person, had been issued without a formal complaint under oath, and, thus, had been issued without probable cause. When the case came before the full court, Chief Justice Charles Pratt held that the warrant's authority for general search and general arrest violated Magna Carta.[24]

The successful *North Briton* cases inspired earlier victims of government warrants to bring suit. In the most famous of these cases, *Entick* v. *Carrington* of 1765, the reformers' attack focused on the powers of seizure. Justice Pratt, by then earl Camden, condemned the use of seized personal papers as self-incrimination. Private property was inherently sacred, and any invasion of it was a trespass. While Camden conceded that officials could inspect private papers, he insisted that the disclosure of personal information was wrong. In a 1763 decision Pratt had condemned all general warrants, even those authorized by statute, but an appellate decision by William Murray, earl of Mansfield, upheld statutory warrants and denounced

Secretary Conway, Boston, 1 Oct. 1765, Massachusetts Archives, 26:155, Massachusetts State Archives, Boston.

23. John Almon, *History of the Late Minority* (London, 1765; reprint, 1766), 143–147; Raymond William Postgate, *That Devil Wilkes*, rev. ed. (London, 1956), 51.

24. Rev. Mr. Birch to Lord Royston, London, 9 July 1763, in Philip C. Yorke, *Life and Correspondence of Philip York, Earl of Hardwicke* (Cambridge, 1913), 3:510; *Huckle* v. *Money* (K. B. 1763), *Cases Argued and Adjudged in the Court of King's Courts at Westminster. By George Wilson, Esq.*, 2:206–207, in *English Reports*, 95:768–769. See also *John Wilkes, Esq.* v. *Wood* (C. P. 1763), *Reports of Cases Adjudged in the Court of King's Bench. . . . By Capel Lofft, Esquire, of Lincoln's Inn. 1790*, 18–19, in *English Reports*, 98:498–499.

only those based on custom. Camden adopted the same argument in his *Entick* v. *Carrington* decision, so in effect by 1765 only general warrants based on custom remained under attack in Britain.[25]

In the colonies, hostility to general warrants intensified between 1768 and 1774 as the courts in most colonies disobeyed instructions under the Townshend Acts of 1767 to issue writs of assistance. In Pennsylvania Chief Justices William Allen and in Connecticut Chief Justice Jonathan Trumbull declared that they categorically opposed all general warrants, not just those in the form of writs of assistance.[26]

Between 1762 and 1775, scores of American pamphlets and newspaper articles joined the chorus against general searches and warrants. Wilkes became a hero to colonial Americans. Provincial newspapers printed his speeches, summaries of the trials, and his account of the famous search that had started it all. John Dickinson condemned writs of assistance as "dangerous to freedom and contrary to the common law, which ever regarded a man's house as his castle, or a place of perfect safety." Dickinson's *Letters from a Farmer in Pennsylvania, to the Inhabitants of the British Colonies* went through seven pamphlet editions and was reprinted at least once in every colony that had a newspaper. The argument eventually reached the national level when, in 1774, the Continental Congress unequivocally condemned customs and excise law provisions for warrantless general searches.[27]

---

25. *Wilkes* v. *Wood* (C. P. 1763), Lofft, 3–4, 18–19, *English Reports*, 98:490, 498–499; *Money and Others* v. *Leach* (K. B. 1765), *Reports of Cases Determined . . . from 1746 to 1799, by the Honourable Sir William Blackstone*, 1:561–562, in *English Reports*, 96:323; *Money et al.* v. *Leach* (1765), *Reports of Cases Argued and Adjudged in the Court of King's Bench. . . . By Sir James Burrow*, 3:1762–1767, in *English Reports*, 97:1085–1088; *Entick* v. *Carrington* (1765), *State Trials*, 19:1045–1046, 1052, 1058–1067, 1073.

26. John Swift and Loring [to Commissioners], 30 Nov. 1771, and John Patterson and Zachariah Hood to Commissioners, 3 July 1773, PRO, Treasury 1/491, 220 and 1/501, 174; William S. Johnson to Richard Johnson, 26 Feb. 1773, William S. Johnson Papers, Connecticut Historical Society, Hartford; Oliver M. Dickerson, "Writs of Assistance as a Cause of the Revolution," in *Era of the American Revolution*, ed. Richard B. Morris (New York, 1939), 48–75.

27. Wilkes's accounts of the searches appeared in *Boston Post-Boy, Providence Gazette, New York Mercury* and *Pennsylvania Gazette* during July and August 1767, and coverage of the leading trials appeared in the same newspapers during September 1763 and February 1764. John Dickinson, *Letters from a Farmer in Pennsylvania* (Philadelphia, 1768), 45–46 (Dickinson's language occurs in letter 9 as reprinted in newspapers such as the *Boston Chronicle*, 8–15 Feb. 1768, and the *Annapolis Maryland Gazette*, 18 Feb. 1768); Dickinson, *Letter to the Inhabitants of the Province of Quebec* (Philadelphia, 1774), 43; *Petition of the Grand American Continental Congress to the King's Most Excellent Majesty* (Boston, 1774), 3.

•

American opposition to general search warrants culminated in their formal repudiation in eight state constitutions written between 1776 and 1784. One group of states led by Virginia, the first state to define constitutional restrictions for search and seizure, simply denounced general warrants. Another group, led by Maryland, declared them illegal. The third position, taken by Pennsylvania and Massachusetts, foreshadowed the Fourth Amendment by announcing a general right against unreasonable search and seizure.[28]

Impetus for an equivalent national guarantee surfaced shortly after the Convention of 1787. Virginia's Richard Henry Lee, the Bay State's Mercy Otis Warren, James Otis's sister, and other Antifederalists objected that the proposed constitution made citizens vulnerable to general warrants issued by the tyrannical hands of a mighty central government. After the new constitution was submitted to conventions of the states for ratification, Virginia, New York, and North Carolina asked for protections against abuses of search warrants.[29]

To a substantial degree, the Fourth Amendment was an effort by the states to deprive the federal government of search and seizure procedures that some states wished to retain for their own use. Despite all the rhetoric and constitutional pronouncements, all of the American colonies and states except Delaware used general searches between 1761 and 1789, when James Madison introduced the prototype of the Fourth Amendment in the House of Representatives. In 1777, for example, officials searched at least six Philadelphia houses and detained forty persons in a roundup of suspected loyalists. When the Fourth Amendment was ratified in 1791, only Virginia,

---

28. Benjamin Perley Poore, comp., *Federal and State Constitutions* (Washington, D.C., 1877), 1:819, 959; 2:1282, 1409, 1542, 1860, 1909. The texts are also printed in Lasson, *History and Development of the Fourth Amendment*, 79–82. The Delaware statement appears in *Proceedings of the Convention of the Delaware State . . . the Twenty-seventh of August, 1776* (Wilmington, Del., 1776), 17.

29. Richard Henry Lee, *An Additional Number of Letters from the Federal Farmer to the Republican* ([New York], 1788; reprint, Chicago, 1962), 32, 52–53, 149; Mercy Otis Warren, *Observations on the New Constitution . . . by a Columbian Patriot* (Boston, 1788), 12. For other examples *see* "A Son of Liberty," *New-York Journal*, 8 Nov. 1787; "A Farmer," *Baltimore Maryland Gazette*, 15 Feb. 1788; David Robertson, ed., *Debates and Other Proceedings of the Convention of Virginia* (Petersburg, 1788–1789), 2:220; Robertson, ed., *Proceedings and Debates of the Convention of North-Carolina* (Edenton, N.C., 1789), 272; *Journal of the Convention of the State of New York* (Poughkeepsie, N.Y., 1788), 73.

Massachusetts, New Jersey, and Rhode Island had already abandoned the general warrant entirely.[30]

"To enter a man's house by virtue of a nameless warrant," declared Charles Pratt in a 1763 Wilkes case, "is worse than the Spanish Inquisition; a law under which no Englishman would wish to live for an hour."[31] The freedom guaranteed by the Fourth Amendment had both British and colonial roots. Specific warrants were devised in Massachusetts, while arguments against general searches were mostly a British contribution. Merged and thereby expanded for the first time in the Fourth Amendment, these developments made freedom from unreasonable search and seizure more extensive in America than anywhere else in the world.

---

30. Israel Pemberton, Journal, 1 Sept. 1777, fols. 2–3, Pemberton Papers, 31:79, Historical Society of Pennsylvania, Philadelphia; Samuel Hazard, ed., *Minutes of the Provincial Council of Pennsylvania . . . 1683–1776* (Harrisburg, Pa., 1851–1852), 11:287–289; *Pennsylvania Archives*, 1st ser., 5 (1853): 574. *See also* Cuddihy and Hardy, "A Man's House Was Not His Castle," 398–400; *Acts and Laws of . . . Massachusetts, 1782–1783*: 131–132, 527; *Acts and Laws . . . of Massachusetts, 1784–1785*: 28, 34; {*Acts Passed October 1785*}, [Rhode Island], 28, 34; *Acts of the Sixth General Assembly of . . . New Jersey*, 101; Hening, *Statutes*, 12:308.

31. *Huckle* v. *Money* (K. B. 1763), 2 Wilson 206–207, *English Reports*, 95:768–769.

No person shall be held to answer for a capital or otherwise infamous crime, unless on a presentment or indictment of a Grand Jury, except in cases arising in the land or naval forces, or in the Militia, when in actual service in time of War or public danger; nor shall any person be subject for the same offence to be twice put in jeopardy of life or limb; nor shall be compelled in any criminal case to be a witness against himself, nor be deprived of life, liberty, or property, without due process of law; nor shall private property be taken for public use, without just compensation.
—Fifth Amendment to the United States Constitution, *1791*

•

That in all Capital or Criminal Prosecutions a Man hath a right to demand the Cause and Nature of his Accusation to be confronted with the Accusors and Witnesses to call for Evidence in his favour and to a speedy Trial by an impartial Jury of his Vicinage without whose unanimous consent He cannot be found guilty nor can he be compelled to give Evidence against himself that no Man be deprived of his liberty except by the Law of the Land or the Judgment of his Peers.
—Article 8, Virginia Declaration of Rights, *1776*

The Bill of Rights

Chapter Eight

Putting Silence Beyond the Reach of Government

The Fifth Amendment and Freedom from Torture

JON KUKLA

IN 1951 before a United States Senate committee, Jake ("Greazy Thumb") Gusik, a former associate of Al Capone, relied on the Fifth Amendment and "refused to tell the investigators if he had taken a train or had flown to Washington." Today, culprits and crooks come first to mind when we think about the Fifth Amendment. The legal safeguard against compulsory self-incrimination originated, however, with steadfast religious men and women who believed, in the words of martyr William Tyndale, that it was "a crule thing to break up into a man's heart, and to compel him to put either soul or body in jeopardy, or to shame himself."[1]

Through the past three centuries, the protection against self-incrimination has been a shield against torture and coerced confessions. "For a man to accuse himself," claimed the clerk of Queen Elizabeth I's Privy Council in 1590, "was and is utterlie inhibited" by Magna Carta. Although the English did not entirely abandon the use of torture until 1640, by the end of the seventeenth century, lawyers, judges, and Parliament all agreed it was illegal. "In other countries," a legal scholar boasted in 1730, "Racks and Instruments of Torture are applied to force from the Prisoner a Confession, sometimes of more than is true; but this is a practice which Englishmen are happily unacquainted with, enjoying the benefit of that just and reasonable Maxim, *Nemo tenetur accusare seipsum*" (no one is bound to accuse himself).[2]

---

1. "Guzik, 'Payoff' Man For Capone, Is Dead," *New York Times*, 22 Feb. 1956, 18; William Tyndale, "The Obedience of a Christen Man," in *Doctrinal Treatises and Introductions to Different Portions of the Holy Scriptures*, ed. Henry Walter (Cambridge, 1848), 335.

2. Robert Beale quoted in Leonard W. Levy, "The Right Against Self-Incrimination: History and Judicial History," *Political Science Quarterly* 84 (1969): 22; Sollom Emlyn quoted in Levy, *Origins of the Fifth Amendment: The Right Against Self-Incrimination* (New York, 1968), 327.

On 14 June 1788, in their debate over ratifying the Constitution, Patrick Henry, George Nicholas, and George Mason explained the connection between self-incrimination and torture. Unless restrained by a bill of rights, Henry warned, the national government might "introduce the practice of France, Spain, and Germany—of torturing, to extort a confession of the crime." Nicholas replied grimly, "If we had no security against torture but our declaration of rights, we might be tortured to-morrow" for written guarantees of rights can be "infringed and disregarded." Mason answered that the Virginia Declaration of Rights, which he had written, "expressly provided that no man can give evidence against himself; and that the worthy gentleman must know that, in those countries where torture is used, evidence was extorted from the criminal himself."[3] In short, while there is a danger that written guarantees will be ignored, the right against self-incrimination removes the motive for coercion or torture by preventing the state from convicting people on the basis of illegally obtained confessions.

•

Despite its ancient roots, full acceptance of the right against self-incrimination is attributable to one man, John Lilburne, "one of the most flinty, contentious men who ever lived." Suspected of shipping seditious religious books into England from Holland, Lilburne was hauled before Archbishop William Laud's ecclesiastical Court of High Commission in 1637. Lilburne denied any wrongdoing and declared that he would answer no "impertinent questions, for fear that with my answer I may do myself hurt." After two weeks in jail, Laud's agents brought him before the secular Court of Star Chamber, which confronted Lilburne with the oath ex officio. This oath—a favorite of inquisitors—required an accused man to swear, without being told the identity of his accusers or the nature of the allegation against him, that he would answer all questions truthfully.[4]

The Star Chamber officials presented Lilburne with a Bible and told him to swear.

"To what?"
"That you shall make true answer to all things that are asked of you."
"Must I so Sir? But before I sweare, I will know to what I must sweare."
"As soon as you have sworne, you shall."

---

3. Elliot, *Debates*, 3:445–452.

4. Levy, *Origins of the Fifth Amendment*, 272–275; M. A. Gibb, *John Lilburne, The Leveller: A Christian Democrat* (London, 1947), 45–66; Pauline Gregg, *Free-born John: A Biography of John Lilburne* (London, 1961), 52–63.

Lilburne refused the oath, and he refused to answer "ensnaring" questions. The court found him guilty of contempt, and on 18 April 1638 Lilburne was whipped through the streets of London and imprisoned. His courage and eloquence in this ordeal made a popular hero. "Freeborn John," the crowds called him.[5]

For two years Lilburne lay in the Fleet Prison, sustained only by food smuggled through the floorboards by his fellow inmates. England was drifting toward civil war, and in desperation Charles I summoned Parliament. On 9 November 1640 a new member, Oliver Cromwell, rose to make his first speech in the House of Commons: he called for John Lilburne's release. John Lilburne was free within weeks, and events soon moved against Laud, who was impeached and imprisoned. Lilburne's final vindication came in July 1641 when Parliament outlawed the oath ex officio and abolished the Courts of Star Chamber and High Commission.[6]

•

The Virginia colony had been established before Lilburne's victory, but there is reason to suspect that the early colonists felt themselves protected against self-incrimination by the common law. In Massachusetts Bay in 1637—the same year that Lilburne began his struggle with Laud—the Reverend John Wheelwright, brother-in-law of Anne Hutchinson, preached a controversial sermon denying the validity of a key doctrine of New England puritanism. Summoned before the General Court, Wheelwright bristled at the court's mention of an oath ex officio and refused to answer questions lest "the Court . . . ensnare him, and . . . make him to accuse himselfe." In the end, armed with the text of Wheelwright's sermon and testimony from those who had heard him, the Massachusetts General Court convicted Wheelwright for "sedition and contempt of the Civill authority" and banished him from the colony. Nevertheless, Wheelwright's claim shows that early colonists knew when and how to protect themselves against self-incrimination. The General Assembly of Virginia, in answer to a motion from the Accomack County burgesses, declared in 1677 "that a person summoned as a witnes against another, ought to sweare upon oath, but noe law can compell a man to sweare against himselfe in any matter wherein he is lyable to corporall punishment."[7]

---

5. Gregg, *Free-born John*, 56–57.

6. Levy, *Origins of the Fifth Amendment*, 281–282.

7. Ibid., 336–348; A. E. Dick Howard, *Commentaries on the Constitution of Virginia* (Charlottesville, 1974), 129–130; Charles Francis Adams, ed., *Antinomianism in the Colony of Massachusetts Bay* (Boston, 1894), 195, 201; Hening, *Statutes*, 2:422.

By the beginning of the eighteenth century, Englishmen took their right against self-incrimination for granted. Benjamin Franklin in 1735 called it one of "the common Rights of Mankind," and Sir Geoffrey Gilbert, a leading English authority on criminal procedure, said it was part of the "Law of Nature."

In the era of the American Revolution, England and the colonies "differed little, if at all, on the right against self-incrimination." James Otis, Jr., and John Hancock, of Massachusetts, and Henry Laurens, of South Carolina, referred obliquely to the right against self-incrimination when they protested the actions of British admiralty and customs officials in the 1760s, but these leading colonists argued more vehemently about illegal searches than self-incrimination. When an overeager customs officer in Philadelphia sought to question under oath seamen suspected of smuggling tea, the crown's attorney general warned in 1770 "that the Court of Admiralty cannot with propriety oblige any persons to answer interrogatories which may have a tendency to criminate themselves, . . . it being contrary to any principle of Reason and the Laws of England."[8]

In practice, respect for the right against self-incrimination during the American Revolution was mixed. Celebrating the repeal of the Stamp Act, the New York Sons of Liberty offered a toast "No Answer to Interrogatories, when tending to accuse the Person interrogated." But ten years later, during the American War of Independence itself, law-abiding Tories often were tarred and feathered by mobs that observed no niceties of legal procedure. George Rome, a Rhode Island tory, vigorously criticized the revolutionaries in a private letter that fell into their hands and was published in the provincial newspaper. Summoned before the legislature and grilled about the opinions expressed in his letter, Rome invoked "the privilege of an Englishman" and declined to answer, saying, "I cannot be legally called to the bar of this house to accuse myself." The legislature promptly imprisoned him for the remainder of its session. For captured British spy Major John André and corrupt diplomat Silas Deane, on the other hand, the Americans honored the right against self-incrimination. In 1778 when Deane was under investigation for corruption, he claimed protection against self-incrimination and the Continental Congress allowed him to do so.[9]

8. Leonard W. Labaree et al., eds., *Papers of Benjamin Franklin* (New Haven, 1959–), 2:44; Sir Geoffrey Gilbert, *Law of Evidence* (London, 1756), 140; Levy, *Origins of the Fifth Amendment*, 404; Oliver M. Dickerson, *Navigation Acts and the American Revolution* (Philadelphia, 1951), 247.

9. David S. Lovejoy, *Rhode Island Politics and the American Revolution, 1760–1776* (Providence, R.I., 1958), 175–176; Levy, *Origins of the Fifth Amendment*, 413–414.

•

After the Declaration of Independence, every state that wrote a bill of rights protected the right against self-incrimination, but it was such a widely accepted inheritance from the common law that authors of state constitutions sometimes forgot it altogether (as happened in New York) or defined it carelessly. Thomas Jefferson overlooked self-incrimination in a constitution that he proposed for Virginia, and he never referred to it in the 1780s when he recommended provisions for a national bill of rights.[10]

When George Mason hastily drafted article 8 of the Virginia Declaration of Rights, he put the statement about self-incrimination among the protections afforded accused parties. Pennsylvania, North Carolina, and Vermont copied Virginia's clause in 1776 and 1777, and Massachusetts in 1780 and New Hampshire in 1784 protected a criminal defendant from being compelled to "accuse, or furnish evidence against himself." Delaware and Maryland in 1776 gave the protection against self-incrimination separate sections in their statements of rights instead of lumping it together with other procedural safeguards for trials.[11]

Unlike either the Virginia precedent or the Sixth Amendment (which explicitly protects the accused alone), the Fifth Amendment was not restrictive. James Madison, who drafted it, provided that no person should be compelled to bear witness against himself. Congress may have added the phrase "in any criminal case" to avoid any misunderstandings about a court's power to subpoena documents in civil suits. Promptly after its ratification in 1791, federal courts ruled that the Fifth Amendment was intended to protect all persons, not just those accused of crimes.[12]

The Fifth Amendment's protection of witnesses in civil suits was affirmed by the Supreme Court in the famous 1803 case of *Marbury* v. *Madison*, which is better known for John Marshall's decision establishing the doctrine of judicial review. Levi Lincoln, attorney general of the United States, was called as a witness to William Marbury's suit against President Madison, and Chief Justice Marshall asked Lincoln what happened to Marbury's missing commission as justice of the peace, which Lincoln had when he was acting secretary of state. When the attorney general (who probably had burned the

---

10. Levy, "The Right Against Self-Incrimination," 10.

11. Richard L. Perry, ed., *Sources of Our Liberties: Documentary Origins of Individual Liberties in the United States Constitution and Bill of Rights* (Chicago, 1959), 376; Levy, "The Right Against Self-Incrimination," 17.

12. "Amendments to the Constitution, 8 June 1789," in *Madison Papers*, 12: 196–211; Levy, "The Right Against Self-Incrimination," 19–20; Levy, *Origins of the Fifth Amendment*, 422–425.

document) refused to incriminate himself by answering, the Supreme Court sustained his right to silence.[13]

Until after the Civil War, the Bill of Rights did not extend to state and local governments. Nineteenth-century state courts often put restrictive interpretations on the ancient common-law right against self-incrimination, and, as Americans dealt with rapid changes in society, abuses by law enforcement authorities of the principles of the Fifth Amendment were not uncommon. In many localities, North and South, fearful authorities responded to change with repressive measures. Slavery ended after the Civil War, but many states played fast and loose with personal liberties in their efforts to control the newly free black Americans or the increasing numbers of immigrants from the Eastern European and Mediterranean countries. The rise of industrialism and of cities, conflict between labor unions and capitalists, and fears of subversion by late-nineteenth-century anarchists or early-twentieth-century communists—all of these forces in modern American life had similar effects. By the early twentieth century, neglect of the history of our right against self-incrimination had become so widespread that lawyers and jurists—reflecting practices at the state level—commonly called it a privilege, not a right.[14] In 1936 the Supreme Court overturned the murder convictions of two black Mississippians because they had been beaten with the buckle end of a leather belt until they confessed. This torture, according to Chief Justice Charles Evans Hughes, was "a wrong so fundamental that it . . . rendered the conviction and sentence wholly void." Even in a state action so "revolting to the sense of justice," however, Hughes carefully noted in 1936 that "the privilege against self-incrimination is not here involved."[15]

●

In theory, as with other personal liberties secured by the Bill of Rights, the Fifth Amendment prohibition against compulsory self-incrimination became applicable to state and local governments with the ratification of the Fourteenth Amendment to the United States Constitution in 1868. In fact, however, it took a century for this to happen. The Supreme Court first applied the eminent domain clause of the Fifth Amendment to the states in 1897, for example. And, not until its 1969 decision in *Benton* v. *Maryland*

---

13. Levy, *Origins of the Fifth Amendment*, 429, 516n.

14. Howard, *Commentaries on the Constitution of Virginia*, 129–143, 189–197.

15. Richard C. Cortner, *Supreme Court and the Second Bill of Rights: The Fourteenth Amendment and the Nationalization of Civil Liberties* (Madison, Wis., 1981), 135–136; Richard Harris, *Freedom Spent* (Boston and Toronto, 1976), 377–379.

did the Court extend the double jeopardy clause of the Fifth Amendment (which embodies a protection against harassment by multiple prosecutions that dates at least to 355 B.C.) to the states on the basis of the Fourteenth Amendment. Finally, by a five-to-four decision on 15 June 1964 the Supreme Court ruled that "the Fifth Amendment's exception from compulsory self-incrimination is also protected by the Fourteenth Amendment against abridgement by the states."[16]

Two years later, in 1966, the Court handed down its decision in *Miranda v. Arizona*, a ruling many people feared would hinder the apprehension and trial of criminals. The *Miranda* ruling declared that before any interrogation took place, a suspect must be told: first, that he or she has the right to remain silent; second, that anything he or she says may be used in court; third, that he or she has a right to consult a lawyer and to have a lawyer present during police questioning, and finally, that if he or she cannot afford legal counsel, a lawyer will be appointed by the government. These warnings, which Americans see recited every evening by actors on police-action television shows, are rooted in the Fifth Amendment. Protection of a suspect's "Miranda rights"—as they have come to be called—is an absolute prerequisite before any defendant's statements, or any evidence obtained as a result of an interrogation, can be admitted as evidence in court. The prosecutor who introduces such evidence must prove that a defendant knowingly and intelligently waived his right to silence and to counsel. Questioning must stop if a defendant wishes to remain silent, and a lawyer must be present if the defendant asks for counsel. (Physical evidence such as photographs, voice samples, lineup results, fingerprints, footprints, or urinalysis and handwriting tests are protected by the Fourth Amendment prohibition of unreasonable search or seizure.)[17]

Mid-1960s critics of the *Miranda* case called it, in the words of Senator Sam Ervin, Jr., "a decision based on excessive and visionary solicitude for the accused." Later in that decade, however, Leonard W. Levy's Pulitzer Prize–winning *Origins of the Fifth Amendment* traced our right against self-incrimination from Old Testament times to the present and put the weight of history behind the Court's generous interpretation of the right. Since the seventeenth century, England and its colonies have extended the

16. Cortner, *Supreme Court and the Second Bill of Rights*, 214; Yale Kamisar, "Equal Justice in the Gatehouses and Mansions of American Criminal Procedure," in *Criminal Justice in Our Time*, ed. A. E. Dick Howard (Charlottesville, 1965), 47; Howard, *Commentaries on the Constitution of Virginia*, 129–138.

17. Howard, *Commentaries on the Constitution of Virginia*, 132–135.

right both to witnesses and to the accused. By the eighteenth century its place in grand jury proceedings was clear. Its protection of witnesses in civil suits was affirmed by the Supreme Court in 1803, and its use in American legislative investigations had begun in 1778 with Silas Deane.[18]

•

In light of recent events, it seems a vicious irony that the Fifth Amendment, which protects against compulsory self-incrimination, also provides for grand juries in capital offenses. In modern America the grand jury has become, as a federal district court put it, "but a convenient tool for the prosecutor. . . . Any experienced prosecutor will admit that he can indict anybody at any time for almost anything." Within the past decade several innocent American women—heirs in spirit to John Lilburne—have spent months in Connecticut and Kentucky prisons for insisting on their right to silence when asked unfair and ensnaring questions before grand juries by well-meaning but zealous prosecutors.[19]

Today, the ghosts of Laud and of Lilburne stalk among us, challenging us to affirm or deny an elemental freedom that distinguishes free and civilized society from the Gulag archipelagoes of the left or right. Even as this essay went to press, presidential aides John M. Poindexter and Oliver L. North invoked the Fifth Amendment and refused to answer congressional questions about arms sales to Iran and diversions of money to Central America, while the Justice Department and attorney general of the United States announced their intention to find a case with which to challenge the Supreme Court's 1966 *Miranda* decision.[20] Laud's ghost recoils at arrogant men like Greazy Thumb Guzik and shouts, "Throw out the rules so you can throw the book at him!" Lilburne's spirit speaks in words such as those of Erwin N. Griswold, former dean of the Harvard Law School, who in 1955 reminded us that the Fifth Amendment is "a lone sure rock in a time of storm, . . . a symbol of the ultimate moral sense of the community, upholding the best in us, when otherwise there was a good deal of wavering under the pressures of the times."[21]

---

18. Sam J. Ervin, Jr., "Miranda v. Arizona: A Decision Based on Excessive and Visionary Solicitude for the Accused," *American Criminal Law Quarterly* 5 (1967): 125; Levy, *Origins of the Fifth Amendment*; Levy, "The Right Against Self-Incrimination," 1–29.

19. Federal Judge William Campbell quoted in Harris, *Freedom Spent*, 394.

20. "2 Ex-Reagan Aides Maintain Silence in House Hearing," *New York Times*, 10 Dec. 1986, A1; "Justice Dept. Study Calls For Overturning Miranda: 'Essential' Change Has Meese's Support," *Washington Post*, 23 Jan. 1987, A17.

21. Erwin N. Griswold, *The Fifth Amendment Today* (Cambridge, Mass., 1955), 73.

In all criminal prosecutions, the accused shall enjoy the right to a speedy and public trial by an impartial jury of the state and district wherein the crime shall have been committed, which district shall have been previously ascertained by law, and to be informed of the nature and cause of the accusation; to be confronted with the witnesses against him; to have compulsory process for obtaining witnesses in his favor, and to have the assistance of counsel for his defence.

•

In suits of common law, where the value in controversy shall exceed twenty dollars, the right of trial by jury shall be preserved; and no fact, tried by a jury, shall be otherwise reexamined in any court of the United States than according to the rules of the common law.
—Sixth and Seventh Amendments to the United States Constitution, *1791*

•

That in all Capital or Criminal Prosecutions a Man hath a right to demand the Cause and Nature of his Accusation to be confronted with the Accusors and Witnesses to call for Evidence in his favour and to a speedy Trial by an impartial Jury of his Vicinage without whose unanimous consent He cannot be found guilty nor can he be compelled to give Evidence against himself that no Man be deprived of his liberty except by the Law of the Land or the Judgment of his Peers.

•

That in Controversies respecting Property and in suits between Man and Man the antient Trial by Jury is preferable to any other and ought to be held sacred.
—Articles 8 and 11, Virginia Declaration of Rights, *1776*

Trial by Jury

The Virginia Paradox

JOHN M. MURRIN AND A. G. ROEBER

AMERICAN LIBERTY owes a huge debt to four Virginia patriots. George Washington secured the tradition of military subordination to the civil power and contributed mightily to defining the presidency. Thomas Jefferson wrote the Declaration of Independence and the Virginia statute on religious liberty, started the process that led finally to the Northwest Ordinance of 1787, and guided the Democratic-Republican party to victory over the Federalists. George Mason won almost equal esteem in the eyes of contemporaries as the primary author of the Virginia Declaration of Rights and the commonwealth's first written constitution, both widely copied by other states. And James Madison contributed more than any other person to the federal Constitution of 1787 and the Bill of Rights.[1]

Article 6 of the federal Bill of Rights, emulating section 8 of Mason's declaration, guarantees to anyone accused of a federal crime a speedy and public trial by jury and the right to summon witnesses and to engage an attorney. Article 7, somewhat narrower than Mason's section 11, upholds civil juries in federal suits worth at least twenty dollars. Some Virginians probably hoped for more. In his proposed constitution of 1776, for example, Jefferson had tried to secure trial by jury "whether of Chancery, Common, Ecclesiastical, or Marine law." Traditionally only the common law had been the domain of juries. On the surface, these facts suggest a passionate commitment to juries among educated Virginians during the

---

1. Mason's role is the least appreciated today despite excellent efforts by Helen Hill Miller, *George Mason, Gentleman Revolutionary* (Chapel Hill, 1975); Robert Allen Rutland, *George Mason, Reluctant Statesman* (Williamsburg, 1961); and Jack P. Greene, "Character, Persona, and Authority: A Study of Alternative Styles of Political Leadership in Revolutionary Virginia," in *Revolutionary War in the South: Power, Conflict, and Leadership*, ed. W. Robert Higgins (Durham, N.C., 1979), 3–42.

American Revolution. If we look further back than the 1760s, however, the picture is less clear.[2]

During the Stamp Act Crisis of 1764–1766, most colonies protested British policy on two constitutional grounds: "no taxation without representation" and the vice-admiralty courts' threat to trial by jury. Every colony that complained in 1765 named juries in its protest except Rhode Island, where Governor Stephen Hopkins briefly raised the issue in a semiofficial pamphlet, and Virginia. Virginia adopted resolutions against the Stamp Act in 1764 and again in 1765, but neither set of Virginia resolves mentioned juries. Nor did Richard Bland mention them in his influential pamphlet of 1766.[3]

•

Trial by jury had remarkably weak roots in Virginia soil. On this issue, unlike many others, Virginia had to catch up with the rest of the colonies. As late as 1750, juries probably held a less conspicuous position in Virginia than in any other mainland province.

Consider Virginia's historical experience in the light of John Locke's famous triad of life, liberty, and property. Were juries considered essential in trials for life? Were they involved in trials of lesser criminal offenses (liberty)? Did the settlers insist upon juries to decide civil disputes (property)? If Virginia's experience was exceptional, how can we explain the differences in jury usage from one colony to another? Did not most seventeenth-century settlers bring from England a common legal heritage?[4]

The last question requires a brief exploration before we can proceed to the others. To judge from their behavior, the colonists recognized several competing traditions, not a single legal heritage. The two extremes were marked by the New Haven Colony and West Jersey. Dominated by righteous Puritans, New Haven abolished juries altogether, even for capital trials. Criminal procedure was inquisitorial; all judicial power resided in the magistrates, whose mission was "to find out the trueth" and punish sin. They accused suspects, grilled them before trial, examined witnesses, passed judgment, and imposed sentences. Once brought to court, a suspect had

2. For the three drafts of the Virginia Declaration, *see Mason Papers*, 1:274–291, especially 288; *Jefferson Papers*, 1:343, 352, 362 (quotation).

3. Edmund S. Morgan, ed., *Prologue to Revolution: Sources and Documents on the Stamp Act Crisis, 1764–1766* (Chapel Hill, 1959), 14–16, 44–69; Merrill Jensen, ed., *Tracts of the American Revolution, 1763–1776* (Indianapolis, 1967), 41–62, especially 53 (Hopkins), and 108–126 (Bland).

4. John Locke, *Two Treatises of Government*, ed. Peter Laslett, rev. ed. (Cambridge and New York, 1963), 395. In any other edition of Locke's *Second Treatise, see* para. 123.

almost no chance of acquittal. Judicial retribution in the name of the just God was efficient, swift, and severe.[5]

At the opposite pole stood Quaker West Jersey, where the magistrates had almost no discretionary powers. By the Concessions and Agreements of 1677 (the most radical constitutional document put into practice in colonial America), each West Jersey court had three judges "who shall sitt with the twelve men of the Neighbourhood . . . and . . . pronounce such Judgment as they shall receive from . . . the said twelve men in whom only the Judgment resides and not otherwise." In other words, without a jury a court could punish only those offenders who pleaded guilty. More powerful than the judges, juries decided both fact and law. Magistrates presided at court and occasionally offered advice to the jury upon request. Dire penalties awaited any judge who exceeded these limitations. No society has ever loaded its jury system with greater expectations than did West Jersey. The system functioned well in the colony for about fifteen years and then, for complicated reasons, disintegrated into judicial chaos during the 1690s. It yielded to a conventional common-law system when the two Jerseys were united as a single royal colony in 1702.[6]

Other colonies fell between these "magisterial" and popular extremes. New Netherland, organized under a Dutch variant of Roman law, never used juries but lacked the millennial urgency of New Haven. Virginia had scant respect for juries until the late seventeenth century. Maryland used civil juries but rarely employed a jury for a noncapital offense before the late 1670s. Massachusetts and Connecticut relied upon civil juries even for trivial disputes and appeals, but before 1660 had confined criminal juries almost exclusively to capital offenses. Plymouth Colony began with a strong commitment to both civil and criminal juries, but as the decades passed it followed the pattern of its orthodox neighbors. Even Maine, never intensely Puritan in the seventeenth century, resembled Massachusetts in this respect. In all New England, the ordinary criminal jury flourished only in Rhode Island, a colony whose settlers had fled from the wrath of godly magistrates outside its borders.[7]

---

5. John M. Murrin, "Settlers, Sinners, and a Precarious Liberty: Trial by Jury in Seventeenth-Century New England," in *Saints & Revolutionaries: Essays on Early American History*, ed. David D. Hall, John M. Murrin, and Thad W. Tate (New York, 1984), 152–206, especially 170–182.

6. Mary Maples Dunn et al., eds., *Papers of William Penn* (Philadelphia, 1981–), 1:398, chap. 19; Henry Clay Reed and George J. Miller, eds., *Burlington Court Book: A Record of Quaker Jurisprudence in West New Jersey, 1680–1709* (Washington, D.C., 1944).

7. Murrin, "Settlers, Sinners, and a Precarious Liberty," passim.

The arrival of the Quakers, first in West Jersey in the 1670s and then in Pennsylvania in the 1680s, created an intercolonial competition for settlers in the Middle Atlantic region. English liberty, with juries as one important component, was a lure to immigrants. Both Maryland and New York responded quickly by expanding their use of juries. North Carolina served as a similar prod to Virginia—the Old North colony's fragmentary early records suggest wide use of juries from the start, and Virginia began to move in the same direction after Bacon's Rebellion in 1676.[8]

We can explain this astonishing variety only by realizing that the early settlers inherited a thoroughly ambiguous tradition from the mother country. In 1600 the English jury already had a four-century history. Twelfth-century juries had provided judges with the information they needed to administer the law; judges applied the law. In time, petit juries evolved from active knowers of local events to passive receivers of sworn testimony made available to them only in court. Grand juries remained more flexible, relying upon both kinds of information. When bench and jury heard the same evidence, conflict between the two became common in both England and the colonies. One solution was the elimination of juries. Canon law, merchant law, and equity law (in chancery courts) did without juries. The Tudor and early-Stuart monarchs favored this approach, creating conciliar courts such as Star Chamber, the Council of the North, and the Council of Wales. These tribunals rapidly expanded until abolished by the Long Parliament of 1641. In addition, Parliament itself had expanded the role of summary justice at the county level by supplanting the role of juries in misdemeanor cases and allowing noncapital crimes to be tried by one or more justices of the peace sitting "out of sessions" (or in "petty sessions") without juries. By the eighteenth century, as Sir William Blackstone warned, this trend posed a massive threat to the traditional criminal jury, though juries continued in ordinary civil disputes.[9]

---

8. Charles County Court Records, V–VII, Maryland State Archives, Annapolis; John M. Murrin, "English Rights as Ethnic Aggression: The Dutch, the English, and Leisler's Rebellion in New York," in *New Approaches to the History of Colonial and Revolutionary New York*, ed. Conrad Wright and William Pencak (Charlottesville, forthcoming); Mattie Erma Edwards Parker, ed., *North Carolina Higher-Court Records, 1670–1696* in *The Colonial Records of North Carolina*, 2d ser., 1 (Raleigh, N.C., 1968).

9. Among an extensive literature, *see* Barnaby C. Keeney, *Judgment by Peers* (Cambridge, Mass., 1949); Catharine Hamilton Kappauf, "Early Development of the Petty Jury in England, 1194–1221" (Ph.D. diss., University of Illinois at Urbana—Champaign, 1973); Thomas Andrew Green, *Verdict According to Conscience: Perspectives on the English Criminal Trial Jury, 1200–1800* (Chicago, 1985); Richard H. Helmholz and Thomas A. Green, *Juries, Libel, & Justice: The Role of English Juries in Seventeenth- and Eighteenth-Century Trials for Libel*

•

The various North American colonies explored most gradations along the spectrum of jury usage. Colonies organized by powerful and self-conscious magistrates embraced the trend toward conciliar and summary justice. Provinces created by ordinary settlers without strong magisterial direction (Rhode Island, early Plymouth, West Jersey, and North Carolina stand out) reflected popular veneration for juries in England. Virginia fixed its judicial institutions just as the influence of conciliar justice was peaking in England. Not surprisingly, the province also took longer than any other to escape from that shadow. In effect, Virginia settlers had to discover an older England before they could herald the new republican America.[10]

White Virginians welcomed juries in three stages. Jury trials for capital offenses were secure by the 1630s. Civil juries had a more checkered history. Seldom used until the 1640s, they were at least available thereafter. By the late seventeenth century, a typical county had witnessed a few civil trials by jury each year, but its justices dispatched the bulk of civil business. The noncapital criminal jury was the last to win general approval. After a halting growth in the late seventeenth century, the criminal jury virtually disappeared in the first half of the eighteenth century (at least in the twelve tidewater counties whose records we have examined), and won a significant place for itself only after 1750 in the final decades before independence.

Until 1624 Virginia had been governed by the Virginia Company of London, and until the reforms of 1618–1619, martial law was the model for justice, particularly under Dale's Code, the *Lawes Divine, Morall and Martiall*.[11] Settlers did not remember this period fondly. They denounced its excesses: the execution of recaptured deserters "by hanginge, shooting and breakinge uppon the wheele," and the punishment of a thief who "had

---

and Slander (Los Angeles, 1984); John H. Langbein, "Origins of Public Prosecution at Common Law," *American Journal of Legal History* 17 (1973): 313–335; and Felix Frankfurter and Thomas G. Corcoran, "Petty Federal Offenses and the Constitutional Guaranty of Trial by Jury," *Harvard Law Review* 39 (1925–1926): 917–1009 (which is mostly a study of the statutory basis of English summary justice). *See also* Sir William Blackstone, *Commentaries on the Laws of England: A Facsimile of the First Edition of 1765–1769*, ed. Stanley N. Katz (Chicago, 1979), 4:277–278.

10. This paragraph and the next rest on the reading of most published and many manuscript court records of the mainland colonies for the seventeenth century by John M. Murrin, and of eighteenth-century Virginia court records by A. G. Roeber; *see also* Roeber, *Faithful Magistrates and Republican Lawyers: Creators of Virginia Legal Culture, 1680–1810* (Chapel Hill, 1981).

11. William Strachey, *For the Colony in Virginea Britannia: Lawes Divine, Morall and Martiall, etc.*, ed. David H. Flaherty (Charlottesville, 1969).

a bodkinge thrust through his tounge and was tyed with a chaine to a tree untill he starved" for stealing a few pints of oatmeal. Recalling their "misery under most severe and Crewell lawes," the colonists in 1624 rejoiced that things had greatly improved and prayed that no one would try to restore the earlier regime.[12]

The substitution of English law for Dale's Code had indeed been a cardinal reform instituted by the London Company in 1618 to end the military regime in which people could be "mercylessly executed, often tymes without tryall or Judgment." Yet in practice the change was neither as complete nor as dramatic as the assembly claimed. Virginia no longer endured the *Lawes Divine, Morall and Martiall,* but the system that evolved in its place was not English common law either, at least not for a long time. On the civil side, it may have drawn upon Star Chamber or the juryless law merchant, perhaps reflecting the commercial background of many settlers and stockholders. Civil business consisted overwhelmingly of suits for debt, and the courts almost automatically gave quick judgment for the plaintiffs. On the criminal side, Virginia justice corresponded fairly well to the emerging practice of summary justice in English counties, which is probably how the government interpreted the company's injunction to rule by "Magistracy and just laws."[13]

Common law won its first big victory in trials for life, but it did not come immediately. Although no settler was burned or deliberately starved to death after 1618, nineteen-year-old Thomas Hayle was "found guilty by the Judge" and executed for raping four children in 1627. His crime was shocking and perhaps for that reason no one thought of a jury trial. Richard Cornish, a Welsh ship captain, was put to death for sodomizing a member of his crew in Virginia waters. The record of his trial has not survived, but we know that his brother and at least one other man thought he was condemned "wrongfully." Were they protesting his innocence or had he also been convicted summarily? Was he denied a jury?[14]

From these cases of the 1620s until Bacon's Rebellion half a century later, every capital case for which we have documentation was tried by a jury. Governor John Harvey attempted to reimpose martial law in the mid-1630s as a terror to his enemies but instead found himself thrust from office and

---

12. "Tragical Relation of the Virginia Assembly, 1624," in *Narratives of Early Virginia, 1606–1625,* ed. Lyon Gardiner Tyler (New York, 1907), 423, 422.

13. Ibid., 422; Wesley Frank Craven, *Dissolution of the Virginia Company: The Failure of a Colonial Experiment* (New York, 1932), 70.

14. *MCGC,* 149 (Hayle), 34, 78, 81, 93 (Cornish).

shipped back to England. Governor William Berkeley, after subduing Bacon's forces, hanged twelve men under martial law in January 1677, but thereafter he used juries against his opponents. Finally, all of the colony's known executions between 1630 and the end of the century were for homicide or treason. All those convicted of manslaughter escaped the executioner by pleading "benefit of clergy" with the sole exception of Margaret Hatch, who claimed to be pregnant but, after failing to convince a jury of matrons, was hanged in 1633.[15]

•

The civil jury has a more complex and confusing history in the seventeenth century. The records of Eastern Shore courts show no use of juries before the 1640s, but the fragmentary materials that have survived from the General Court indicate that civil juries at least existed in that body from the 1630s. None of the evidence suggests widespread use until the legislation of the early 1640s.

In 1642, for the last time, Virginia faced the danger that the Virginia Company of London might be restored. Newly arrived Governor Berkeley and the General Assembly complained to London in April that reimposition of company rule might destroy trial by jury in the colony. That June the legislature specifically authorized juries in the county courts. Litigants promptly took advantage of this opportunity. On the Eastern Shore, twenty-one civil cases went before juries in the next three years, only a minority of those tried but a significant departure from earlier practice.[16]

Whatever it had said in 1642, the assembly did not like this trend. By 1645–1646, the old company really was dead, and England was too distracted by civil war to interfere directly in the colony. Without explaining its motives, the legislature weakened the jury system in July 1646. It permitted many cases slated for a jury to be heard in chancery (equity), and required litigants who requested juries to pay their costs regardless of the outcome of the cases. (Under customary English procedure the loser, whether plaintiff or defendant, paid costs.)[17]

---

15. Based on all capital trials in *MCGC*, passim; *see* 456–462 for the Baconian trials and 480 for Hatch. On Harvey, *see* Warren M. Billings, ed., *Old Dominion in the Seventeenth Century, 1606–1689* (Chapel Hill, 1975), 251–257; and J. Mills Thornton III, "The Thrusting Out of Governor Harvey: A Seventeenth-Century Rebellion," *VMHB* 76 (1968): 11–26.

16. *MCGC*, 481, 482; Hening, *Statutes*, 1:231, 271; Susie M. Ames, ed., *County Court Records of Accomack-Northampton, Virginia, 1640–1645* (Charlottesville, 1973), from which a tabulation of all jury trials has been compiled.

17. Hening, *Statutes*, 1:303–304, 313–314.

The loss of most early seventeenth-century Virginia court records may prevent historians from satisfactorily gauging the effect of these discouragements, but shortly after the Restoration in 1660, the assembly conceded that the colony had restricted juries in a manner "quite contrary to the law of England." At the county level, the extremes are probably represented by Surry and Northumberland. A poor southside county, Surry scarcely ever used juries before Bacon's Rebellion. Northumberland, a dynamic Northern Neck community across the Potomac from Maryland where civil juries had taken hold by the 1650s, set a pace that the rest of Virginia could not match until late in the century. In fourteen years from 1652 to 1666, sixty-two cases went to juries. Excluding five verdicts that are either unknown or too complex to classify, the jurors supported the defendant about forty percent of the time. In civil litigation decided by the bench, on the other hand, plaintiffs nearly always won.[18]

After the Restoration, the legislature required that juries be available at every county court. The overall pattern of response is still far from clear, nor have historians exhausted the available manuscript sources on this question. Clearly, however, the reaction was mixed. Cases appealed to the General Court in the 1670s often had been decided by juries at the county level, although in 1677 one county complained that juries were a useless and expensive encumbrance "when often times in 3 or 4 Courts not one Cause is put to a Jury." On the other hand, the General Court itself rarely used civil juries within the Council chambers. More often it ordered sheriffs to assemble local juries and report their decisions, especially in land-title and estate cases. Northumberland used juries as often after 1660 as before, and except when the General Court ordered local juries to report their findings on specific questions, Surry still ignored them—until Bacon's Rebellion.[19]

That upheaval badly divided Surry County, which had already witnessed a tax revolt among the settlers of the Lawnes Creek Parish in 1673. Arthur Long, a poor householder without tithables before 1676, became one of Nathaniel Bacon's southside captains and evidently enjoyed plundering his social betters. The county elite fled with the governor, except for Colonel

---

18. Ibid., 2:73–74. All jury trials have been tabulated from Surry County Deeds, Wills, Etc., 1, 1652–1672, Reel 1; Surry County Orders, 1671–1691, Reel 28; and Northumberland County Order Book, 1652–1665, Reel 47, VSL.

19. *MCGC*, 322, 323, 336, 337 for juries within the General Court, and 224, 228–229, 255, 293, 351 for use of local juries; on one occasion the General Court named the county bench as the local jury; *see* 287, 299. The complaint is number 13 among the Northampton County grievances of 1677 printed in "Causes of Discontent in Virginia, 1676," *VMHB* 2 (1894–1895): 289–292.

Thomas Swann, whose equivocal behavior alienated Berkeley and earned Swann the epithet Old Toad among unsympathetic small planters. After Bacon's death some ordinary settlers whispered about fleeing through the wilderness to North Carolina, where they thought their kind would be welcomed more sympathetically. They had reason for fear. The county magistrates returned in a vindictive mood and used juries to sanction their revenge. In a series of about twenty lawsuits extending into 1679, they exacted retribution from Bacon's followers. The juries found for the plaintiffs in each of these cases. Because the sheriff selected the jury and was himself a member of the elite, we suspect that he chose the panels with care. Only after 1679 did the county settle into a conventional, less partisan pattern.[20] The jury's survival in Surry County civil suits, despite its counterrevolutionary local beginnings, suggests a popular fondness for the institution. Between 1679 and 1691, juries found for the defendant about half the time.

By the last two decades of the seventeenth century, the civil jury was secure though hardly predominant in the county courts of Virginia. In Surry from 1683 to 1685, only three of fifty-five civil cases went to a jury, but for the entire period from 1677 to 1691 the average was closer to three per year. Those who sought a jury trial could get one, but most litigants preferred to leave adjudication to the bench, where undoubtedly it was cheaper, at least for the loser.[21]

●

Juries touched life and property, but they also touched liberty in misdemeanor cases, although the early Virginia courts prosecuted few malefactors. If one uses only court records to measure the per capita crime rate, the seventeenth-century Chesapeake colonies appear more law-abiding than Puritan New England. Four considerations warn us against believing any such statistic (which no one has yet compiled anyway). First, in 1632 alone Virginia had two homicides in a population struggling to exceed five thousand, and between 1672 and 1674 the colony had five homicide trials. By contrast, New Haven had no homicides in its entire history except a settler killed by an Indian. Second, fornication, the most common criminal

---

20. *See* Surry County Deeds, Wills, Etc., 1, 1652–1672, Reel 1, pp. 192–193 for an early jury case. Jury practice after Bacon's Rebellion has been tabulated from Surry County Deeds, Wills, and Orders, 1671–1684, Reel 1; *see* 227–228 (Swan), 192–193 (North Carolina), 137, 195, 196, 201–205 (Long), VSL. Documents about the 1673 tax revolt are printed in Billings, *Old Dominion in the Seventeenth Century*, 258–267.

21. Jury behavior has been tabulated from Surry County Deeds, Wills, and Orders, 1671–1684, Reel 1; and Surry County Orders, 1671–1691, Reel 28, VSL.

offense in New England, seems not to have been prosecuted in the seventeenth century Chesapeake unless bastardy was involved. Modern demographic studies show that bastardy and bridal-pregnancy rates remained low in seventeenth-century New England, but that nearly one in five immigrant servant women in the Chesapeake region conceived an illegitimate child, and within the same group every third bride was pregnant on her wedding day. Third, defamation suits in Virginia and Maryland reveal much casual violence and theft that seems not to have been prosecuted. A favorite slander throughout the region was some variant of "hog thief." Finally, with much of the early Chesapeake population bound as indentured servants, the primary responsibility for public order rested with their masters, not the courts.[22]

Three cases, the first extreme, illustrate the private enforcement of public order. In the first, Elizabeth Abbott died after her master gave her five hundred lashes with a whip decorated with fishhooks. The court did not punish him. Nor, half a century later, did it prosecute a master who had compelled a seriously ill servant to return to work tending cattle in the woods, where, according to the coroner's jury, the weakened servant either was killed by wolves or else starved to death first and then was partially devoured by wolves. In the third case, James Bruce happened upon his female servant making love outdoors with James Savage, servant or hired laborer. Bruce did nothing until later in the day when Savage abandoned his chores, lay down in the field, and contentedly announced, "goodman Bruce I am weary, the ground is hard I can worke noe longer." Bruce stormed into the house and thrashed, not Savage, but the woman. Work, not fornication, mattered.[23]

When the courts did prosecute minor crimes, they nearly always proceeded summarily. Governor Berkeley, for instance, commissioned an Eastern Shore court "to doe and execute what one Justice of peace or two or

---

22. For homicides, *see MCGC*, 480, 300, 329, 353, 380. On pregnancy patterns, *see* Lois Green Carr and Lorena S. Walsh, "The Planter's Wife: The Experience of White Women in Seventeenth-Century Maryland," *WMQ*, 3d ser., 34 (1977): 542–571. On livestock theft, *see* Susie M. Ames, ed., *County Court Records of Accomack-Northampton, Virginia, 1632–1640* (Washington, D.C., 1954), 47–48, 55–56, 59, 107. As one example of popular sentiment about regional standards of proper behavior, Anthony Cotton was sued for defamation in Maryland in 1638 for saying that James Cloughton deserved to be "whippt at virginea" for actions that if Cotton "had his deserts he had been hanged in new England" (William Hand Browne et al., eds., *Archives of Maryland* [Baltimore, 1883–1972], 4:18–19).

23. *MCGC*, 22–24; Surry County Deeds, Wills, Etc., 1, 1652–1672, Reel 1, pp. 199–200; Ames, *Accomack-Northampton Records, 1640–1645*, 292.

more Justices of the Peace may doe or execute." In English procedure these phrases described what justices did out of sessions, without juries.[24]

Our research about juries is far from complete, but it does suggest a pattern. Criminal juries were rarer than civil ones. Accomack-Northampton used more than twenty civil juries before 1645 but none for crime, and Northumberland impaneled sixty-two civil juries and no criminal juries before 1666. So far, we have encountered only one noncapital case before 1690 in which someone was both indicted by a grand jury and tried by a separate petit jury. Virginia perhaps mirrored the English practice in some locales in which grand jurors were still knowers of local events. Their indictment was tantamount to conviction.[25]

Surry County provides an interesting exception to the overall pattern. Between 1677 and 1691, eleven criminal trials, all for theft, went before juries. In every instance, the proceeding was initiated by the victim, not by a grand jury, and where the record is specific enough to tell, either the victim or the court, not the accused, requested the jury. Because victims derived benefits proportionate to the official evaluation of their losses in these cases, this assessment (not the determination of guilt) was probably the jury's main purpose. Criminal juries began to thrive where their roles most closely approximated their established civil function.[26]

As the seventeenth century closed, white Virginians had secured their right to trial by jury for capital crimes. (Blacks participated in the jury process in the seventeenth century, but in the eighteenth were excluded.) Juries were also available for civil suits, although most litigants did not use them. In misdemeanor trials, juries very rarely participated even when the vigorous development of grand juries after the 1670s greatly expanded the volume of criminal business at the county level.

•

Had the American Revolution begun in 1700, few Virginians would have listed encroachment upon juries as a grievance against English rule. Local governments in the Old Dominion did not yet value the institution highly, even though juries were popular in other colonies. This situation changed little during the first half of the eighteenth century. Juries mattered only in

---

24. Ames, *Accomack-Northampton Records, 1640–1645*, 178.

25. For the use of distinct grand and petit juries in the same Northampton case, *see* Warren M. Billings, "Pleading, Procedure, and Practice: The Meaning of Due Process of Law in Seventeenth-Century Virginia," *Journal of Southern History* 47 (1981): 569–584, especially 575–576.

26. The criminal juries are in Surry County Orders, 1671–1691, Reel 28, passim.

trials for life. They seemed at best marginally important to the protection of liberty or property.

For the white men and women of eighteenth-century Virginia, juries still functioned in the two basic English modes of their sixteenth- and seventeenth-century forebears: the grand jury, which served as a collective conscience regulating behavior and manners; and the petit jury, which was not often used in Virginia trials before 1750. In a 1705 revision of the colony's statutes, the General Assembly set the qualifications for jurors and specified how juries were to be called. These regulations stood unaltered until 1748: twenty-four prospective grand jurors were summoned two months in advance of the May and November meetings of the county courts, at which fifteen were impaneled to hear information and make presentments to the court. County grand jurors had to be worth £50 in "visible real and personal estate." One needed an estate worth £100 to sit as a grand juror before the General Court in Williamsburg. In both instances, jurors had to be free white males and could not be tavern keepers, constables, surveyors of highways, millers or mill owners. These occupations were politically sensitive and their practitioners susceptible to bribery or pressure. Moreover, grand juries might have occasion to present *them* for dereliction of duty.[27]

Both county and General Court grand juries kept a close watch on Virginians' public and private behavior during the first half of the century. Owing to the destruction of the General Court records in April 1865, we do not know in detail how grand juries in Williamsburg handled misdemeanors brought to their attention. In the counties, we know that grand juries presented and courts punished people who failed to attend church, swore profane oaths, sold liquors without a license, or gave birth to bastard children, as well as overseers of the roads who failed to keep the roads clear and in good repair. We know, too, that before 1750 few Virginians contested grand jury presentments; they paid their fines or were whipped if they could not afford the fine. After midcentury, however, this deference to the collective judgment of the freeholders of the county changed, as did Virginians' use of the petit jury.[28]

---

27. Hening, *Statutes*, 3:367–371.

28. For an overview of court day and the use of the jury in fifteen tidewater counties, *see* Roeber, *Faithful Magistrates*, 41–47, 73–95, 102–105, 127–129. Juries performed other duties, including the assessment for taxation of controverted property (York County Orders, Wills, Etc., 14, 1709–1716, Reel 6, pp. 141–142, 17 Mar. 1712, VSL) and determining the amount of a lawyer's fee in certain cases when "the judge may direct what in his opinion is a reasonable fee, but this is not binding and conclusive on the party who may insist on it's being

When we remember the right to a trial by a jury of one's peers, we immediately think of a criminal case where reputation, freedom, and perhaps even life itself are at risk. And we assume that just such a concern must have motivated George Mason to write into the Virginia Declaration of Rights, or James Madison into the Bill of Rights, guarantees that protect us in such perilous cases. In eighteenth-century Virginia, however, most colonists probably never experienced the spectacle of a criminal case tried before a jury. Only the governor and his Council, sitting as the General Court in April and November, heard capital cases for felony or treason. After 1711, the same officials also met in June and December as a court of oyer and terminer to rule in cases involving prisoners who otherwise might languish in the public jail in Williamsburg. Crowded in the small General Court chamber of the Capitol, and nowhere else in the colony, could Virginians witness a petit jury called to render its verdict for serious crimes.[29]

For these trials, the clerk of the General Court instructed the sheriff of the county in which the alleged offense was committed to send six names back to Williamsburg. Four of the six freeholders were summoned to appear on the fourth day of the General Court session, when the court chose eight other jurors from bystanders in Williamsburg. In 1734 the procedures of the General Court and the court of oyer and terminer were streamlined: six days before the courts met, the sheriffs of James City and York counties (the line ran down Duke of Gloucester Street) each summoned six men from his county. These twelve freeholders constituted the grand jury inquiring into treasons and felonies in the colony. Petit juries for the Williamsburg high courts were composed of twelve men from the county in which the alleged crime occurred. The right to legal counsel (honored informally in felony and treason trials) was guaranteed by statute in 1734, and the same law reiterated what had been true since 1705: once a petit or grand juror had been sworn,

---

tried by a jury on a quantum meruit—and if the jury find it a reasonable [fee] it then becomes an established fee" (David John Mays, ed., *Letters and Papers of Edmund Pendleton, 1734–1803* [Charlottesville, 1967], 1:83; Frank L. Dewey, *Thomas Jefferson, Lawyer* [Charlottesville, 1986], 105).

29. Hugh F. Rankin, *Criminal Trial Proceedings in the General Court of Colonial Virginia* (Charlottesville, 1965), provides the best survey of what we believe went on in the General Court, but *see also* Warren M. Billings, ed., "*Temple* v. *Gerard*, 1667–1668: An Example of Appellate Practices in Colonial Virginia," *VMHB* 94 (1986): 88–107; Dewey, *Thomas Jefferson: Lawyer*, 1–8, 18–25.

no one could challenge his right to sit because of insufficient personal or real estate.[30]

Scant evidence survives of the verdicts juries reached in the courts at Williamsburg, but historians do know from the notices in the *Virginia Gazette* and from surviving fragments of the General Court records that fewer than one-third of the persons accused of felony suffered death as the penalty. Nearly as many seem to have been acquitted, and a large number received reduced punishments. These figures tell something about the importance of judicial discretion in Virginia; they tell nothing at all about the nature of jury deliberations or decisions.[31]

•

Fortunately, historians know more about what went on in the counties, where juries were sometimes used in the courtroom. At first, any defendant could demand a petit jury trial in practically any case. Debt-collection cases were the most common, however, and in the 1730s the General Assembly set a lower limit that prevented the use of juries when the dispute was valued at less than £5. This restriction is somewhat puzzling, however, for county court records show that few juries were used in debt cases—or any cases for that matter—in early-eighteenth-century Virginia. Virginians got along well month after month, year after year, without using petit juries. On the average, between 1700 and 1750 most tidewater Virginia counties used fewer than five juries a year for any reason. Law required the county court to select a jury for each court session, which normally lasted one to three days, but this imposed no burden on freeholders who, in any event, gathered on court days to visit and talk about the weather, crops, and the odds at nearby horseraces. Occasionally the influence of a local ordinary seeped into court, though liquor was banned from jury rooms, which were located near the main entrances to most courthouses. John Plant, of Caroline County, was fined in November 1737 "two hundred pounds of tobacco for Misbehaving himself in the Jury room and afterwards in Court."[32]

At midcentury, Virginians regarded their fellow jurors as "the most able men of the county" and relied on them to monitor social behavior but rarely used them in trials. Instead, Virginians trusted the wisdom of the gentlemen justices of the county court, and if presented by the grand jury they rarely contested the charges. Typical was the Henrico County man who declined to

---

30. Hening, *Statutes*, 4:403–405; 5:523–526.

31. Rankin, *Criminal Trial Proceedings*, 89–122.

32. Roeber, *Faithful Magistrates*, 127–128; Hening, *Statutes*, 4:426–428; Caroline County Order Book, 1732–1740, Reel 13, p. 457, 12 Nov. 1737, VSL.

"contest with our said Lord the King," and who admitted that he was "guilty in manner & form as in the Indictment against him is alleged and puteth himself upon the Grace & Mercy of the Court."[33]

Virginia justices could determine whether a suspect would be tried in the county or remanded over to Williamsburg for felony trial. More often than not, criminals were tried locally, sometimes by lowering the appraisal of stolen goods, sometimes by deciding that the evidence was insufficient "to touch his life." Prisoners relied on the discretion of the justices to save them from being put on trial for their lives and usually preferred to be dealt with immediately. In Essex County in 1747, William Cropsley was suspected of stealing cloth. Ordered to come before the grand jury at the next court, and alarmed at the prospect of languishing (and possibly dying) in a drafty and ill-kempt county jail from February to May, Cropsley "openly begg'd the said Court to take the matter now alleg'd against him into their further Consideration and inflict such Corporeal punishment as they Judge the nature of the Crime deserves. Upon which the Prisoner hearing the Judgment of the Court on the aforesaid motion was satisfied and willing to suffer accordingly." The maximum penalty was thirty-nine lashes. He received thirty-one, which he evidently thought preferable to spending the winter in jail only to be tried and whipped, if he had survived.[34]

Of course, eighteenth-century Virginians had repeat offenders who exhausted the patience of justices and jurors alike. Even allowing for sympathy to a woman accused and judged in an all-male system, one suspects that Mary Baker (alias Moll Harvey) and her husband Samuel vexed many a freeholder. Sent by York County Court to Williamsburg in 1741 to stand trial for a felony, the pair was either acquitted (apparently by a jury) or served a reduced sentence. They surfaced in Essex in 1743, where "Mary Baker alias Moll Harvey behaving herself in an abusive manner in Court It is therefore ordered that the Sheriff do take her from the Barr and Put her in the Stocks & there keep her the Space of an hour." Samuel posted bond, and the Bakers left for Henrico. There, on 12 March 1744, Mary, Samuel, and another woman came before the justices charged with stealing "a mulatto wench and child" in King and Queen County. Acquitted, Moll was in trouble again in April for "coming into Court & behaving her Self in a most Contemptuous manner" and was punished by being ducked in a nearby stream. Finally, on 9 May 1747 she completed the circle, winding up again in York County Court, which sent her to Williamsburg for having stolen the

---

33. Henrico County Court Minute Book, 1752–1755, Reel 67, 5 Nov. 1754, VSL.

34. Essex County Orders, No. 14, 1745–1747, Reel 71, p. 347, 17 Feb. 1747, VSL.

altar and pulpit linens from the church of Charles Parish. Here, alas, the county records fall silent and the General Court records are missing. Perhaps the Bakers finally stopped troubling their fellow colonists.[35]

•

When Virginians revised their laws in 1748, they made an important change involving juries. The statute of 1705 had required jurors in Williamsburg to possess property valued at £100, and county jurors £50. The new measure substituted Virginia money for sterling, which at midcentury stood at an exchange rate of roughly four to three. Until someone undertakes an elaborate study of the jurors themselves, we shall not know whether this action lowered the property qualifications for jurors. Possibly the law only confirmed informal practices and prevented the disqualification of men who were already serving on juries. Confusion about monetary standards did provoke criticism of Virginia jurors after 1748. As Virginians increasingly used juries to settle debts, recover goods, or win damages in cases of assault and battery, their frustrations mounted over what they regarded as poor verdicts.[36]

What was happening to make juries the institution that George Mason defended as a bulwark of liberty? First, the use of grand juries declined after 1750. They sat less frequently than they were supposed to, their presentments often were dismissed by the justices, and their indictments contested by the accused. Again and again one finds persons formally accused of misdemeanors—illegal sale of liquor, adultery, absence from church, or theft—demanding trial before a petit jury. In Richmond county from 1711 to 1754 only six defendants (all were persons of means) requested juries, and five of them were convicted. Between 1754 and 1776, criminal jury trials became commonplace in the county. Strangely enough, however, formal trials with attorneys and a petit jury usually resulted in convictions and fines. People presented for misdemeanors were not getting more lenient

---

35. York County [Orders], Wills, and Inventories, 19, 1740–1746, Reel 10, 10 Nov. 1741; Essex County Orders, 1742–1743, Reel 70, p. 301, 20 Dec. 1743; Henrico County Order Book, 1737–1746, Reel 66, pp. 252–253, 12 Mar, 1744; p. 366, 7 Apr. 1746; York County Judgments and Orders, 1746–1752, Reel 29, pp. 10–11, 9 May 1747; for other references to the Harveys, *see also* Lancaster County Orders, No. 10, 1752–1756, Reel 28, pp. 376–377, 25 Aug. 1755, and Caroline County Order Book, 1746–1754, Reel 15, p. 18, 14 Feb. 1747, VSL. We have been unable to determine the relationship of John and William Harvey to "Moll Harvey."

36. Hening, *Statutes*, 5:523–526; John J. McCusker, *Money and Exchange in Europe and America, 1600–1775: A Handbook* (Chapel Hill, 1978), 205–214.

treatment after going through the time and expense of a jury trial.[37]

Second, after 1750 the county justices seem to have grown impatient with grand jury presentments and to have dismissed many of them because court sessions were being prolonged by days of tedious argument and the proliferation of jury trials. Courts that had dispensed judgments in leisurely one- or two-day sessions now held four- and five-day sessions. The justices faced an increase in litigation far out of proportion to the modest population growth in Virginia's eastern counties. Whether in Norfolk and Richmond or in Culpeper, Charles City, Essex, and Richmond counties, Virginians were demanding juries.[38]

What were the cases and the results? The overwhelming majority involved debt. And, if one examines the results of jury trials, it appears that the plaintiffs (or creditors) almost always won. When the amount of debt was not in dispute, the parties often waived the jury at the last minute and either settled out of court or asked the justices for summary judgment. Cases in which the amount of the debt was contested, or in which assault and battery or unlawful detention of property was alleged, almost always went to the jury. Even when juries found for the creditors, the amount of their award sometimes seemed a victory for the defendant. Virginia's counties averaged only three to five jury trials a year during the first half of the eighteenth century, but from 1750 to the American Revolution the number rose to between seventeen and twenty a year.[39]

---

37. On grand juries *see* Roeber, *Faithful Magistrates*, 137–145. Richmond County was peculiar in keeping a separate record of its criminal proceedings; all counties were ordered to do so, but only Sir Marmaduke Beckwith, clerk of Richmond County, complied. Civil causes far outnumbered criminal proceedings in the county (and everywhere else we know of in Virginia); Peter Charles Hoffer and William B. Scott, eds., *Criminal Proceedings in Colonial Virginia* (Athens, Ga., 1984), xvi–xviii.

38. Roeber, *Faithful Magistrates*, 128–145; E. Lee Shepard, "Administration of Justice in Revolutionary Virginia: The Norfolk Courts, 1770–1790," (M.A. thesis, University of Virginia, 1974), 45–46, 65, 115 n. 58; A. M. Pritchard, comp., *Abstracts from the County Court Minute Book of Culpeper County, Virginia, 1763–1764* (Dayton, Va., 1930), 7–58. These only surviving records for Culpeper County reveal twenty-one jury trials in ten months; plaintiffs won in seventeen, a defendant in only one, and in three cases decisions were set aside or appealed after being awarded to the plaintiffs.

39. Roeber, *Faithful Magistrates*, 131–132. A complete analysis of the York County Court's performance is being conducted by David Konig, of Washington University, for the Colonial Williamsburg Research Department. Our examination of York records for the years 1759–1783 reveals an increase in jury trials in the 1760s and 1770s with the peak year in 1772 (113 causes going to a jury or begun with a jury impaneled but settled by arbitration). Even in York, arguably the most efficient court in all of Virginia, only about half of the pending causes were dispatched within a given year; plaintiffs won in almost every instance

At first no one paid much attention to the lowered property qualifications for jurors that had been enacted in 1748, in part no doubt because the Seven Years' War distracted attention from such matters. In the 1760s, however, creditors began complaining that they could not obtain justice before county court juries. Inevitably, they groused, the local small landholders who sat on juries favored their fellow debtors. Juries, an irate newspaper correspondent complained in 1771, were "composed mostly of Knaves, Villains, and Blockheads, by whom honest Mens Properties and Estates were frequently forced from them, without Redress." Virginia, he concluded, needed juries composed of intelligent and substantial freeholders with terms of service to extend for one to three years. Wealthy planters and merchant creditors believed that lowered property qualifications for Virginia jurors had wrought havoc with justice in the colony. Pessimistic about collecting lawful debts in most courts, merchants began turning in particular to Yorktown, where, it was rumored, the county court diligently heard cases and juries sternly upheld creditors' just demands for payment. Was this true? Were most Virginia jurors people of modest means who favored debtors against creditors? On the eve of Virginia's struggle with Great Britain, was resistance brewing in the jury rooms of the Old Dominion? Did George Mason sense this in July 1774 when he drafted the tenth article of the Fairfax County resolves, protesting "the taking away our Trials by Jurys, the ordering Persons upon Criminal Accusations, to be tried in another Country than that in which the Fact is charged to have been committed"? Was this in his mind as he wrote the Virginia Declaration of Rights?[40]

Sadly, the evidence one would need to examine—the complete record of jury trials in Fairfax County where Mason had sat as a justice of the peace—has been destroyed. We shall never know what Mason's experience with jury trials had been. Clearly, in the aftermath of the Boston Tea Party, Mason's fears for jury trials focused upon criminal procedure, not the mundane use of juries in civil disputes. Yet perhaps he had cause for alarm about several broader issues. Parliament's Intolerable Acts of 1774 directly raised the question of change of venue. Should a royal official accused of a crime in one

---

when a civil cause went before a jury. Amounts awarded in York ranged from forty shillings and costs to the spectacular award of £10,000 won by Francis Jerdone in a debt suit on 20 February 1764. The more ordinary awards fell in the range between £12 and £30 Virginia current money; Roeber, "The Most Able Men of the County ...': Trial by Jury in Eighteenth-Century York County, Virginia," forthcoming.

40. *Virginia Gazette* (Purdie & Dixon), 12 Dec. 1771; Roeber, *Faithful Magistrates*, 135–137; *Mason Papers*, 1:204 for the Fairfax Resolves citation; 1:274–291 for texts of drafts and commentary upon the Declaration of Rights.

colony be permitted a jury trial in another? Parliament said yes. Patriots thought not, and Mason expressed their anxiety.[41]

But in the decade before 1776, as a whole, juries more often became a political issue when property, not life or liberty, was at stake. British policy since 1763 had threatened civil, not criminal, juries. The vice-admiralty courts, whose powers were expanded in 1764 and 1765, acted against vessels and cargoes. The Quebec Act of 1774 allowed that province to retain French civil law (with no provision for juries) but imposed English criminal law. Revolutionary spokesman had more occasion to defend civil than criminal juries.

The uneasiness of Virginia creditors and merchants simply was not well-founded. Close examination of the York County records demonstrates unmistakably that merchants and creditors who brought suit invariably recovered lawful debts. Plaintiffs who took debtors before juries always won. The Yorktown court was particularly efficient (usually managing to clear its docket within three days even though it heard twenty to twenty-five jury trials per year between 1760 and 1774), but whether in the Norfolk borough court or the Essex County Court, the pattern of creditors winning suits prevails, though not as consistently.[42]

•

What, then, is one to make of the Virginia Declaration of Rights and its two articles defending the right to trial by jury? Curiously, although Virginians had been arguing about the quality of juries since the 1760s, these articles

41. Joseph Horrell, "George Mason and the Fairfax Court," *VMHB* 91 (1983): 418–439. Mason must have observed at least some jury trials at the county level, though his attendance was sporadic. In this, he resembled Thomas Jefferson, who never practiced as an attorney in the county courts but attended Augusta's sessions and may have served as justice in Albemarle (though we have no evidence that he did so because of the destruction of that county's records); Dewey, *Thomas Jefferson: Lawyer*, 27–28, 122–126.

42. *See* note 39, above. On the problem of indebtedness, *see* T. H. Breen, *Tobacco Culture: The Mentality of the Great Tidewater Planters on the Eve of Revolution* (Princeton, 1985). Apparently, younger merchants, traders, and planter-lawyers like Jefferson were those who had most recently fallen into deepest debt. On Jefferson's practice in caveats and petitions in lapsed lands, *see* Dewey, *Thomas Jefferson: Lawyer*, 30–44; Jacob M. Price, "The Last Phase of the Virginia-London Consignment Trade: James Buchanan & Co., 1758–1768," *WMQ*, 3d ser., 43 (1986): 64–98. Parliament and the Privy Council began using law as a policy tool increasingly by the 1750s. Alison Gilbert Olson's speculation that by 1765 Crown authorities were viewing jury verdicts, hitherto a barometer of local opinion, with suspicion requires qualification (Olson, "Parliament, Empire, and Parliamentary Law, 1776," in *Three British Revolutions: 1641, 1688, 1776*, ed. J. G. A. Pocock [Princeton, 1980], 289–322, especially 303–312). Judging from the figures we have uncovered, Virginians, at least, had not regarded jury verdicts before the 1750s as particularly significant.

elicited no debate. Modern commentators usually single out the sections dealing with the right to trial by one's peers in criminal cases (article 8 of the Virginia Declaration of Rights), and yet Virginians had little experience with such matters. Most Virginians had encountered juries in the modest, nonheroic cases of debt collection and personal assaults; their voice speaks in article 11: "in controversies respecting property, and in suits between man and man, the ancient trial by Jury is preferable to any other, and ought to be held sacred."[43]

In light of what had happened since 1750, perhaps one should not be surprised that Virginians applauded George Mason's defense of the right to trial by jury. Indeed, they took the right for granted. Because articles 8 and 11 of the Virginia Declaration of Rights were the antecedents of articles 6 and 7 of the Bill of Rights, they must be understand in the local context of Virginia's legal history. One need not look for stirring and sensational issues to explain why eighteenth-century farmers and merchants were sensitive about an institution that only recently they had begun using frequently. The revolutionary generation may have defended the right to a jury trial with references to a remote past, for they embraced an Anglo-American prefer-ence for "ancient and immemorial" institutions, but in fact Virginians' extensive use of the jury was very recent.[44]

Does such a revelation mar our carefully polished image of America's founders? It need not. The defense of the right to a trial by one's peers—even in debt settlements—sprang from real life. Today trial by jury faces a precarious, and ironic, future. The firm constitutional guarantees such as those written by Mason and Madison sometimes make judicial proceedings cumbersome or counterproductive. Legal experts despair of unfolding to jurors the complexities of modern civil cases, while others argue the merit of compelling courtroom technicians to explain themselves, once in a while, before ordinary mortals. In criminal cases, jury trials can consume weeks of already overloaded court dockets, while guilty pleas now account for more than 90 percent of completed cases. The result has been plea bargaining, in

---

43. *Mason Papers*, 1:288.

44. J. G. A. Pocock, *Ancient Constitution and the Feudal Law: English Historical Thought in the Seventeenth Century* (New York, 1967), 30–55. In the eighteenth century, William Blackstone defined custom as something that has "been used so long, that the memory of man runneth not to the contrary" (Blackstone, *Commentaries*, 1:76). Virginians may have doubted their ability to press this argument too far; *see* for example Pendleton's remark in the crisis surrounding the closing of the courts in 1774: "gentlemen object that we are not antient enough to establish any point upon custom," but this legal scruple did not deter the patriots from continuing to invoke custom (Mays, *Letters and Papers of Edmund Pendleton*, 1:82–85).

which defendants plead guilty to reduced charges and save the state the time and expense of jury trials.[45]

More than 90 percent of the world's jury trials occur in the United States. The British, by contrast, abolished grand juries in 1933 as redundant formalities once the nation had acquired a professional police force, and reserve jury trials for only the most serious crimes (and in civil litigation since 1937, fraud and libel suits). Their goal is speedy justice, another aspiration of eighteenth-century Virginians. Comparable reforms in the United States would require constitutional amendments, a lengthy process. Will Americans, like the settlers of West Jersey, ignore practicality and bury noble aspirations in mountains of procedure? Or are there Masons and Madisons among us who can distill the central lessons of our time and frame practical measures that respect our most cherished values? Preserving trial by jury as it enters its ninth century requires a reexamination of our priorities of life, liberty, property, and of the delicate balance between social justice and public order.

---

45. For example, Warren E. Burger, "Is Our Jury System Working ," *Reader's Digest* 118 (Feb., 1981): 126–130.

Excessive bail shall not be required, nor excessive fines imposed, nor cruel and unusual punishments inflicted.
—Eighth Amendment to the United States Constitution, *1791*

•

That excessive Bail ought not to be required nor excessive Fines imposed nor cruel and unusual Punishments inflicted.
—Article 9, Virginia Declaration of Rights, *1776*

The Bill of Rights

Chapter Ten

Bail, Fines, and Punishment

The Eighth Amendment's Safeguards

RICHARD A. WILLIAMSON

DEEPLY ROOTED in Anglo-American jurisprudence, the Eighth Amendment's restraints on excessive bail, excessive fines, and cruel and unusual punishments date from before Magna Carta. Affirmed in practice by many of the American colonies and reaffirmed in law by the Eighth Amendment, these ancient protections are among the most important contained in the Bill of Rights. Only the provisions about bail and punishments, however, arouse occasional contemporary controversy. Fines receive virtually no judicial attention because the maximum fines allowed by law in criminal cases are modest. The United States Supreme Court has never used the Eighth Amendment to invalidate a fine.

Society's need to ensure that accused persons are present for trial undergirds the concept of bail, for routine incarceration of persons only *accused* of crime is unacceptable in Anglo-American jurisprudence. Bail initially meant that someone accepted custody of an accused before trial and promised to surrender himself if the accused failed to appear. In time, property or money was placed at risk in the event of flight as an incentive to ensure that, if released, the accused would not flee before trial. A monetary bail system can be hard on the poor, especially when bail bondsmen charge 10 percent of the bail for their services and sometimes require cash and collateral for the remainder. Bondsmen, in turn, guarantee, or post, the full amount. Recently, most states have attempted to soften the financial inequities of the bail system by releasing persons on their simple promise to forfeit a sum of money if they fail to appear for trial.

•

The English antecedents for our right to bail are well documented. Chapter 39 of Magna Carta provides that "no freeman shall be captured or imprisoned . . . except . . . by the law of the land," and the Statute of Westminster in 1275 enumerated specific criminal offenses that were bailable. Three centuries passed before *Darnell's Case* (1627) made the next advance in the development of bail. Several knights imprisoned without bail in 1627 by

Charles I brought a habeas corpus action for their release. The Crown argued that Magna Carta did not confer a right to bail, and the royal judges agreed. Parliament in 1628 responded in the Petition of Right by providing that "no freeman . . . be imprisoned or detained" as the knights had been.[1]

In practice, seventeenth-century English courts continued to imprison people without bail until 1679, when the Habeas Corpus Act provided an effective means for prisoners to challenge unlawful detention. Even after 1679, however, a judge could frustrate the law by setting terms of bail that an accused person could not meet. "Excessive bail hath been required of persons committed in criminal cases," Parliament complained in 1689, "to elude the benefit of laws made for the liberty of the subjects." Accordingly, the English Bill of Rights contained a declaration that "excessive bail ought not to be required." Substituting *shall not* for *ought not to be*, this is the language of the Eighth Amendment.[2]

The path from Magna Carta to the Eighth Amendment's bail provision is clear, but significant constitutional issues do remain unresolved. Nowhere does the Constitution expressly confer an absolute right to bail in all criminal cases. It is possible, therefore, to construe the Eighth Amendment as conferring a right to bail only for cases declared eligible by statute or court decision and, thus, to assert that a fundamental human right is vulnerable to legislative or judicial denial. The absence of an explicit constitutional guarantee, Caleb Foote has explained in his seminal work on the American bail system, was an oversight resulting from the cursory manner in which the Bill of Rights was written and debated.[3]

Both English experience and colonial American history suggest that the Eighth Amendment does implicitly guarantee a right to bail for most offenses. The Massachusetts Body of Liberties of 1641 provided that

> No mans person shall be restrained or imprisoned by any Authority whatsoever, before the law hath sentenced him thereto, If he can put in sufficient securitie, bayle, or mainprise, for his appearance, and good behaviour in the meane time, unlesse it be in Crimes Capital, and Contempts in open Court.[4]

---

1. Schwartz, *Roots*, 1:12, 19 n. 1, 21; 3 Edward I, chap. 15 (1275); *State Trials*, 3:1 (1627).

2. 31 Charles II, chap. 2 (1679); Schwartz, *Roots*, 1:40–43. The U.S. Constitution itself provides that "the Privilege of the Writ of Habeas Corpus shall not be suspended, unless when in Cases of Rebellion or Invasion the Public Safety may require it" (art. 1, sec. 9).

3. Caleb Foote, "The Coming Constitutional Crisis in Bail: I," *University of Pennsylvania Law Review* 113 (1964–1965): 959, 986.

4. Schwartz, *Roots*, 1:71 n. 1, 73–74.

The New York Charter of Libertyes and Priviledges of 1683 has a similar statement. In 1785 the General Assembly of Virginia adopted a bill authored by Thomas Jefferson that eliminated judicial discretion about bail except for crimes "punishable in life or limb" or manslaughter where there was "good cause to believe the party guilty," and in the Northwest Ordinance of 1787 Congress provided that "all persons shall be bailable unless for capital offenses where the proof shall be evident, or the presumption great." Such examples suggest, but cannot irrefutably prove, that the Eighth Amendment intended a right to bail in most cases, but unfortunately the little we know about the adoption of the amendment sheds faint light on the question.[5]

George Mason, for both the Virginia Declaration of Rights and the amendments proposed by the Virginia Convention of 1788, lifted the wording of his bail provision from the English Bill of Rights. Perhaps because he was not a lawyer, Mason failed explicitly to state the right to bail. Perhaps he did not fully appreciate the structure of the English bail system as expressed in the "technical jargon" of the law.[6] Mason's mistake, if such it was, breezed unnoticed into the Bill of Rights. The only recorded mention of bail in the congressional debate on the Bill of Rights is this statement by Samuel Livermore, of New Hampshire:

> The clause seems to express a great deal of humanity, on which account I have no objection to it; but as it seems to have no meaning in it, I do not think it is necessary. What is meant be the terms excessive bail? Who are to be the judges?[7]

The Supreme Court answered Livermore's question thirty years ago in the case of *Stack* v. *Boyle*: "The right to release before trial is conditioned upon the accused's giving adequate assurance that he will stand trial," the court ruled. "Bail set at a figure higher than an amount reasonably calculated to fulfill this purpose is '*excessive*' under the Eighth Amendment."[8] By this standard, use of bail for anything except ensuring presence at trial would violate the Eighth Amendment.

Today, concern about the public danger of releasing persons accused of violent crimes has brought the Eighth Amendment to the edge of a public debate. Preventive detention laws are a major development in American

---

5. Ibid., 162, 166; 2:386 n. 1, 395; Foote, "Coming Constitutional Crisis," 976–977 n. 8.

6. Schwartz, *Roots*, 2:234 n. 1; 4:766 n. 1, 776–845; Foote, "Coming Constitutional Crisis," 986 n. 8.

7. *Annals of Congress*, 1:782.

8. *Stack* v. *Boyle*, *U.S. Reports*, 342:4–5 (1951).

criminal jurisprudence, but their constitutionality has yet to be resolved. They assume that release before trial may be denied outright, or effectively denied by high bail, if a court believes the accused poses a continuing threat to society. The objections to preventive detention are both theoretical (it relies on "probable cause" rather than conviction "beyond reasonable doubt") and practical (it forces court to predict the future and guess which people are likely to commit additional crimes). Preventive detention laws challenge our assumed right to bail and the Eighth Amendment's prohibition of excessive bail, and it seems likely that the Supreme Court will eventually be asked to rule on them.[9]

•

The cruel and unusual punishment clause also has a well-documented history in English law. As early as the tenth century, Anglo-Saxon law prescribed maximum punishments for specified crimes. Three chapters of Magna Carta treat punishment, and chapter 20 provides that "a freeman shall be [punished] for a small offence only according to the degree of the offence; and for a grave offence . . . according to the gravity of the offence." In 1689 the English Bill of Rights limited the Crown's authority to impose punishments unauthorized by statute and required that punishments be proportionate to offenses. Nevertheless, Anthony Granucci's authoritative studies of the Eighth Amendment show that the English Bill of Rights was not meant to outlaw punishments we consider inhumane, but was, instead, designed to prevent punishments unauthorized by law and those disproportionate to the seriousness of the offense. Indeed, the prevalence of cruelty in seventeenth- and eighteenth-century England is well known—from bearbaiting as a sport to executions by disemboweling, drawing and quartering (which continued until 1814), or be beheading and quartering (which continued until 1870).[10]

---

9. John N. Mitchell, "Bail Reform and the Constitutionality of Pretrial Detention," *Virginia Law Review* 55 (1969): 1223; *District of Columbia Code Annotated, 1981 Edition* (Charlottesville, 1981–1986), vol. 5, sec. 23–1322, pp. 763–766; *United States Code Annotated* (Saint Paul, Minn., 1985), Title 18, sec. 3142, pp. 172–192, and sec. (e), p. 175; *United States* v. *Edwards*, *Atlantic Reporter*, 2d ser. (Saint Paul, Minn., 1939–), 430:1321, 1370 (D.C. App. 1981) (en banc) (Mark, J., dissenting). The Supreme Court has upheld a limited preventive detention system for juvenile offenders; *Schall* v. *Martin*, *Supreme Court Reporter* (Saint Paul, Minn., 1883–), 104:2403 (1984). *See also* Paul B. Wice, *Bail and Its Reform: A National Survey* (Washington, D.C., 1973), 4–32.

10. Larry Charles Berkson, *The Concept of Cruel and Unusual Punishments* (Lexington, Mass., 1975), 3–4; Anthony F. Granucci, "'Nor Cruel and Unusual Punishments Inflicted': The Original Meaning," *California Law Review* 57 (1969): 839–865; Schwartz, *Roots*, 1:10 n. 1, 43.

The American concept of cruel and unusual punishment was quite different. Even though they used the language of the English Bill of Rights, the statesmen who proposed and debated the Bill of Rights in state ratifying conventions and the First Congress sought to prohibit barbarous forms of punishment. In the Massachusetts ratifying convention, Abraham Holmes worried that Congress had the power to determine punishments without being "restrained from inventing the most cruel and unheard-of punishments. . . . There is no constitutional check on them but the racks and gibbets may be amongst the most mild instruments of their discipline." Patrick Henry echoed this in the Virginia convention:

> When we come to punishments, no latitude ought to be left, nor dependence put on the virtue of representatives. What says our [Virginia] bill of rights?—"that excessive bail ought not to be required, nor excessive fines imposed, nor cruel and unusual punishments inflicted." Are you not, therefore, now calling on those gentlemen who are to compose Congress, to . . . define punishments without this control? . . . What has distinguished our ancestors?—That they would not admit of tortures, or cruel and barbarous punishment.[11]

Scant additional evidence of the founders' intent is recorded in congressional debates on the Bill of Rights. William L. Smith, of South Carolina, objected to the words "nor cruel and unusual punishments" because he thought they were "too indefinite." Samuel Livermore, of New Hampshire, thought the Eighth Amendment expressed "a great deal of humanity" but had "no meaning in it." "It is sometimes necessary to hang a man," he continued,

> villains often deserve whipping, and perhaps having their ears cut off; but are we in future to be prevented from inflicting these punishments because they are cruel? If a more lenient mode of correcting vice and deterring others from the commission of it could be invented, it would be very prudent in the Legislature to adopt it; but until we have some security that this will be done, we ought not be restrained from making necessary laws.[12]

American punishments did not parallel English experience. In *The Concept of Cruel and Unusual Punishment* (Lexington, Mass., 1975), Larry Berkson demonstrated that particularly cruel punishments—beheading, boiling, breaking on the wheel, gibbeting, pressing to death, burning at the stake, and mutilating—had been rare in colonial America. The ducking stool, collar

---

11. Elliot, *Debates*, 2:111, 3:447.
12. *Annals of Congress*, 1:782–783.

of torment, dung cart, and whipping—punishments considered cruel to-day—were used, but colonial American punishments were mild compared to those applied in Europe.[13]

Not until 1878 did the Supreme Court decide a major case involving the cruel and unusual punishment clause. In *Wilkerson* v. *Utah*, the Supreme Court unanimously upheld execution by firing squad as a punishment for premeditated murder and noted the difficulty of defining "with exactness" the meaning of "cruel and unusual punishments." This decision is important because by reviewing writings about capital punishment and methods used in other countries, the Court committed itself to interpreting the cruel and unusual punishment clause as an evolving concept that limited the severity as well as the form of punishment.[14]

Twelve years later, when it upheld the use of electrocution in the case of *In re Kemmler*, the Court again faced the question of cruelty and declared that punishments were cruel if they involved "torture or lingering death; but the punishment of death is not cruel, within the meaning of that word as used in the Constitution." Two years later, three dissenting justices in *O'Neil* v. *Vermont* (1892) argued that cruelty was also present when "punishments . . . by their excessive length or severity are greatly disproportioned to the offenses charged." Their view won acceptance by the Court in 1910, when in *Weems* v. *United States* the Court disallowed fifteen years of hard labor in ankle chains—the penalty prescribed by state law—as punishment for falsifying a public document. The Court found the sentence excessive in relation to the offense, to other crimes, and to the practices of other places.[15]

The *Weems* decision also said that cruel and unusual punishment was an evolving and "progressive" concept that could "acquire meaning as public opinion becomes enlightened by a humane justice." The Court used this evolutionary idea again in *Trop* v. *Dulles*, declaring in 1958 that deprival of citizenship for wartime desertion violated the Eighth Amendment and "evolving standards of decency that mark the progress of a maturing society." The Eighth Amendment, Justice Potter Stewart wrote in a similar 1962 decision, is always to be seen "in the light of contemporary human knowledge."[16]

---

13. Berkson, *Cruel and Unusual Punishments*, 4.

14. *Wilkerson* v. *Utah*, U.S. *Reports*, 99:130, 135–136 (1878).

15. *In re Kemmler*, U.S. *Reports*, 136:436, 446–447 (1890); *O'Neil* v. *Vermont*, U.S. *Reports*, 144:323, 339 (Field, J., dissenting) (1892); *Weems* v. *United States*, U.S. *Reports*, 217:349 (1910).

16. *Weems* v. *United States*, U.S. *Reports*, 217:378 (1910); *Trop* v. *Dulles*, U.S. *Reports*, 356:86, 101 (1958); *Robinson* v. *California*, U.S. *Reports*, 370:666 (1962).

In noncapital cases, the Supreme Court's recent rulings about cruel and unusual punishment have created uncertainty. In 1980 the *Rummel* v. *Estelle* ruling upheld life imprisonment for a repeat offender's third conviction for nonviolent fraud and declared that setting terms of imprisonment was "properly within the province of legislatures, not courts."[17] In 1982 the Supreme Court also upheld a Virginia jury's sentence of forty years in prison and a $20,000 fine for the distribution of nine ounces of marijuana. Acting from conscience, the commonwealth's attorney who originally prosecuted that case urged the offender's immediate release "in view of the lack of any semblance of uniformity of sentencing," and later the Virginia legislature reduced the maximum sentence for the same offense to less than half that upheld by the Court's decision.[18] The Court's most recent cruel and unusual punishment case, *Solem* v. *Helm* (1983), reviewed a sentence for writing a hundred-dollar bad check. The maximum punishment for the offense was five years and a $5,000 fine, but because the defendant had three previous convictions for third-degree burglary and one each for grand larceny, false pretenses, and driving while intoxicated, the court in South Dakota sentenced him to life imprisonment without parole. The Supreme Court found the sentence was "grossly disproportionate" and in violation of the Eighth Amendment.[19]

•

Capital punishment raises the most controversial modern Eighth Amendment issue. "The penalty of death," the Supreme Court has declared,

> differs from all other forms of criminal punishment, not in degree, but in kind. It is unique in its total irrevocability. It is unique in its rejection of rehabilitation of the convict as the basic purpose of criminal justice. And it is unique, finally, in its absolute renunciation of all that is embodied in our concept of humanity.[20]

Until very recently, many death sentence appeals argued that the sentence of death was excessive punishment for a specific offense; because most

---

17. *Rummel* v. *Estelle*, *U.S. Reports*, 445:263, 272, 275–276 (1980).

18. *Hutto* v. *Davis*, *U.S. Reports*, 454:370, 377–378 n. 7 (1982) (per curiam); *see Code of Virginia, 1950, 1979 Cumulative Supplement Annotated*, 4, *1975 Replacement* (Charlottesville, 1976), sec. 18.2–248.1 (a) (2), p. 153. The maximum penalty for the distribution of less than five pounds of marijuana, a class 5 felony, was ten years in jail and a $1,000 fine (*Code of Virginia*, 4, *1975 Replacement*, sec. 18. 2–10, p. 112). The governor of Virginia commuted Davis's sentence to twenty years and he was paroled in 1984.

19. *Solem* v. *Helm*, *U.S. Reports*, 463:277, 292–300 (1983).

20. *Rummel* v. *Estelle*, *U.S. Reports*, 445:272 (1980) (quoting *Furman* v. *Georgia*, *U.S. Reports*, 408:238, 306 [Stewart, J., concurring] [1972]).

American states use electrocution, gas chambers, hanging, or firing squads, few petitioners claim that the method of execution is inhumanely cruel.

On the question of excessiveness, the Supreme Court's decisions make it reasonably clear that a death sentence for a crime other than murder violates the cruel and unusual punishment clause. In *Coker* v. *Georgia* (1977) the Court found the death penalty for rape "grossly disproportionate and excessive," and in 1982 the Court spared the life of a man who had participated in a robbery in which a victim was killed, although he was not the killer. The Supreme Court held that the imposition of the death sentence on a person who did not actually take or intend to take life constituted cruel and unusual punishment.[21]

The question of capital punishment was temporarily cast in doubt by the Court's 1972 landmark decision of *Furman* v. *Georgia*, which invalidated Georgia's discretionary death penalty statute. At the time, public opinion seemed to be moving toward abolition of the death penalty. Only one person was executed in 1966, and of sixty-seven death sentences issued in 1965 sixty-two were commuted or reversed. Justices William Brennan and Thurgood Marshall saw this as evidence for society's rejection of capital punishment and argued that death itself constituted cruel and unusual punishment. Three other justices (William O. Douglas, Potter Stewart, and Byron R. White) voted to invalidate Georgia's death penalty because it was being applied "arbitrarily and capriciously." Georgia's death sentences were "cruel and unusual in the same way that being struck by lightening is cruel and unusual," they argued, for only "a capriciously selected random handful" of convicted criminals were executed for their crimes. Any discretionary death sentence in a system without standards was unconstitutional.[22]

The states reacted to the *Furman* decision in three ways. Some abolished the death penalty altogether. Others enacted *mandatory* death sentences for some crimes—a practical impossibility since prosecutors determine the charges and juries can find defendants guilty of lesser offences. Still others constructed death penalty statutes with standards and procedural safeguards. In 1976 the Supreme Court made another major review of the death penalty in *Gregg* v. *Georgia*, and a seven-member majority upheld Georgia's new laws. "Evolving standards have influenced juries in recent decades to be

---

21. *Coker* v. *Georgia, U.S. Reports*, 433:584, 593–600 (1977); *Enmund* v. *Florida U.S. Reports*, 458:782 (1982).

22. *Furman* v. *Georgia, U.S. Reports*, 408:238, 291–292 nn. 40–42 (Brennan, J., concurring), 309–310 (Stewart, J., concurring) (1972) (per curiam).

more discriminatory in imposing the death sentence," the Court acknowledged,

> but the relative infrequency of jury verdicts imposing the death sentence does not indicate rejection of capital punishment *per se*. Rather, the reluctance of juries in many cases to impose the sentence may well reflect the humane feelings that this most irrevocable of sanctions should be reserved for a small number of extreme cases.

That same day the Court invalidated North Carolina's and Louisiana's mandatory death penalties.[23]

Since the *Gregg* decision, at least thirty-five states have enacted capital punishment laws like Georgia's, with elaborate procedures and carefully defined standards, and by July 1984 more than fourteen hundred murderers have been sentenced under these new statutes. Today, executions are still national news when they occur, and many believe that the states will not execute all those who have been condemned. Others disagree, believing that as appeals run their slow courses, executions will resume in substantial numbers.

•

The Eighth Amendment's protections against prerevolutionary English practices are among the most important in the Bill of Rights. They embody the founders' wariness of human frailties that can affect the enforcement of law and the imposition of criminal sanctions. But by 1791 the traits advocated in the Eighth Amendment were firmly established, and during the ensuing centuries United States courts have relatively rarely had to apply its provisions. Preventive detention and the death sentence arouse contemporary controversy, but the Eighth Amendment is not frequently at the center of criminal litigation. This limited judicial attention suggests not failure but success. Compared with other places and other times, the various levels of government in the United States have rarely committed the abuses that the Eighth Amendment was written to prevent.

---

23. *Gregg* v. *Georgia, U.S. Reports*, 428:153, 181–183 (1976); *Woodson* v. *North Carolina, U.S. Reports*, 428:280 (1976); *Roberts* v. *Louisiana U.S. Reports*, 428:325 (1976).

The enumeration in the Constitution of certain rights shall not be construed to deny or disparage others retained by the people.
—Ninth Amendment to the United States Constitution, *1791*

The
Bill of
Rights

Chapter Eleven

Restoring the Declaration of Independence

Natural Rights and the Ninth Amendment

JOHN P. KAMINSKI

THE AMERICAN REVOLUTION and the war for independence were not synonymous, Benjamin Rush wrote in January 1787. The war was only "the first act of the great drama." Americans had yet "to establish and perfect" their government. Eight months later in Philadelphia the Convention of 1787 promulgated its new Constitution. To this day, Americans have argued whether the Founders preserved or overthrew the Spirit of '76, whether their new government was revolutionary or counter-revolutionary. Pennsylvania Federalist James Wilson thought the Constitution was based upon "the same certain and solid foundation" as the Declaration of Independence, and A Jerseyman told readers of the *Trenton Mercury* that while the declaration "opened the door by which our entrance into national importance was first made," the Constitution offered America a government strong enough to secure the rights won in the war for independence.[1]

Other Americans saw the proposed constitution in a different light. To Boston's Helvidius Priscus (thought to be Samuel Adams) the document violated "the principles of the late glorious revolution." To Philadelphiensis it "defeat[ed] the intention of the revolution . . . [for] nothing short of pure liberty is consistent with revolution principles." The Constitution was sure to bring despotism "as darkness brings the night." Elbridge Gerry, one of three delegates at Philadelphia who had refused to sign the Constitution, believed it was "neither consistent with the principles of the Revolution, or of the Constitutions of the several States." Gerry saw in the new plan only "fœderal Chains," while A Georgian begged his readers

---

1. *Philadelphia American Museum*, Jan. 1787, *Ratification*, 13:46; James Wilson, Pennsylvania convention, 4 Dec. 1787, *Ratification*, 2:472–473; *Trenton Mercury*, 6 Nov. 1787, *Ratification*, 3:146.

to call to mind our glorious declaration of independence, read it, and compare it with the federal constitution; what a degree of apostacy will you not then discover: Therefore, guard against all encroachments upon your liberties so dearly purchased with the costly expence of blood and treasure.[2]

Centinel was astonished at the "Incredible transition!" People willing to give up their lives for liberty were "about to sacrifice that inestimable jewel . . . to the genius of despotism." "Scarcely have four years elapsed since the United States [were] rescued from the domination of foreign despots," the essayist concluded, "when they are about to fall a prey to the machinations of a profligate junto at home." George Mason, one of two Virginia delegates who refused to sign the Constitution, agreed that government under the Constitution would "commence in a moderate aristocracy," then "vibrate some years between" monarchy and aristocracy, and terminate in one or the other. "Here is a revolution as radical as that which separated us from Great Britain," Patrick Henry warned. "Our rights and privileges are endangered, and the sovereignty of the States . . . relinquished." Many Americans agreed with Thomas Tredwell, of New York, that the Constitution "departed widely from the principles and political faith of '76. . . . Sir, in this Constitution we have not only neglected,—we have done worse,—we have openly violated, our faith,—that is, our public faith."[3]

Other Antifederalists believed Americans would never accept so dangerous a constitution. Connecticut Federalist Stephen Mix Mitchell thought it unlikely that "those indomitable Spirits, who have stood forth in the foremost Ranks, in this Revolution, will ever give up so much of their natural or acquired Liberty as is absolutely necessary in order to form a strong & efficient fœderal Government." The Reverend James Madison, president of the College of William and Mary, wrote his cousin James Madison that Americans wanted good government at the "least possible Expence to Natural Liberty."[4]

2. *Boston Independent Chronicle*, 27 Dec. 1787, *Ratification*, 15:332n; *Philadelphia Freeman's Journal*, 23 Jan. 1788, *Ratification*, 15:461; Elbridge Gerry to John Wendell, Cambridge, 16 Nov. 1787, *Ratification*, 14:128; *Gazette of the State of Georgia*, 15 Nov. 1787, *Ratification*, 3:243.

3. *Pennsylvania Packet*, 25 Dec. 1787, *Ratification*, 15:98; *Philadelphia Independent Gazetteer*, 29 Dec. 1787, *Ratification*, 15:178; *Massachusetts Centinel*, 21 Nov. 1787, *Ratification*, 14:151–152; Patrick Henry, speech in Virginia convention, 5 June 1788, *Debates and Other Proceedings of the Convention of Virginia*, ed. David Robertson (Petersburg, 1788–1789), 1:56; Thomas Tredwell, speech in the New York convention, 2 July 1788, Elliot, *Debates*, 2:401.

4. Samuel Mix Mitchell to William Samuel Johnson, Wethersfield, 18 Sept. 1787, *Ratification*, 3:347; James Madison to James Madison, Williamsburg, 9 Feb. 1788, *Madison Papers*, 10:487–488.

Antifederalists read one threat to natural rights in the provision that the Constitution, federal laws, and treaties have precedence over state laws and constitutions. Despite the Federalists' assertions to the contrary, state bills of rights seemed helpless to preserve liberty against the proposed central government. Worse, many Antifederalists thought, were two clauses empowering federal legislation for "the general welfare" and things "necessary and proper." Some Antifederalists, doubtful that even a federal bill of rights could rein these three constitutional provisions, predicted civil war if the new government were established. The Antifederalist minority of the Pennsylvania convention warned that the people of America were not "willing to resign every privilege of freemen, and submit to the dominion of an absolute government, that will embrace all America in one chain of despotism . . . they will with virtuous indignation, spurn at the shackles prepared for them, and confirm their liberties by a conduct becoming freemen." What man, Philadelphiensis asked, was "so base, that [he] will peaceably submit to a government that will eventually destroy his sacred *rights and privileges?*"[5]

•

Why this animosity toward the new Constitution? Without being strictly limited to specific powers, the national government could coerce both the states and the people, which had not been possible under the Articles of Confederation. Half the population believed that the proposed central government was little more than a domestic version of British rule that, without a bill of rights, seriously endangered the natural and acquired rights of all Americans. "When power is given to this Government," Patrick Henry charged, "the language . . . is clear, express, and unequivocal; but when this Constitution speaks of privileges, there is an ambiguity, Sir, a fatal ambiguity;—an ambiguity which is very astonishing."[6]

Antifederalists demanded explicit protection for their rights. Thomas B. Wait, who published the *Cumberland Gazette* of Portland, Maine, summarized the Antifederalist argument:

> No people under Heaven are so well acquainted with the natural rights of mankind, with the rights that ever ought to be reserved in all civil compacts,

---

5. *Pennsylvania Packet*, 18 Dec. 1787, *Ratification*, 15:22; *Philadelphia Freeman's Journal*, 23 Jan. 1788, *Ratification*, 15:461.

6. Patrick Henry, speech in Virginia convention, 5 June 1788, *Debates of the Convention of Virginia*, 1:56, 58.

as are the people of America—Nor perhaps will Americans, themselves be so well acquainted at a future day with those rights as they now are.—During the last fifteen or twenty years, it has been the business of the ablest politicians (politicians too, who were contending for the liberties of the people) to discover, "and draw a line between, those rights which must be surrendered, and those which may be reserved"—If not the whole truth, yet, many great truths have been discovered, are now fresh in our minds, and I think OUGHT TO BE RECORDED.

The people are now masters of the subject, and should be as explicit with respect to those rights they mean to reserve, as were the Convention with regard to those rights that are to be given up—The same instrument that conveys the weapon, should reserve the shield—should contain not only the powers of the rulers, but also the defence of the people.[7]

What are these natural rights about which Americans were so concerned? One very influential American statement is the Virginia Declaration of Rights:

That all Men are by Nature equally free and independent, and have certain inherent Rights, of which, when they enter into a State of Society, they cannot, by any Compact, deprive or divest their Posterity; namely, the Enjoyment of Life and Liberty, with the Means of acquiring and possessing Property, and pursuing and obtaining Happiness and Safety.

The self-evident truths of the Declaration of Independence are another, more popular statement: "That all men are created equal, that they are endowed by their Creator with certain unalienable Rights, that among these are Life, Liberty and the pursuit of Happiness."[8]

Antifederalists knew that state bills of rights secured these liberties and feared that the Constitution did not. The state constitutions, said Virginia's Richard Henry Lee, protected "that residuum of human rights, which is not intended to be given up to society, and which indeed is not necessary to be given for any good social purpose." In New York, Brutus (perhaps Melancton Smith) maintained that "there are certain rights which mankind possess, over which government ought not to have any controul." The Antifederalists of Pennsylvania summed it up: "Without the full, free, and

---

7. Thomas B. Wait to George Thatcher, Portland, Me., 15 Aug. 1788, Thatcher Papers, Chamberlain Collection, Boston Public Library.

8. Hening, *Statutes*, 9:109; *Jefferson Papers*, 1:429.

secure enjoyment" of the "unalienable and personal rights of men, . . . there can be no liberty."[9]

Several delegates to the Convention of 1787 had unsuccessfully proposed that individual rights be protected in the draft constitution, and on 12 September 1787 George Mason recommended the establishment of a committee to prepare a bill of rights. Elbridge Gerry moved that a committee be appointed, Mason seconded the motion, and the convention rejected the proposal. The convention's refusal to put a bill of rights in the Constitution almost killed the new plan of government. Antifederalists throughout the country opposed the Constitution for many reasons—some of them contradictory—but all Antifederalists agreed that natural rights had to be protected by a bill of rights.

•

When the Constitution was published, the demand for a bill of rights put Federalists immediately on the defensive. James Wilson, in a speech in Philadelphia on 6 October 1787 that was the first public defense of the Constitution by a former delegate to the convention, attempted to answer this criticism by enunciating a concept of reserved powers. In state constitutions, Wilson argued, all powers and rights not expressly reserved to the people are given up, but in the new constitution "the congressional authority is to be collected, not from tacit implication, but from the positive grant expressed in the instrument of union. Hence it is evident, that . . . every thing which is not given, is reserved." Congress, Wilson declared, could not restrict the freedom of the press, for example, because the Constitution gave Congress no power over the press.[10]

James Madison agreed with Wilson's reasoning in a letter to Thomas Jefferson, explaining that he favored a bill of rights if one could be written without giving the federal government more powers by implication. Then, in the Pennsylvania ratifying convention, Wilson elaborated his argument. A bill of rights would be dangerous because the positive declaration of *some* rights would imply that rights not listed were given up to the central government.

> Who will be bold enough to undertake to enumerate all the rights of the people? and when the attempt to enumerate them is made, it must be remembered that if the enumeration is not complete, every thing not expressly

---

9. Richard Henry Lee to Edmund Randolph, New York, 16 Oct. 1787, *Ratification*, 14:368; *New York Journal*, 17 Jan. 1788, *Ratification*, 15:393; *Pennsylvania Packet*, 18 Dec. 1787, *Ratification*, 15:25.

10. *Pennsylvania Herald*, 9 Oct. 1787 (extra), *Ratification*, 13:339.

mentioned will be presumed to be purposely omitted. So it must be with a bill of rights, and an omission in stating the powers granted to the government, is not so dangerous as an omission in recapitulating the rights reserved by the people.[11]

Federalists adopted Wilson's theory of reserved power as their official explanation for the Constitution's omission of a bill of rights, which made it a target for Antifederalist attacks. Arthur Lee, writing in New York City over the pen name Cincinnatus, accused Wilson of sophistry, and his brother Richard Henry Lee described Wilson's reasoning as "clearly a distinction without difference." A Democratic Federalist in Philadelphia found Wilson's efforts "extremely *ingenious*" but "*futile*." If the theory of reserved power was sound, why wasn't *it* expressly stated in the Constitution, especially if it was "the only security that we are to have for our natural rights"?[12]

A number of Antifederalists found the obvious inconsistency of Wilson's position—the Constitution itself reserved several rights. According to Richard Henry Lee, every one of the reservations "proves the Rule in Conventional ideas to be, that what was not reserved was given." Jefferson, abroad as American minister to France, held that Wilson's theory was "a gratis dictum, opposed by strong inferences from the body of the instrument." The Constitution prohibited denial of habeas corpus, bills of attainder, ex post facto laws, and grants of nobility. "Now, how absurd—how grossly absurd is all this," Thomas B. Wait exclaimed, "if Congress, in reality, have no powers but those particularly specified in the Constitution! It will not do, my friend—for God's sake let us not deny self-evident propositions—let us not sacrifice the truth." The Federal Farmer, America's most widely read Antifederalist pamphleteer, declared that "the 9th and 10th Sections in Art[icle] 1. in the proposed constitution, are no more nor less, than a partial bill of rights," and counseled "that this bill of rights ought to be carried farther . . . as a part of this fundamental compact between the people of the United States and their federal rulers."[13]

---

11. James Madison to Thomas Jefferson, New York, 17 Oct. 1788, *Madison Papers*, 11:297; James Wilson, Pennsylvania convention, 28 Nov. 1787, *Ratification* 2:391.

12. *New York Journal*, 1 Nov. 1787, *Ratification*, 13:530; Richard Henry Lee to Samuel Adams, New York, 27 Oct. 1787, *Ratification*, 13:484–485; *Pennsylvania Herald*, 17 Oct. 1787, *Ratification*, 2:193.

13. Lee to Adams, *Ratification*, 13:485; Thomas Jefferson to James Madison, Paris, 20 Dec. 1787, *Madison Papers*, 10:336; Thomas B. Wait, Portland, Me., to George Thatcher, 8 Jan. 1788, *Ratification*, 15:284–285; Federal Farmer letters to the Republican, letter 4, 12 Oct. 1787, *Ratification*, 14:45–46.

Federalists sprang to Wilson's defense. James Iredell, writing as Marcus in the *Norfolk and Portsmouth Journal*, reiterated the danger of not listing every single right. Remarker in the *Boston Independent Chronicle* maintained that "notwithstanding all that hath been said of it," the theory of reserved power was "perfectly true," and the omission of a bill of rights "was wisdom itself, because it implies clearly that the people who are at once the *source* and *object* of power, are already in full possession of all the rights and privileges of freemen. Let the people retain them forever."[14]

Federalists also explained why some rights were protected in the Constitution. Lawyer Thomas Hartley, of York, Pennsylvania, proclaimed that the definition of treason, habeas corpus, and trial by jury in criminal cases laid a "solid foundation" and secured "the great cardinal points of a free government . . . without the useless enumeration of privileges under the popular appellation of a bill of rights." James Madison in *The Federalist*, No. 44, acknowledged that bills of attainder and ex post facto laws already were contrary to the social compact theory, the principles of sound legislation, some of the state bills of rights, and the spirit of all of the state constitutions. Nevertheless he contended "that additional fences against these dangers ought not to be omitted. Very properly therefore have the Convention added this constitutional bulwark in favor of personal security and private rights." George Nicholas believed that Virginians would not give up "any greater share of their natural rights and privileges" under the new Constitution; power already delegated to the state and the Confederation governments simply was being redistributed between the states and the new federal government. Despite these protests, Federalists soon realized that the Constitution could not be ratified by key states without at least the promise a federal bill of rights.[15]

Indeed, Federalists found that their willingness to support a bill of rights and the possibility of other amendments to the Constitution was a convenient tactic to blunt the weapons of the virulent Antifederalists. In this approach the state of Virginia again took the lead. Writing in the *Virginia Independent Chronicle* on 20 February 1788, the Impartial Examiner insisted that the federal government needed "a positive unequivocal declaration in favor of the rights of freemen. . . . The more general [a government's]

---

14. James Iredell, *Norfolk and Portsmouth Journal*, 20 Feb. 1788; *Boston Independent Chronicle*, 27 Dec. 1787.

15. *Pennsylvania Herald*, 2 Jan. 1788, *Ratification*, 2:430–431; *The Federalist*, No. 44, *New York Packet*, 25 Jan. 1788, *Ratification*, 15:470; George Nicholas, Charlottesville, 16 Feb. 1788, Burnett Collection, Southern Illinois University, Carbondale.

influence, the more extensive the powers, with which it is invested, the greater reason there is to take the necessary precaution for securing a due administration, and guarding against unwarrantable abuses." Then, on 7 June 1788 Patrick Henry anticipated the Ninth Amendment by proposing to the Virginia Convention "that a general positive provision should be inserted in the new system, securing to the States and the people, every right which was not conceded to the General Government." When Virginia ratified the Constitution, its convention proposed

> That there be a Declaration or Bill of Rights asserting and securing from encroachment the essential and unalienable Rights of the People in some manner as the following;
>
> First, That there are certain natural rights of which men, when they form a social compact cannot deprive or divest their posterity, among which are the enjoyment of life and liberty, with the means of acquiring, possessing and protecting property, and pursuing and obtaining happiness and safety.

Guided by this example, New York, North Carolina, and Rhode Island each proposed similar amendments when they ratified the Constitution.[16]

•

On 8 June 1789, when James Madison introduced a number of proposed amendments to the Constitution in the United States House of Representatives, the precursor of the Ninth Amendment read:

> The exceptions here or elsewhere in the constitution, made in favor of particular rights, shall not be so construed as to diminish the just importance of other rights retained by the people; or as to enlarge the powers delegated by the constitution; but either as actual limitations of such powers, or as inserted merely for greater caution.

This amendment, Madison explained, answered the objection "against a bill of rights, that, by enumerating particular exceptions to the grant of power, it would disparage those rights ... which were not singled out" by putting them "into the hands of the general government" where they "were consequently insecure." Madison agreed that the objection had been "one of the most plausible arguments I have ever heard urged against the admission of a bill of rights into this system; but, I conceive, that may be guarded against. I have attempted it."[17]

---

16. *Debates of the Convention of Virginia*, 1:153; Edward Dumbauld, *The Bill of Rights and What It Means Today* (Norman, Okla., 1957), 182.

17. *Madison Papers*, 12:201–202, 206.

On 28 July 1789 a House committee reported a revised wording of Madison's amendment: "The enumeration in this Constitution of certain rights shall not be construed to deny or disparage others retained by the people." Only slightly altered by House and Senate action, this wording went to the states for approval and was ratified as the Ninth Amendment in 1791.[18]

•

For many years the Ninth Amendment remained unused as the Supreme Court steered clear of the untested reserved rights while steadily building upon the firmer foundation of other amendments. In 1965, however, several of the justices considered the Ninth Amendment in the case of *Griswold* v. *Connecticut* when the Court struck down an anticontraceptive law as an infringement of the right of marital privacy. Justice William O. Douglas, writing for the majority, described the Bill of Rights as having penumbrae, or shadows, "formed by emanations from those guarantees that help give them life and substance." While there was no specific amendment that guaranteed the right of privacy, the Court ruled that such a right was protected by the Third, Fourth, and Fifth amendments. Justice Douglas also referred to the text of the Ninth Amendment to demonstrate the existence of natural rights other than those specifically mentioned in the amended Constitution. Justice Arthur Goldberg's concurring opinion considered the Ninth Amendment in more detail.

> The language and history of the Ninth Amendment reveal that the Framers of the Constitution believed that there are additional fundamental rights, protected from governmental infringement, which exist alongside those fundamental rights specifically mentioned in the first constitutional amendments. . . . To hold that a right so basic and fundamental and so deep-rooted in our society as the right of privacy in marriage may be infringed because that right is not guaranteed in so many words by the first eight amendments to the Constitution is to ignore the Ninth Amendment and to give it no effect whatsoever. . . . The Ninth Amendment shows a belief of the Constitution's authors that fundamental rights exist that are not expressly enumerated in the first eight amendments and an intent that the list of rights included there not be deemed exhaustive.

Neither justice based his opinion upon the Ninth Amendment, for other specific amendments were broad enough to provide a constitutional basis for this decision. Rather than upholding unenumerated rights with the Ninth

---

18. Dumbauld, *Bill of Rights*, 211.

Amendment, the Supreme Court has often gone to great lengths to expand the application of other amendments to protect unenumerated rights.[19]

The Founders realized that no statesman could list every liberty in a bill of rights, so they wrote the Ninth Amendment to affirm the natural rights doctrines of the Declaration of Independence. As a statement that unspecified natural rights exist that are not to be abrogated, the Ninth Amendment stands as a silent sentinel guarding liberties not otherwise named in the Constitution. Perhaps it is still too early to judge the effectiveness of this two-hundred-year-old clause. Quite possibly, in a future marked by astonishing technological development, the ancient wisdom of the Ninth Amendment may protect as yet undefined rights from as yet uninvented dangers.

---

19. Lester S. Jayson et al., eds., *Constitution of the United States of America: Analysis and Interpretation* (Washington, D.C., 1973), 1258–1259.

The powers not delegated to the United States by the Constitution, nor prohibited by it to the States, are reserved to the States respectively, or to the people.
—Tenth Amendment to the United States Constitution, *1791*

The Tenth Amendment and the New Federalism of 1789

CHARLES F. HOBSON

THE TENTH AMENDMENT SEEMS DIFFERENT from the other nine. It speaks not of safeguards for the *rights* of individual citizens but of the distribution of *powers* between the United States and the states or people. In the twentieth century, when judicial enforcement of the Bill of Rights often voids state laws or state court decisions that violate individual rights, this reserved powers amendment has served as a text for the assertion of state rights against the spirit of the Bill of Rights. In 1789, however, the reserved powers amendment was recognized as an essential part of the Bill of Rights. Of all the amendments proposed for the Constitution, none was more frequently recommended: seven state ratifying conventions, along with the minority of the Pennsylvania convention, called for an explicit declaration reserving to the states the powers not delegated to the general government. Setting limits on the exercise of power by the federal government was to Samuel Adams "a summary of a bill of rights."[1]

In 1789, few Americans expected any danger that the states would violate fundamental liberties. Amendments protecting individual rights were intended to restrict only the federal government; an amendment reserving undelegated powers to the states simply reinforced the guarantees of personal liberty found in the state declarations of rights. The omission of a bill of rights was not the only reason Antifederalists opposed the Constitution in 1788 and 1789. Their demand for a bill of rights was but one part—and by no means the most important part—of their campaign to alter the Constitution in the direction of the discarded Articles of Confederation. They wished to restore the sovereignty of the states, the foundation of the old system, by limiting the central government's substantive powers over taxation, commerce, and treaty making.

The Antifederalists won protections for individual rights, but they failed in their larger aim. The enactment of the Bill of Rights was, in truth, a bitter

---

1. Edward Dumbauld, *The Bill of Rights and What It Means Today* (Norman, Okla., 1957), 163; Schwartz, *Bill of Rights*, 2:697.

disappointment, a second and decisive defeat for the unreconciled opponents of the Constitution. Friends of the Constitution, at first hostile to a bill of rights, preempted the campaign for amendments and turned it to their own purposes. Credit for this brilliant political statesmanship belongs to James Madison, who drafted the amendments and then shepherded them through Congress. Madison saw an opportunity to appease the large group of Americans who except for its omission of a bill of rights favored the Constitution. The addition of a bill of rights, he shrewdly calculated, would separate the well-meaning from the hostile critics and broaden popular support of the Constitution without sacrificing anything essential to the power and energy of the new government.

•

Like the first nine amendments, the Tenth Amendment directly answered fears that the proposed national government would destroy the state governments. The Antifederalists saw no other way to unite the states than in a league of free and equal states, each retaining full sovereignty, like the Articles of Confederation. Strictly speaking, the Confederation Congress was not a government but an instrument subordinate to the states for specific military and diplomatic objectives. It acted through the states, not directly upon individual citizens, and passed resolutions and ordinances but not laws. Law-making authority—sovereignty—remained with the states. There was no national executive or judiciary.

In practice the states under the Confederation were not completely sovereign, and Congress did act like a real government in war and diplomacy. Yet the experience of the American Revolution did not alter the essential structure of the Confederation as a league of independent states (the commonly accepted definition of a "federal" polity). The second article of the Confederation declared that "each state retains its sovereignty, freedom and independence, and every Power, Jurisdiction and right, which is not by this confederation expressly delegated to the United States, in Congress assembled." This article, a perfect summary of the federal system of the Confederation, was the parent of the Tenth Amendment. The offspring, however, has no mention of the "sovereignty, freedom and independence" of the states. Significantly missing, too, is the word "expressly" before "delegated." The Tenth Amendment, so it seemed, was a husk without a kernel. Its framers, to be sure, had consciously conformed the second article to the spirit of the new Constitution. As the second article expressed the "old" federalism of the Confederation, so the Tenth Amendment expressed the "new" federalism of the Constitution.

The most striking change proposed by the Constitution was the creation of a real central government with legislative, executive, and judicial departments. A republican government like those of the states, it would embrace the whole United States, deriving its powers from the people and acting directly upon them. The American people henceforth would be citizens of two governments, each with its proper sphere. Sovereignty was divided between a central government with jurisdiction over the entire nation and state governments with local jurisdiction. The Constitution embodied a new definition of *federalism*, the one we are familiar with today in our civics textbooks.

•

Antifederalists who indicted the Constitution for its vague, equivocal expressions applied the same charge to the final text of the Tenth Amendment, which did nothing to clarify the meaning of the Constitution. The difference between the second article of the Confederation and the Tenth Amendment to the Constitution was the difference between the old federalism and the new. It was a measure of the political distance Americans had traveled since 1776, of how they had transformed their ways of thinking about "federalism," "sovereignty," and "republican" government. The heart of the Antifederalists' critique of the Constitution was their adamant refusal to surrender the old federalism of the Articles of Confederation. They claimed to be the true spokesmen for federalism; they denied that the Constitution was *federal* in the accepted meaning of the word; and they denounced the friends of the plan for appropriating the *Federalist* label. This confusion of political terminology, Antifederalists said, masked a conspiracy to replace the state governments with a consolidated national government and suppress the rights and liberties of the people.

For all their exaggerated rhetoric, the Antifederalists correctly perceived that the Constitution was a radical departure from their existing government. The framers offered a government that defied precise description: a strange, unwieldy hybrid of a unitary government and a confederacy of state governments without precedent in history or in the writings of the ablest philosophers. Luther Martin, of Maryland, expressed the bewilderment of the Antifederalists when he protested that he was unable to discover

anything in the history of mankind or in the sentiments of those who have favoured the world with their ideas on government, to warrant or countenance the motley mixture of a system proposed: a system which is an innovation in government of the most extraordinary kind; a system neither wholly federal, nor wholly national—but a strange hotch-potch of both.

Federalists, too, described the plan as "partly federal, and partly national" to reassure the people that the states would continue to be essential parts of the system and that the federal features would predominate. These assurances fell upon deaf ears among Antifederalists who insisted that a government could either be federal or consolidated but not both. The Constitution, they said, unmistakably "squinted" in the latter direction.[2]

Consolidation was a word Antifederalists repeatedly used against the Constitution. What did they mean? And why did they regard it as dangerous? Consolidated governments held supreme political and legal authority within their jurisdictions. In this sense state governments with no federal relationships to their counties, townships, or cities were consolidated governments. The alarming implication of the Constitution was that the states would be reduced to the petty status of counties and corporations. Antifederalists took no comfort in knowing that the proposed new government was republican in form, for they contended that any government with such an extensive territory as the United States would necessarily degenerate into monarchy or despotism. While the friends of the Constitution repeatedly argued that it was both federal and republican, Antifederalists saw only consolidation and eventual tyranny.

Consolidation pervaded the whole system, beginning with the opening words of the preamble: "The question turns, sir, on that poor little thing— the expression, We, the *people*, instead of the *states*, of America," said Patrick Henry at the Virginia Convention of 1788. This preamble betrayed an intention to make "this alarming transition, from a confederacy to a consolidated government." To Pennsylvania Antifederalist Robert Whitehill these words showed that "the old foundation of the union is destroyed, the principle of confederation excluded, and a new and unwieldy system of consolidated empire is set up, upon the ruins of the present compact between the states."[3]

Then, if further proof were needed that the framers intended "to absorb and abolish the efficient sovereignty and independent powers of the several States, in order to invigorate and aggrandize the general government," one only had to turn to the body of the Constitution. Powers of the central government were stated in general terms that left opportunity for expansion

2. Alpheus Thomas Mason, ed., *The States Rights Debate: Antifederalism and the Constitution*, 2d ed. (New York, 1972), 116; James Madison, *The Federalist*, No. 39, in *The Federalist Papers: Alexander Hamilton, James Madison, John Jay*, ed. Clinton Rossiter (New York, 1961), 240–246.

3. Kenyon, *Antifederalists*, 239; Mason, *States Rights Debate*, 135.

by interpretation or implication. The power to levy taxes and raise armies—the purse and sword—were themselves sufficient to destroy the states, and the clause giving Congress power to pass all laws "necessary and proper" seemed to give the legislature authority to do whatever it wished. Under close scrutiny by the Antifederalists, every clause of the Constitution seemed calculated toward a consolidated government that would leave the states as subordinate administrative units only. Who could misunderstand a statement that the Constitution and the laws and treaties made under it would be the "supreme law," state constitutions and laws "to the contrary notwithstanding"?[4]

•

All these objections to the Constitution rested on the Antifederalists' belief that, sovereignty being indivisible, the Federalists' claim that the Constitution distributed portions of sovereign power between the general and state governments was absurd. Did not all the respected political thinkers agree that there could be only one supreme law-making authority in a state? It was inconceivable that one government could exist within another (*"imperium in imperio"*), said William Grayson, of Virginia; the absurdity surpassed "everything that I have read of concerning other governments." "The idea of two distinct sovereigns in the same country, separately *possessed* of sovereign and supreme power, in the same matters at the same time," a New York Antifederalist sneered, "is as supreme an absurdity, as that two distinct separate circles can be bounded exactly by the same circumference."[5]

Such logic left no middle ground. Either the general government or the states would predominate, and the tendency of the Constitution left no doubt where supremacy would eventually reside. The minority of the Pennsylvania convention believed

> that two co-ordinate sovereignties would be a solecism in politics; that . . . it would be contrary to the nature of things that both should exist together—one or the other would necessarily triumph in the fulness of dominion. However, the contest could not be of long continuance, as the State governments are divested of every means of defence, and will be obliged by "the supreme law of the land" *to yield at discretion.*

---

4. John Smilie in the Pennsylvania convention, in Mason, *States Rights Debate*, 140.

5. William Grayson quoted in Gordon S. Wood, *The Creation of the American Republic, 1776–1787* (Chapel Hill, 1969), 527; Kenyon, *Antifederalists*, 401.

The doctrine of sovereignty proved that the Constitution "was calculated to abolish entirely the state governments, and to melt down the states into one entire government."[6]

Montesquieu's idea that republican government was suitable only for small territories with homogeneous populations gave Antifederalists additional reasons to worry about consolidated government. "Is it to be supposed," asked George Mason, author of the Virginia Declaration of Rights,

> that one national government will suit so extensive a territory, embracing so many climates, and containing inhabitants, so very different in manners, habits, and customs? It is ascertained by history, that there never was a government, over a very extensive country, without destroying the liberties of the people.[7]

The minority in the Pennsylvania convention dissented from the Constitution because it was "the opinion of the most celebrated writers on government, and confirmed by uniform experience, that a very extensive territory cannot be governed on the principles of freedom, otherwise than by a confederation of republics." How could such a government simultaneously represent the interests of New England farmers, New York merchants, Pennsylvania artisans, and South Carolina planters? First the national government would degenerate into a type appropriate for an extensive territory—either monarchy or despotism. Then, unity would require military coercion and the dreaded scourge of free governments—a standing army—would be needed to enforce obedience to the general government. In short, the reasoning went, the proposed national government could not possibly remain republican. To the Antifederalists, the Constitution could have but one result: the annihilation of the states and the accompanying destruction of the rights and liberties of the people.[8]

To explain the new system's "strange hotch-potch" of federal and national features, the Federalists modified the idea that sovereignty was indivisible. Unlike the Antifederalists, who equated sovereignty with government, the Federalists asserted that ultimate power resided not with the general or state governments but with the people themselves. The people could allocate portions of their undivided supreme authority to be exercised by different governments. This redefinition of sovereignty, which had emerged during

---

6. Kenyon, *Antifederalists*, 42–43; Robert Yates, "Letters of Brutus," in Mason, *States Rights Debate*, 113.

7. George Mason, speech in the Virginia convention, in Mason, *States Rights Debate*, 149.

8. Kenyon, *Antifederalists*, 39.

the period of constitution making and political experimentation between 1776 and 1787, made possible the new federalism of the Constitution.[9]

Popular sovereignty had been largely an abstraction in 1776. In practice, in the act of forming their governments the people had always surrendered power to them. During the American Revolution, however, the novel concept of the people actively exercising power "out of doors" developed. The most important tangible form of this idea was the convention of the people. By writing a constitution in a general convention and by ratifying it in special conventions, the people truly acted as the "constituent power" and wrote their own fundamental laws. According to this new way of thinking, the people did not surrender ultimate power when forming governments. The Constitution became the concrete expression of their permanent claim of supreme authority. The people, said James Wilson, of Pennsylvania, "can distribute one portion of power to the more contracted circle called State governments; they can also furnish another proportion to the government of the United States." The powers of each were only "so many emanations of power from the people." Federalists argued that this relocation, or restoration, of sovereignty in the people answered the charge of consolidation, for both the general and state governments were held in check by the will of the people embodied in the Constitution.[10]

The Antifederalist objection that republican government was practicable only in small territories had, in truth, been undermined by the factious politics of the state governments since 1776. Republican government as exercised in the states had come to mean government by majority factions whose laws reflected narrow self-interests rather than the public good. James Madison observed in *The Federalist*, No. 10, that the very smallness of the state jurisdictions had made it relatively easy for factions to gain control. His solution to the problem of faction was not to abandon principle but to enlarge the jurisdiction: "Extend the sphere, and you take in a greater variety of parties and interests; you make it less probable that a majority of the whole will have a common motive to invade the rights of other citizens." Madison's great insight was to realize that enlarging the republic could promote moderation and justice. By distributing powers and functions between the general and state governments, the new federalism made it feasible to enlarge the jurisdiction of a republic. "And happily for the *republican cause*," he wrote, "the practicable sphere [of republican govern-

9. Much of the discussion that follows draws heavily from Wood, *Creation of the American Republic*, 524–532.

10. Ibid., 530–531.

ment] may be carried to very great extent, by a judicious modification and mixture of the *federal principle*." The new federalism of the Constitution provided "a Republican remedy for the diseases most incident to Republican Government." Just as the notion of divided sovereignty gave new meaning to federalism, so the redefinition of federalism made possible the reformation of republican government.[11]

These fundamentally different assumptions held by the Federalists and Antifederalists shaped their quarrel over the necessity of a bill of rights. Seizing upon the new conception of sovereignty, Federalists such as James Wilson contended that the government under the Constitution was only a partial delegation of the people's original supreme power and, therefore, adding a bill of rights would be "superfluous and absurd." Retaining everything not delegated, said Alexander Hamilton, "the people surrender nothing; and as they retain every thing, they have no need of particular reservations." Adhering to the traditional notion of sovereignty, Antifederalists found this stock reply unacceptable. They warned that the people delegated all "rights not expressly reserved" (a principle that had made state declarations of rights necessary) and that the proposed federal government was in this respect no different from the states. Antifederalists thought that an explicit reservation of powers to the states was the most effective guarantee for individual liberty. If the Constitution had included an express reservation in terms similar to the second article of the Confederation, North Carolinian Samuel Spencer concluded, "it would have superseded the necessity of a bill of rights."[12]

Thus, the reserved powers amendment was the very foundation of a bill of rights. By agreeing to amend the Constitution to safeguard individual rights, the Federalists wisely sacrificed their theory to keep the Constitution's original delegation of powers intact. The legislative history of the Tenth Amendment illustrates this fact. James Madison presented a declaration of reserved powers to the House of Representatives in June 1789 that read: "The powers not delegated by this Constitution, nor prohibited by it to the states, are reserved to the States respectively." In his accompanying speech the Virginia representative noted that several state ratifying conventions were

---

11. Rossiter, *Federalist Papers*, 83, 84, 325.

12. Schwartz, *Bill of Rights*, 1:529; *The Federalist*, No. 84, in Rossiter, *Federalist Papers*, 513; "Letters of Agrippa" [James Winthrop?], in Schwartz, *Bill of Rights*, 1:515; speech in the North Carolina convention, in Schwartz, *Bill of Rights*, 2:945.

particularly anxious that it should be declared in the constitution, that the powers not therein delegated, should be reserved to the several states. Perhaps words which may define this more precisely, than the whole of the instrument now does, may be considered as superfluous. I admit they may be deemed unnecessary; but there can be no harm in making such a declaration, if gentlemen will allow that the fact is as stated. I am sure I understand it so, and do therefore propose it.

Madison cleverly implied that his draft reflected the wording recommended by the state conventions. In fact, most of those conventions copied the second article of the Confederation by reserving all powers not "expressly delegated." Madison deliberately omitted "expressly," for he intended the amendment only as an explicit statement of a principle that he regarded as implied in the original Constitution.[13]

The significance Madison attached to "expressly" was revealed in a brief debate in the committee of the whole on 18 August when Thomas Tudor Tucker, of South Carolina, moved to add the word. Madison immediately objected that "it was impossible to confine a government to the exercise of express powers. There must necessarily be admitted powers by implication, unless the constitution descended to recount every minutiæ." The doctrine of implied powers, which Madison fully accepted, would have been foreclosed from the beginning. Years later Chief Justice John Marshall confirmed Madison's understanding of the omission of "expressly." The Constitution, said Marshall, contained no phrase

> which, like the articles of confederation, excludes incidental or implied powers; and which requires that every thing granted shall be expressly and minutely described. Even the 10th amendment, which was framed for the purpose of quieting the excessive jealousies which had been excited, omits the word "expressly." . . . The men who drew and adopted this amendment had experienced the embarrassments resulting from the insertion of this word in the articles of confederation, and probably omitted it to avoid those embarrassments.[14]

On 21 August, Elbridge Gerry, of Massachusetts, again moved for "expressly." The motion lost on a roll-call vote, thirty-two to seventeen. Three days later the House adopted the reserved powers amendment as written by Madison. When the amendments were taken up by the Senate, that body on 7 September defeated a third and final attempt to insert

---

13. *Madison Papers*, 12:202, 209.
14. Ibid., 346; *McCulloch* v. *Maryland, U.S. Reports*, 17:406–407 (1819).

"expressly." Two days later the reserved powers amendment passed the Senate in the form that Congress formally approved on 25 September 1789 and sent to the states for ratification: "The powers not delegated to the United States by the Constitution, nor prohibited by it to the States, are reserved to the States respectively, or to the people." The Senate had added two phrases to the amendment: "to the United States" and "or to the people." The reasons for these additions were not recorded (for the Senate then met behind closed doors), but a few conjectures may be offered to suggest why they were made. The additional words gave balance and symmetry not only to the amendment itself but also to its relationship with the Constitution as a whole. The final wording explicitly recognized the three constituent elements of the new American federalism—the United States, the states, and the people—and the inclusion of "or to the people" reaffirmed the distinction that was central to this new definition of popular sovereignty. Fittingly, too, this change meant that a document that opened with "We the people" now concluded with "the people."[15]

•

The Tenth Amendment offered cold comfort to the Antifederalists for it did little to remove the specter of consolidation. Yet these "men of little faith" were more successful than they realized. In the debate over the Constitution, they had compelled the Federalists to deny consolidation and to explain a new federalism in which both the national and state governments were subordinate to the supreme authority of the people. This process of explaining the Constitution to make it acceptable to the American people and consistent with their historical experience effectively foreclosed the possibility of a unitary national government for the United States. As a declaration of the "federal" construction of the Constitution, the Tenth Amendment *was* in one sense superfluous, as Madison had said, but only because its purpose had been accomplished in the clarification of terms by which the Constitution was presented and justified to the people before its enactment.

Contrary to the worst fears of the Antifederalists, the federal republic that came into being in 1789 represented a true middle ground between consolidation and a confederacy of sovereign states. The nature of the relationship between the federal and state governments was not clear in 1789 and would never be fully clarified. The Tenth Amendment, as Marshall observed, left "the question, whether the particular power which may become the subject of contest has been delegated to the one government, or

---

15. Schwartz, *Bill of Rights*, 2:1127, 1150–1151; Dumbauld, *Bill of Rights*, 219, 222.

prohibited to the other, to depend on a fair construction of the whole instrument."[16]

The Constitution, as subsequent events have shown, is ambiguous enough to support almost diametrically opposing constructions. Over the course of two centuries it has been invoked both to enlarge and to restrict the scope of national powers. Interestingly, when the Tenth Amendment has been cited to narrow the scope of federal power, judges have frequently altered its text by interpolating "expressly."[17] While the net result since 1789, and especially since 1865, has been a vast increase in the powers and jurisdiction of the national government, the system is still recognizably federal. The Tenth Amendment stands as a constant reminder, if one is needed, that political authority in the United States is not concentrated in one central government but divided and dispersed among many jurisdictions.

16. *McCulloch* v. *Maryland, U.S. Reports*, 17:406 (1819).

17. Walter Berns, "The Meaning of the Tenth Amendment," in *A Nation of States: Essays on the American Federal System*, ed. Robert A. Goldwin (Chicago, 1963), 133–137.

Notes on Contributors

Lawrence Delbert Cress is professor of history and chair of the history department at the University of Tulsa and author of *Citizens in Arms: The Army and the Militia in American Society to the War of 1812* (Chapel Hill, 1982). He was associate professor of history and assistant provost at Texas A & M University when his essay was initially published in the Autumn 1983 issue of *Virginia Cavalcade.*

William Cuddihy is coauthor of "A Man's House Was Not His Castle: Origins of the Fourth Amendment to the United States Constitution," *William and Mary Quarterly*, 3d ser., 37 (1980): 371–400, and is completing a dissertation on constitutional history at the Claremont Graduate School. His essay was initially published in the Spring 1984 issue of *Virginia Cavalcade.*

B. Carmon Hardy is professor of history at California State University at Fullerton and coauthor of "A Man's House Was Not His Castle: Origins of the Fourth Amendment to the United States Constitution," *William and Mary Quarterly*, 3d ser., 37 (1980): 371–400. His essay was initially published in the Winter 1984 issue of *Virginia Cavalcade.*

Charles F. Hobson is editor of *The Papers of John Marshall* at the College of William and Mary in Virginia. He is author of "The Negative on State Laws: James Madison, the Constitution, and the Crisis of Republican Government," *William and Mary Quarterly*, 3d ser., 36 (1979): 215–235, and was an editor of *The Papers of James Madison* at the University of Virginia. His essay was initially published in the Winter 1986 issue of *Virginia Cavalcade.*

John P. Kaminski is editor of the multivolume *Documentary History of the Ratification of the Constitution* (Madison, Wis., 1976–   ) and director of the Center for the Study of the American Constitution at the University of Wisconsin. His essay was initially published in the Autumn 1985 issue of *Virginia Cavalcade.*

Jon Kukla has directed the publications program of the Virginia State Library since 1976. He edited *The Bill of Rights: A Lively Heritage* and is author of *Speakers and Clerks of the Virginia House of Burgesses, 1643–1776* (Richmond, 1981) and "Order and Chaos in Early America: Political and Social Stability in Pre-Restoration Virginia," *American Historical Review* 90

(1985): 275–298. His essay was initially published in the Summer 1984 issue of *Virginia Cavalcade*.

Martin E. Marty is Fairfax M. Cone Distinguished Service Professor of the History of Modern Christianity at the University of Chicago and associate editor of *The Christian Century*. His books include *The Irony of It All, 1893–1919* (Chicago, 1986), volume one of his projected four-volume *Modern American Religion*, and *Righteous Empire: The Protestant Experience in America* (New York, 1970), which won the National Book Award. His essay was initially published in the Spring 1983 issue of *Virginia Cavalcade*.

John M. Murrin is professor of history at Princeton University and author of such major essays as "Political Development" in *Colonial British America: Essays in the New History of the Early Modern Era*, ed. Jack P. Greene and J. R. Pole (Baltimore and London, 1984), "Feudalism, Communalism and the Yeoman Freeholder: The American Revolution Considered as a Social Accident" with Rowland Berthoff in *Essays on the American Revolution*, ed. Stephen G. Kurtz and James M. Hutson (Chapel Hill, 1973), and "The Great Inversion, or Court versus Country: A Comparison of the Revolution Settlements in England (1688–1721) and America (1776–1816)" in *Three British Revolutions: 1641, 1688, 1776*, ed. J. G. A. Pocock (Princeton, 1980). He has edited *Saints & Revolutionaries: Essays on Early American History* (New York, 1984) with David D. Hall and Thad W. Tate, and *Congress at Princeton: Being the Letters of Charles Thomson to Hannah Thomson, June–October 1783* (Princeton, 1985) with Eugene R. Sheridan. His essay written with A. G. Roeber was initially published in the Autumn 1984 and Winter 1985 issues of *Virginia Cavalcade*.

David M. O'Brien is associate professor of government and foreign affairs at the University of Virginia and his books include *The Public's Right to Know: The Supreme Court and the First Amendment* (New York, 1981) and *Storm Center: The Supreme Court in American Politics* (New York, 1986). His essay was initially published in the Summer 1983 issue of *Virginia Cavalcade*.

A. G. Roeber is associate professor of history at the University of Illinois at Chicago and author of *Faithful Magistrates and Republican Lawyers: Creators of Virginia Legal Culture, 1680–1810* (Chapel Hill, 1981). His essay written with John Murrin was initially published in the Autumn 1984 and Winter 1985 issues of *Virginia Cavalcade*.

Robert A. Rutland was editor of *The Papers of James Madison* at the University of Virginia until his retirement in 1986. His books include *The Birth of the Bill of Rights, 1776–1791* (Chapel Hill, 1955, and Boston, 1983), *The Ordeal of the Constitution: The Antifederalists and the Ratification*

Struggle of 1787–1788 (Norman, Okla., 1966), and *James Madison and the Search for Nationhood* (Washington, D.C., 1981), and he also edited *The Papers of George Mason, 1725–1792* (Chapel Hill, 1970). His essay was initially published in the Winter 1983 issue of *Virginia Cavalcade.*

Brent Tarter is an editor of the *Dictionary of Virginia Biography* project at the Publications Branch of the Virginia State Library. He edited *The Order Book and Related Papers of the Common Hall of the Borough of Norfolk, Virginia, 1763–1798* (Richmond, 1979) and was an editor of volumes 3 through 7 of *Revolutionary Virginia, The Road to Independence: A Documentary Record* (Charlottesville, 1973–1983) for the Virginia Independence Bicentennial Commission. His essay was initially published in the Autumn 1982 issue of *Virginia Cavalcade.*

Richard A. Williamson is vice dean and professor of law at the Marshall-Wythe School of Law at the College of William and Mary in Virginia. His essay was initially published in the Spring 1985 issue of *Virginia Cavalcade.*

The Virginia Declaration of Rights

Enacted on 12 June 1776

A DECLARATION OF RIGHTS made by the representatives of the good people of Virginia, assembled in full and free Convention; which rights do pertain to them, and their posterity, as the basis and foundation of government.

1. That all Men are by nature equally free and Independent and have certain inherent Rights of which when they enter into a state of Society they cannot by any compact deprive or divest their Posterity namely the enjoyment of Life and liberty with the means of acquiring and possessing property and pursuing and obtaining happiness and Safety.

2. That all power is vested in and consequently derived from the People that Magistrates are their Trustees and Servants and at all times amienable to them.

3. That Government is or ought to be instituted for the common benefit protection and Security of the People Nation or Community of all the various Modes and forms of Government that is best which is capable of producing the greatest degree of happiness and Safety and is most effectually secured against the danger of Mal-Administration and that whenever any Government shall be found inadequate or contrary to these purposes a Majority of the Community hath an indubitable unalienable and indefeasible right to reform alter or abolish it in such manner as shall be judged conducive to the publick Weal.

4. That no Man or set of Men are intitled to exclusive or separate Emoluments or Privileges from the Community but in consideration of publick Services which not being descendible neither ought the Offices of Magistrate Legislator or Judge to be hereditary.

5. That the Legislative and Executive powers of the State should be separate and Distinct from the Judicative and that the Members of the two first may be restrained from oppression by feeling and participating the burthens of the People they should at fixed Periods be reduced to a private station return into the Body from which they were originally taken and the vacancies be

supplied by frequent certain and regular Elections in which all or any part of the former Members to be again elegible or inelegible as the laws shall direct.

6. That Elections of Members to serve as representatives of the People in Assembly ought to be free and that all Men having sufficient evidence of permanent common Interest with and attachment to the Community have the right of Suffrage and cannot be taxed or deprived of their Property for Publick Uses without their own Consent or that of their Representatives so Elected nor bound by any Law to which they have not in like manner assented for the public good.

7. That all Power of suspending Laws or the execution of Laws by any Authority without consent of the Representatives of the People is injurious to their rights and ought not to be exercised.

8. That in all Capital or Criminal Prosecutions a Man hath a right to demand the Cause and Nature of his Accusation to be confronted with the Accusors and Witnesses to call for Evidence in his favour and to a speedy Trial by an impartial Jury of his Vicinage without whose unanimous consent He cannot be found guilty nor can he be compelled to give Evidence against himself that no Man be deprived of his liberty except by the Law of the Land or the Judgment of his Peers.

9. That excessive Bail ought not to be required nor excessive Fines imposed nor cruel and unusual Punishments inflicted.

10. That General Warrants whereby any Officer or Messenger may be commanded to search suspected places without evidence of a fact committed Or to seize any Person or Persons not named or whose Offence is not particularly described and supported by evidence are grievous and oppressive and ought not to be granted.

11. That in Controversies respecting Property and in suits between Man and Man the antient Trial by Jury is preferable to any other and ought to be held sacred.

12. That the freedom of the Press is one of the great Bulwarks of liberty and can never be restrained but by despotic Government.

13. That a well regulated Militia composed of the Body of the People trained to Arms is the proper natural and safe Defence of a free State that standing Armies in time of peace should be avoided as dangerous to liberty and that in all Cases the Military should be under strict Subordination to and governed by the Civil power.

14. That the People have a right to Uniform Government and therefore that no Government separate from or Independent of the Government of Virginia ought to be erected or established within the Limits thereof.

15. That no free Government or the Blessing of Liberty can be preserved to any People but by a firm adherence to Justice Moderation Temperance Frugality and Virtue and by frequent recurrence to fundamental Principles.
16. That Religion or the Duty which we owe to our Creator and the manner of discharging it can be directed only by reason and Conviction not by force or Violence and therefore all Men are equally intitled to the free exercise of Religion according to the Dictates of Conscience And that it is the mutual Duty of all to practice Christian Forbearance Love and Charity towards each other.

Index